The **ABC**'s of
Writing Fiction

The ABC's of
Writing Fiction

WITHDRAWN

Ann Copeland

STORY PRESS
CINCINNATI, OHIO

The ABC's of Writing Fiction. Copyright © 1996 by Ann Copeland. Printed and bound in the United States of America. All rights reserved. No part of this book may be reproduced in any form or by any electronic or mechanical means including information storage and retrieval systems without permission in writing from the publisher, except by a reviewer, who may quote brief passages in a review. Published by Story Press, an imprint of F&W Publications, Inc., 1507 Dana Avenue, Cincinnati, Ohio 45207. (800) 289-0963. First edition.

Other fine Story Press Books are available from your local bookstore or direct from the publisher.

00   99   98   97   96   5   4   3   2   1

Library of Congress Cataloging-in-Publication Data

Copeland, Ann.
  The ABC's of writing fiction / by Ann Copeland.
     p.   cm.
  Includes index.
  ISBN 1-884910-12-2 (hc : alk. paper)
  1. Fiction—Technique.   I. Title.
PN3355.C595   1996
808.3—dc20   95-53258
                                                                        CIP

Designed by Clare Finney

The permissions opposite this page constitute an extension of this copyright page.

PERMISSIONS

For Doctor Definition
and my friends at the
Moncton Writers Breakfast.

ACKNOWLEDGMENTS

I wish to thank Jack Heffron, my editor, for his tactful, discerning suggestions which greatly refined and improved these ABC's.

Thanks also to my dear friend Vincent Poirier for his interest and his ongoing support of my efforts to master this challenging alphabet.

TO THE READER

As I write these words, I am visiting a version of Paradise—Cascade Head, a nature conservancy on the Oregon Coast. Before the day is over, I may spot a shy deer leaping into the woods or perhaps a bald eagle circling high above this quiet and beautiful world. I am more than four thousand miles from home.

That kind of distance, though—the kind we measure by miles and clocks—fades to peculiar insignificance as a writer works. How strange that as we call forth words, stare at them, consider their implications, and arrange them to build stories, a new kind of time and space gradually comes into being. The "real world"—the world that frames us—drops off and our imagination discovers, however briefly, a new home. It may not be Paradise, but it is certainly a version of creation.

During the past fifteen years, I've sought ways to teach this strangely beguiling act of creation called fiction writing to a wide range of people. I've met and worked with them in places as distant as Bemidji, Minnesota, and Moscow, Idaho; and in my own small town, Sackville, New Brunswick, Canada. Levels of literary sophistication have varied greatly. I have learned from their questions, explored with them ways of looking at technical problems, puzzled with them through revisions of promising manuscripts.

As I worked with them and labored over my own fictions, I found that often just a word or phrase helped to unlock my stuck imagination or turned a puzzling technical knot so students could see it in a fresh way. Over the years I jotted down these words and phrases, tested them with students, sifted to find what seemed most helpful—both for sustaining a writer's spirit and for suggesting new ways to get past a writing problem.

Fiction writing is a complex process. To teach it or learn it, we break it down into its component parts: beginning, middle, end, plot, scene, and so on. We look for ways to manage these elements with increasing skill. Yet every fine story adds up to so much more than the sum of its parts. I have been struck by how seldom we urge students to consider the complex ways elements of fiction *interconnect*. How might I do this in a book, while covering all the basics as well? I sought a nonhierarchical arrangement that would encourage free association, random discoveries, and the occasional surprise to inspire finer fictions.

This alphabetical arrangement was my solution. While entries are self-contained, they interconnect and resonate with one another in various ways. Cross-references encourage you to browse. As you search out remarks for *Background* under B, for example, you will happen upon the neighboring entry, *Beanbag Chair*. A glance at that may spark you to understand your task in a fresh way. And that insight may affect the fiction you are working on more positively than one more crank-up of its plot.

Now and then I refer to music as a help to better understand what writing fiction is about. I've found such analogies—which spring from my experience as an amateur musician—useful for deepening my own and my students' sense of how a narrative works.

Moments come to every writer, no matter how successful or how experienced, when we seek help—new ways of seeing a problem, tough-minded criticism, supportive advice. Those who work in relative isolation, far from other writers or teachers, occasionally long for a friendly, experienced voice at their elbow, a voice that will address the technical problem of the moment—so far removed from "What shall we have for dinner tonight?" I know. I have been such a writer. And sometimes, more than anything else, as the vision which impelled us fades and the words on the page fall so far short of what we imagined, we need inspiration to keep on trying.

I hope these ABC's will meet such needs and lead to an enlarged sense of your writerly freedom. Perhaps, in this not-so-simple alphabet, you will find what you need and also what you didn't know you needed. Serendipity is a value in fiction writing. See *Serendipity*.

A WAY IN

How do you find your way into a character, especially if his mode of operating, his very being, differs radically from you? Puts you off, in fact. Try several approaches to see what works: sketching (picture-making), daydreaming, writing dialogues and monologues, making lists of his hates and loves, of his secrets. When portrait painter Brett Whiteley was trying to capture the essence of his subject, the Nobel Prize-winning Australian novelist Patrick White—a prickly, elusive, complex subject if ever there was one—he asked White to list his loves and hates, then (to White's annoyance) kept the list pinned to his easel as White sat for him. Such an exercise may help you think about aspects of character.

For me, developing a character's history creates a major way in. As I invent "facts" and think about their implications, they pull me inside that other life. Or sometimes I begin to hear the characters speaking to one another in my head. Often a few words in that distinctive voice of a given character can get me started writing.

Contemporary short story writer Grace Paley, whose several collections include *Enormous Changes at the Last Minute* and *Later the Same Day,* claims her primary way in is through listening to the voices in her head. In a recent interview-discussion in *Green Mountains Review,* Paley was asked how she found her way into an unattractive male character. She declared that it wasn't a case of starting with—or even ending up with—sympathy. It was a case of wanting, as she put it, "to get into that voice so I can see why they're acting the way they are, doing what they're doing." Whatever provides *you* with a way in is something to note and develop for yourself.

Consider also at what pace you'll lead your reader into the story. Despite contemporary pressures to snare your reader immediately with a hook, don't underestimate the power of a subtler approach. You may decide to first prepare the world into which you'll thrust your characters.

Henry James offers us the leisurely approach in the opening of *The Portrait of a Lady*. First, he introduces us to a gathering of three for tea on the lawn of an English country house: an old man, two younger men, a dog at their feet. We learn the history of the house behind them before we even find out who they are: a father, a son, an English Lord. At least five pages (and a leisurely tea) pass before we have a clear sense of what James is setting in motion. Finally, the young woman from America, Isabel Archer, steps onto that prepared English stage to begin her adventure of self-discovery. In this case, setting constitutes a way into character.

One caution: If you arrange a leisurely entry into your story, by the end it must become clear that you were not merely winding up but from the beginning were in control of the shape, arranging things so your reader could feel a connection, deep and important, between end and beginning. See *Beginnings; Character; Frame.*

ABSTRACTION

Avoid abstract language. Select concrete and specific words to tell your story. The more you develop a character as an individual—full of contradictions, specific mannerisms of mind and body, conflicting desires—the greater your chance of creating a character the reader will connect with, a figure he will recognize as "human." Don't, as author, talk about truth, justice, liberty. (Perhaps one of your characters will, but that's another matter. You will create a context so the reader knows how to take his words.) Your task is not to preach truth, goodness, or beauty but to create it through the carefully orchestrated lie of fiction, which may ultimately lead to a deeper truth.

Fiction thrives in a concrete world. See *Detail; Senses; Specific.*

ACTION

Action always involves character change. A character must be in a different place—emotionally, psychologically—at the end of the story from where he was at the beginning. The change may be as subtle as a shift in understanding, as momentous (but quiet) as the loss of a final chance to change. Though the consequences of action are external and visible, the origin of change is always interior. In his *Writing in General and the Short Story in Particular, Esquire* fiction editor Rust Hills offers this rule: *action alters character in fiction.*

Connect *agent* and action in your writing mind. Do not connect *victim* and action. A character struck down by fate is not an agent. Sometimes a writer sets out to show how a character stands no chance against the circumstances that engulf him. Choice is not possible, let alone even a minor triumph. This won't make a satisfying story because any reader wants a ray of hope, some sense of possibility, however slight, to carry her through a book.

Let's say your hero—we'll call him Frederick—suffers a deep loss. He's a virtuoso pianist and he loses his right arm. Through the course of subsequent events, Frederick develops a new attitude toward his loss. That process, that action, opens new possibilities for him. He suffers failures, gives some disastrous concerts, survives bad reviews, and gradually masters the repertoire for left hand. In so doing he transforms his sense of the art that engages him. He even develops a new audience. Though the action manifests itself in Frederick's altered behavior, the source of that behavior is interior. He becomes the agent of his own renewal.

Action does not, therefore, simply mean movement—"Sylvia leapt from the chair and rushed from the room"—although it may involve movement, gesture, physical change, and reaction. Shooting, stabbing, yelling, bombing do not constitute action in fiction—unless thought, choice, perplexity, or frustration animate those activities.

The habitual gestures and movements of a character, his little daily and hourly rituals, help define him. Let's consider a story opening that goes like this:

> When Rob gets up in the morning he always checks his answering machine before he washes his face. Still in his pajamas, he staggers to the office, looks for the telltale flickering red light. If there's no message, his day is off to a bad start.

Rob's movements here help to define his character. Perhaps he's a workaholic; perhaps he's a terribly lonely man, longing for at least that flickering light of connection. By such bits you build a sense of him. Rust Hill calls these habits of a character, in their smaller and larger patterns, "fixed action" to distinguish from "moving action"—that chain of change that impels a narrative forward. "Fixed action" helps to convey character; "moving action" pushes the story forward. In the overall story pattern, as Hills puts it, "moving action alters fixed action."

Action stems from choice, decision, results in some kind of discovery, leads to new choices, decisions. Even if the heroine throws herself beneath a train in the end—like Anna Karenina, the eponymous heroine in Leo Tolstoy's classic study of adultery's consequences—as readers, we avidly follow her tortuous path as she makes her choices, because Tolstoy convinces us that those choices are "in character," and the end toward which they finally lead is "right."

Decision and consequent discovery are central to action. Decision generates discovery. Our one-armed pianist discovers a new repertoire and in himself a new capacity and interest. The subsequent decision to concertize leads him to the discovery of new pitfalls on stage.

As you work out the pattern of events that will dramatize this process, ask yourself: What is the most crucial moment, or sequence of moments, of change for my character? What does that reveal about him? How do I make it show clearly? These questions will help you select scenes. See *Change; Irony.*

ADDICTIONS

Addictions of several kinds threaten fiction writers.

1. Support from writing workshops. Writers function on a fragile psychic platform. We crave reassurance and fear rejection. We need response to our work. We want to find out if we're connecting with anyone out there, if what we're saying is even comprehensible. This anxiety afflicts all writers.

Positive responses from those close at hand—teacher, classmates—can comfort. And distract. Such responses may help sustain motivation to write, but I have known students who would go from workshop to workshop seeking immediate return on their writing, yet stop short of sending anything out. A rejection slip lacks the warmth of other writers at a roundtable discussing the effectiveness of our prose. Much can be learned from such discussions, but at a certain point a real writer needs to let go of workshop support and launch out into the depths of self-sustained writing.

2. Beginnings. Catching one idea and mistaking it for more than it is. One bright idea does not a story make.

3. The idea of writing, of being a writer, as opposed to the daily grind of actually putting words on paper and exposing them to public view.

4. The sound of one's own voice.

5. Perfection. Endless revising, the inability to let go.

Valuable addictions for fiction writers: writing, listening, reflecting, writing, people-watching, writing, silence, writing. I abstain from discussion of obvious addictions: alcohol, drugs, television. Writing fiction is enough of a trip. See *Grandma*.

ADJECTIVES

Adjectives can dilute attention and distract a reader. The power in an English sentence lies in its nouns and verbs. You can often gain clarity and precision by deleting adjectives. Be sensitive to their placement. In the following opening paragraph of the great nineteenth-century Russian storyteller Anton Chekhov's "The Lady with the Pet Dog," note his parsimony with adjectives.

> A new person, it was said, had appeared on the esplanade: a lady with a pet dog. Dmitry Dmitrich Gurov, who had spent a fortnight at Yalta and had got used to the place, had also begun to take an interest in new arrivals. As he sat in Vernet's confectionery shop, he saw, walking on the esplanade, a fair-haired young woman of medium height, wearing a beret; a white Pomeranian was trotting behind her.

"New" becomes important here, implying both a setting in which any new person is observed, and implying as well a particular observer, Gurov, the cynical, worldly and world-weary observer. Indeed, that tiny three-letter word even carries thematic import: the story that follows will explore how a man copes with discovery of something profoundly new to his experience—romantic love.

Strategically placed adjectives can define and deepen visual and sensory appeal. Character in fiction, as in life, is multiple and layered.

Adjectives may help you suggest some of that layering. See *Delete; Detail; Revising.*

ADVERBS

Adverbs are false friends. Avoid using them to suggest feeling: " 'Don't be ridiculous,' he said laughingly." (Is this possible?) " 'I didn't mean to hurt you,' she said apologetically." (Does your reader need it said two ways?) " 'That'll show you,' she shouted gleefully." Put yourself to the test. Place your character on the stage of your mind. Now, show your reader what the character is feeling by his gestures and movements.

> "You're being ridiculous," he said. He turned away and stared out the window.
> "I didn't mean to hurt you." She came near. He felt her touch his shoulder.

See *Dialogue; Gestures.*

AFFIRMATION

Fiction writers build bridges into the lives and thoughts of others, a lonely, arduous task without an excess of affirmation in the process. In her instructional book *Real Writing*, the New Zealand novelist, poet and dramatist Rachel McAlpine offers useful advice to writers. Stand before the mirror every morning, look yourself squarely in the eye, and say in the most persuasive, positive voice you can muster: "Today you are going to complete such and such a part of the fabulous book you're in the process of producing." Repeat it several times a day. It's good advice. See *Goal-Setting; Routine.*

AGE

Mozart wrote his first symphony at eight, composed an opera at twelve, and died at thirty-five. John Keats published his first volume of poems at twenty-two (1817), his final volume of poems in 1820, and died a year later at twenty-six. James Joyce's *Dubliners* was published when he was thirty-two. Leo Tolstoy wrote *Anna Karenina* between the ages of forty-five and forty-nine and his last book, *Resurrection*, at seventy-one. George Eliot's first novel, *Adam Bede*, came out when she was forty. Flannery O'Connor's first novel, *Wise Blood*, was published when she was twenty-seven and she died at thirty-nine. When Eudora Welty won the Pulitzer Prize for *The Optimist's Daughter* (1973), she was sixty-four.

What does all this tell us?

Nothing. *Carpe diem.*

If you think too much about age, it will drive you to despair. Contemporary American writer Harriet Doerr's highly praised novel *Stones for Ibarra* was published when she was seventy-four. Frances Trollope, the indefatigable mother of nineteenth-century British novelist Anthony, started writing when she was past fifty and went on to produce 138 volumes before she died.

There is a connection between age and perspective, youth and daring. I wouldn't push it, however. An eighty-year-old could write an electrifying book, a twenty-year-old could produce a dud. As long as you have your wits, energy, and motivation, forget about age.

A caution about managing age in stories: I have made silly errors in stories because I didn't take the time, first off, to figure out ages. It's hard (or was until recently) to make the pregnancy of a sixty-two-year-old woman convincing. Be careful. Avoid stereotypes of older characters: the limping old guy, the bluehaired lady, the pipe and rocking chair, wrinkles. Vitamin E, body culture, and reconstructive surgery achieve wonders these days. To say nothing of a NordicTrack.

ALLUSION

Allusions can add depth, irony, a new dimension to a line, a title. You may allude to a person, place, event, or to another literary work or passage. Allusion assumes your reader's familiarity with the reference and so, by a kind of shorthand, builds in extra resonance.

Handle allusion with care, though, and be realistic about the world of your reader. For example, "Sorrowful Mysteries" by contemporary short story writer Andre Dubus is a title that will resonate for only a handful of readers today. Don't count on your reader to be familiar with the Bible or the so-called Great Books.

In this example from her story "Point of Departure," National Book Award-nominee Hortense Calisher hopes her reader will remember Odysseus' faithful Penelope, at home every night unweaving the work of her day to stave off suitors until her husband's return.

Here, a man has just left, for the final time, the woman he's been most recently involved with.

> ... Perhaps it is worse for women, he thought, but they *are* the worst—all of them Penelopes, trying to weave you into the fabric of their lives, building on you in one way or the other until you have to get out from under.

In my story "Scoring," a middle-aged mother returns, with her college-visiting son, to her old university. They enter the office of a professor whose secure placement in the universe of learning casts long shadows on her lost connection with that world. Instantly cut by a sense of loss, she thinks:

> I have measured out my life in chocolate chips. Seasons of mothering have transformed me. I see Peter eye the book-shelves, the messy signs of mental industry. Where are the dreams, the ambitions of yesteryear? I'm being seduced again—by pipe-smell, the books, the atmosphere. . . . I always was a pushover. We have interrupted his work. What have I to show? It's standing there, with holes in its jeans.

How much does identifying T.S. Eliot's famous poem "The Love Song of J. Alfred Prufrock" behind those opening words matter? If the reader catches it, he may grasp a secondary irony in the speaker's voice, perhaps gather a deeper sense of what's at issue in the story.

Beware of making television or other topical allusions your reference point. "He looked like JR." How will the next generation of readers imagine a JR?

ALTERNATIVES

Don't be fooled by print on the page. Look "behind" it, as you read. The author *could* have chosen a different way to show something about a character, could have started in a different place, could have developed other scenes. What would have been gained? What lost? The pressure of those felt but unrealized alternatives increases tension and contributes to the reader's experience of a story. See *Choice; Read.*

AMBITION

A tiny ambition will produce a tiny book. Shoot for the stars. David Marr, in *Patrick White: A Life*, his biography of the Nobel laureate, reveals White's ambitions for the epic story of that troubling ego-maniac explorer, Voss: "I wanted to give my book the textures of music, the sensuousness of paint, to convey through the theme and character of *Voss* what Delacroix and Blake might have seen, what Mahler and Liszt might have heard."

Now I ask you.

ANECDOTE

Let me tell you what happened to me this morning.

As I poked through the racks in the women's clothing department in a small store, I overheard the salesman, Gerard. He's been there for years, knows his customers' tastes and sizes. A tall, overweight, kindlooking man, he was talking to a clerk as they stood around waiting for a customer. I kept my nose hidden in the clothes rack.

"Well, I'll have to sing 'The Old Rugged Cross' this Saturday," said Gerard. "That's what they want. They read about a funeral in the paper last week, saw I sang 'The Old Rugged Cross,' then they wanted it. When it comes to funerals, no imagination 'round here."

Clerk: "What time's the funeral at on Saturday?"

Gerard: "Ten. Funny thing. When they called me and asked me to sing, I said: 'Who's dead?' "

"Dave Richardson," they said.

"Dave Richardson!" I said. "Why he's been dead for ten years."

"He's been in the Veterans' Hospital," they said.

"Well, I hadn't seen him 'round for over ten years," I said. "Thought he was dead."

"No," they said. "He's been in the Veterans' Hospital. But I can tell you one thing. He's good and dead now."

It would take some doing to turn this into a story. The doing would involve, at the very least, developing the clerk and the salesman's background, perhaps establishing some relationship with Dave Richardson, some reason why the salesman wanted him dead, some irony in the fact that he's singing at the funeral. Even then, what have we at issue? Not much yet. One anecdote does not a story make. Once you're known as a fiction writer, you become a magnet for other peoples' anecdotes. "Just let me tell you what happened to me this morning. It would make a great story!"

Smile and take it with a grain of salt.

ANXIETY

Anxiety over possible rejection has kept many a good writer from submitting her work. Anxiety over finishing is a special hazard if you're writing a novel. How will I ever reach the end? Anxiety over what people in your immediate world—parents, children, uncles, aunts, friends, colleagues—will think can inhibit you. Anxiety that you may be on the wrong track, in a novel or a story. I could go on, but why make you anxious over anxiety? Generally, writers' anxieties center on time (I've started this trilogy—how long will it take to complete it?), money (what will I live on in the meantime?), talent (do I have enough?).

A particularly virulent virus of anxiety causes the Elsewhere Disease whose primary symptom is a nagging voice that says: "If only I lived somewhere else, or inhabited some other life, I'd have material for fiction." See *Background; Elsewhere; You.*

ARRANGING

You are the Great Arranger. You arrange words in a sentence, sentences in a paragraph, paragraphs into a story; make and arrange scenes, images, symbols, foreshadowings, clues: you do it all, and then make it look almost accidental. You decide beginnings, middles, ends, just desserts. You dish it out, withhold it. Every bit of arranging matters.

A few less obvious kinds of arranging you may find particularly troublesome:

1. Arranging for sequence, physical or temporal:

Physical: Getting the movements right in activities such as bike-riding, dancing, ice skating, can be tricky. I always have to go back and unsnarl my sequences lest my bikerider get off the bike before he puts on the brake.

Andre Dubus—author of stories, novellas, novels and essays—is especially good at getting movements in a physical sequence right, with a care and slow rhythm that sometimes approaches a kind of verbal ballet. In the following excerpt from his novel *Voices from the Moon*, father and daughter dance a slow jitterbug together. Dubus choreographs the long dance passage carefully and concludes it:

> They moved apart, holding both hands, then raised their arms and turned from each other, back-to-back, their twisting hands touching, then he took her right with his left, and they danced sideways, back and forth in their rectangle, to the faster beat. At the song's end he swirled with her, then dipped, his left arm supporting her back as beside her he bent his forward knee and leaned with it, as though to kneel. He pulled her up, and held her, and they danced slowly, silently, to "Little Girl Blue."

Temporal: You may choose to tell your story in chronological order or not, but always your reader needs to understand how the something happening now relates temporally to events that preceded and those that will follow. If you choose to arrange things non-linearly, be careful where you place clues.

2. Arranging for emphasis: The final spot in a sentence, a paragraph, or a story carries special weight. Compare the following two selections. In the first, I simply make a general statement in passive voice. The second, from short story writer and novelist Joanne Greenberg's "Introduction to Seismology," elaborates basically the same statement, in specific terms, with strong verbs, arranged to lead to the surprise, single-word climax and conclusion.

> Many disasters and mysterious happenings are caused by the earth's movement.
>
> versus
>
> The earth moves, shifts, goes to putty or quicksand, slops, heaves, shoots mountains, cleaves asunder, pulls sink holes, and drops canyons sometimes in a day. When he was in college and studying geology, he was sometimes kept awake by the knowledge of the instability of what should be most stable of all: bedrock.

3. Arranging for pacing: Writers sometimes miss a chance to integrate character description with forward movement of a story. In these opening two sentences by American novelist and theorist John

Gardner in his story "Redemption," the narrator sets the story in motion and conveys the inner state of his protagonist.

One day in April—a clear, blue day when there were crocuses in bloom—Jack Hawthorne ran over and killed his brother, David. Even in the last moment he could have prevented his brother's death by slamming on the tractor brakes, easily in reach for all the shortness of his legs; but he was unable to think, or, rather, thought unclearly, and so watched it happen, as he would again and again watch it happen in his mind, with nearly undiminished intensity and clarity, all his life.

Such economy matters especially in the short story with its demands for compression and direction. Once you understand what you're about, what your subject really is, and where your story is going, arranging becomes rearranging to sustain and deepen interest, to make direction clearer, to clarify climax, heighten tension.

The following paragraph closes chapter one of Jane Austen's famous novel *Pride and Prejudice*, about the Bennet family and their five daughters of marriagable age. These deft sentences illustrate masterly arrangement for variety, emphasis, and ironic tone of voice.

Mr. Bennet was so odd a mixture of quick parts, sarcastic humour, reserve, and caprice, that the experience of three and twenty years had been insufficient to make his wife understand his character. *Her* mind was less difficult to develop. She was a woman of mean understanding, little information, and uncertain temper. When she was discontented she fancied herself nervous. The business of her life was to get her daughters married; its solace was visiting and news.

A caution: While you must master English grammar and syntax, *your* designs in arranging and rearranging units of your story may differ from those in grammar texts which urge straightforwardness and clarity. In presenting a fictive situation, you may aim to conceal rather than reveal. Likewise, in orchestrating a climax, your goal may be to delay it as long as tolerable for the reader, to increase suspense. You often choose to present the act *before* the narrative elaboration of the act, thereby reversing the normal sequence of cause and effect.

Rearranging presumes distance and a sense of design. You need distance from material to see its units, rather than feel its flow. Distance enables you to see; seeing enables you to rearrange. As you work, you may feel a contradiction between these two. In the end you want a seamless garment, not one that reveals every stitch. A writer too anxious to "go with the flow," may resist this advice to pull back and look, rearrange. Resist at your peril.

Finally, through arranging and rearranging parts of your story, you are seeking to make light fall in just the right places, so that it suggests shadows along with light. This notion comes from Irish fiction writer Frank O'Connor, in his classic study of the short story, *The Lonely Voice*. Hold it in mind as you rearrange for best effect. See *Density; Revising; Scene*.

ART

Art has the power to command our attention. It enables us to see or hear something in a new or different way. It alters our perceptions, modifies our sensibility, transforms our capacities for feeling. Through a mysterious interplay with receptive minds and hearts, works of art can change us.

Writers have only words to accomplish this daunting end. We choose them with care. As Isaac Bashevis Singer puts it in the introduction to his *The Collected Stories of Isaac Bashevis Singer*, literary art "has the magical power of merging causality with purpose, doubt with faith, the passions of the flesh with the yearnings of the soul."

This is what we seek to achieve as fiction writers—this uniting of opposites to satisfy both mind and heart while illuminating some small part of life's mystery. In the last analysis, art transcends its definitions. See *Attention; Dangers; Language; Paradox*.

ARTIFICE

Although many entries in these ABC's assume fiction aims to make a structure so transparent that the reader sees *through* it, as through clear glass, into the world of the fiction, some writers aim for the opposite: to expose the skeleton of the narrative, to turn the secrets of fiction-making inside out, so to speak. You might read *Tom Jones* or *Tristram Shandy* to see how eighteenth-century British novelists Henry Fielding and Laurence Sterne played with this technique, reminding their readers that the story is merely fiction, not life. More recently, the influential writer and theorist John Barth, in his much-anthologized story "Lost in the Funhouse," creates a tale about a boy trying to piece himself together in the funhouse of adolescence and simultaneously weaves a piece about the process of fictionalizing. You may wish to experiment with this approach, but be warned: to do so successfully requires literary sophistication, not naiveté.

AS IF (AS THOUGH)

These two little words can open up interior dimensions of a character, or the implications of a situation, and offer your reader a sudden glimpse into larger and deeper worlds hidden behind the words of the story. In the following example from Don DeLillo's award-winning novel *White Noise*, the narrator describes a very small child, his son Wilder, who at last—for no evident reason—has stopped crying.

> They watched him with something like awe. Nearly seven straight hours of serious crying. It was as though he'd just returned from a period of wandering in some remote and holy place, in sand barrens or snowy ranges—a place where things are said, sights are seen, distances reached which we in our ordinary toil can only regard with the mingled reverence and wonder we hold in reserve for feats of the most sublime and difficult dimensions.

"As if" and "as though" lead your reader to participate in another's act of imagining, whether that of the narrator or of a character in the story. A narrator often uses "as if" or "as though" to nudge the reader past merely visualizing a character, to imagine that character from within, consider his motivations or inhibitions. In the following description, a grieving young man watches a snowfall in the mountains of southern Bavaria as he mourns his lost wife and son. American writer Mark Helprin uses "as if" to usher us inside the protagonist of his short story "The Schreuderspitze."

> He sat for hours watching the snow, feeling as if he were part of it, as if the diminution of his body were great progress, as if such lightening would lessen his sorrow and bring him to the high rim of things he had not seen before, things that would help him and show him what to do and make him proud just for coming upon them.

Do you want your reader merely to visualize your character (itself an achievement) or to go further and see into him or her? See *Metaphor; Simile.*

ASSOCIATION

To exploit the power of association, cultivate inner quiet. Let your imagination roam, collect, discover connections. Sorting out comes later. Don't hold back from following your powers of imaginative association. You'll be surprised. See *Buried; Clustering.*

ATTENTION

In *The Book of Laughter and Forgetting*, a daring novel that blends essay, philosophical inquiry, anecdote, and narrative experiment, Czech author Milan Kundera says: "All man's life among men is nothing more than a battle for the ears of others."

You are working to seduce a reader's attention. All the technical devices presented in this book are just that: strategies to secure and sustain the attention of a reader. Imagine a hot summer day. Your potential reader is lying outside in a hammock. She's sleepy. She tries to hold open a book propped on her chest. Sun shines through the trees, warming her. The hammock swings to a slight rhythm. Warm. Ummm. Sleepy. Ummmm. Just a hair's breadth from ZZZZZZZZZ. Uh oh. That's *your book* that keeps slipping! See *Art.*

ATTITUDE

Writing fiction involves coming to terms with your attitude toward basic puzzles in life, the big ones: loss, grief, waste, betrayal, faith, money, greed, etc. This ongoing process will filter through your fiction. Not that your fiction is a handy, inexpensive soapbox. You may choose to study a character engaged in actions you abhor: deceit, betrayal, murder. If you are religious, you may want to study a relentlessly secular mentality. If you are faithful in love, you may wish to explore promiscuity. To do this successfully you need a fair degree of self-knowledge about your attitudes. This may be why some experienced fiction writers suggest you not write a novel until you're past thirty. Nonsense. Try when you want to. See *A Way In; Self-Knowledge.*

AUDIENCE

The question is often asked by students and by interviewers: What audience did you have in mind while you were writing this? I can identify two distinguishable, though overlapping stages. In the beginning, the rough-draft stage, my audience is myself: What am I trying to say here? How do I get the words onto the page? How do I show what I'm trying to show? What is that, anyhow? The process is fluid, exploratory, tentative. I take a long time to discover what I'm actually writing.

After several rewrites, I begin to bear down on the material in another way—as if I were an impersonal reader. Come at this cold. Assume nothing. Does the story make sense? What kind of sense? Could an intelligent, sympathetic reader (ah, I begin to imagine a reader) find insight, pleasure, meaning in this? If I dropped out this or that, could he catch the meaning? Would it be clearer to him with a transition added? An imagined audience is becoming a reality, beginning to exert pressure on the material. I want to reach that audience; my aim is bridge-building, not bafflement. Therefore I summon the courage to be ruthless and critical. See *Beanbag Chair; Exposure; Revising.*

AUTOBIOGRAPHY

A friend meets you on the street with a gleam in her eye: "I've just finished reading your book, and I know who that was on page twenty-seven. It was Mary Lou, wasn't it?" Be prepared. They're always wrong, because a character can't duplicate a real-life person and if you tried to you were on the wrong track. In any attempt to write autobiographical fiction, considerations of design, sequence, and holding your reader's interest invariably enter in, to say nothing of memory's will to recreate the past in some new pattern to meet your present needs. So don't worry too much about the inevitable "identifying" that will go on.

In *Afterthought*, Irish novelist and literary critic Elizabeth Bowen's book of essays on writing, she offers a telling metaphor for autobiographical fiction that fails. Bowen compares it to soap bubbles children blow from pipes. Some bubbles float off into the air, free and lovely, while others hang over the lip of the pipe, refusing to disengage. The stuck limp bubble hanging there is like autobiographical fiction that doesn't work. Successful autobiographical fiction leaves the breath of its maker, floats free and whole into the universe, a radiant sphere.

We aim to create and send forth that self-contained iridescent world, a new and beautiful bubble of words afloat in the universe of art. See *Distortion*.

AVOIDING

Suddenly it's crucial to do dishes, clean out files, write a letter, read the latest issue of *Harper's*—for inspiration, of course. Every writer knows the problem, only too well. Writing is hard work. Picking up the pen, turning on the computer, getting down to it, facing the question of where to go from where you left off yesterday. Oh yes, now, where was I? Who were those characters anyway? A writer is one who writes. How inventive we become when faced with that work. Welcome to the human race.

The issue is how to avoid avoiding. Trick yourself by setting a short-term goal. Reread yesterday's work to hear the voice. Look at your bankbook. Glue yourself to the chair. See *Count; Routine*.

BACKGROUND

"What background do I need to become a fiction writer?" beginning writers often ask anxiously. My reply: (1) Do you have a thorough grasp of the language you're writing in and a delight in exploring its resources—grammar, syntax, metaphor, symbol, rhythm? (2) Does reading fiction give you great pleasure? Does it excite you? If so, that will help carry you past prophecies of doom: "Books are on the way out." "There's no money in it." "Your life is too dull." "You should travel first." "Why not become an accountant and find security?"

Beware the Exotic Dream: "If I could just have a hot affair in the Bahamas, or travel on the QE II, or spend a month in Tahiti, I'd have the background I need to write fiction." In 1974 I started my first book of stories with a subject clear in mind: I would try to bring to fictional life some of what I'd seen and learned in thirteen years of convent life. Hardly a riveting topic, you say. But I knew I'd had a rare opportunity to observe close up, in a confined space, many basic drives of human nature: desire, frustration, ambition, commitment, betrayal, love, loss, manipulation, greed. If Jane Austen could dramatize characters in a room, then why not I the convent parlor? That book came out in 1978 and I was surprised at the interest it generated.

So, *look* at what you already have in your background. Think hard on what you believe matters about people. Then: stay home, plumb your experience, observe, and write.

Questions about presenting background in your fiction: How much? When to deliver it? You start dealing with your characters at a spot in their lives where you are going to set them in motion. Yet your reader has to feel their prehistory, somehow. Sometimes direct presentation is the best way.

In the following excerpt from Richard Russo's best-selling novel *Nobody's Fool*, we learn in summary form the background of Sully, the unemployed boarder with Miss Beryl, the shrewd octogenarian and former schoolteacher through whose viewpoint the description is delivered.

> Miss Beryl smiled . . . and it occurred to her, not for the first time, that those who thought of stupid people as literal were dead wrong. Some of the least gifted of her eighth-graders had always had a gift for colorful metaphor. It was literal truth they couldn't grasp, and so it was with Sully. He had been among the first students she'd ever taught in North Bath, and his IQ tests had revealed a host of aptitudes that the boy himself appeared bent on contradicting. Throughout his life a case study underachiever, Sully—people still remarked—was nobody's fool, a phrase that Sully no doubt appreciated without ever sensing its literal application—that at sixty, he was divorced from his own wife, carrying on halfheartedly with another man's, estranged from his son, devoid of self-knowledge, badly crippled and virtually unemployable—all of which he stubbornly confused with independence.

Many contemporary authors are niggardly with backgrounds of their characters. It is the moment, the now, that counts, and that very absence of background may illumine a character's limitations, or the constraints of the narrow stage on which he moves.

Your question as a writer is threefold: (1) How much do I need to know about my character's background? (2) How much does my reader need to know? (3) How shall I deliver it? See *Character; Dialogue; Scene.*

BEANBAG CHAIR

I offer this homely analogy aware that, as with all analogies, it sags. As you move through writing a story, something carries you—an inchoate sense, a pressure, of something that needs to be realized, told. At a certain point you move beyond first or fifth draft and develop a deeper sense of what you're about. You begin to shape the story. Snip, snap, cut, paste, move, cut, rearrange.

What guides your hand? You have units, elements of fiction to deal with; you have a flowing story to achieve. But something else is at work in you. Some unseen sense enables your shaping hand—now tentative, now certain. How to understand it?

Imagine a huge beanbag. You wish to make it into a kind of chair, a specially designed chair, to receive and support a specific body. An invisible body. You've never seen the body, but you're somehow deeply familiar with it. You've come now to the end of the umpteenth revision of your novel. Suddenly you sense that the end is awkward, heavy. Too many beans there. Could you shift some?

You set about shifting around elements—here a scene, there a description—once more. The proportion of space defined by the arrangement of beans is somehow off. You just *know* it. This lumpy thing could accommodate only a seriously deformed monster. No place for an elbow. No width for the fanny. Nothing to support a tired neck.

With a renewed sense of that forever-invisible body, you begin again to shove things around, judging now how comfortable the thigh would be, the bottom, the back. And finally, voilà, the finished chair, ready to hold that body. The articulated shape is just right—comfy, supportive, well-proportioned. Elegant even, if a bean bag can be elegant. You *recognize* it. There it sits at last, the defined invisible form in terms of which, against which, because of which you have persisted, rearranged, cut, and shaped.

The body never appears. It never will. But its known and felt presence has animated your every move. See *Design.*

BEGINNINGS

A glimpsed face, a remembered dream fragment, a newspaper item, a conversation overheard, the quality of light against a building, a half-buried memory, a sharp hurt, the shape of a cloud: story beginnings surround us, fly by waiting to be caught. All writing is, as Henry James remarked in the preface to his novel *The Portrait of a Lady,* "use." He urges the writer to develop an alert readiness to "catch" those "windblown germs" that "are floated into our minds by the current of life."

Trust your instincts about what attracts you and seems to matter in the human situation.

A few technical notes on actual (as opposed to remote) beginnings of fiction: The beginning *sets the story in motion*. It establishes the tone of voice in which the tale will be told, the angle from which it will be told, who the main characters are, what they're up to. Something is set in motion and generates a sense of anticipation in the reader.

First drafts often start too early. It's like the pitcher winding up at the mound. All those antics: spitting on the ball, eyeing the bases, posturing, catching signals. The story begins when the ball leaves his mitt.

When I started a story called "Remembrance Day," I was pretty clear about my subject but got overinvolved in windup. I wanted to write about the troubling question of connection with one's own country when you have lived away from it for a number of years. Though based on my own experience of living for years in Canada, I decided to make this the story of a pacifist during the Vietnam era who goes to Canada, lives there for years, and finds himself tied to that other country in deep ways: wife, children, in-laws, community, job. I would focus on the Veteran's Day ceremony on November 11 to which he'd take his father-in-law, a veteran, and his son, a Cub Scout, both of whom had a role in the ceremony.

I began by showing the father, Ace, at home, upstairs with his son, looking for the misplaced toggle to complete the Cub Scout uniform, then going downstairs, helping "Pops" into his coat, saying good-bye to his wife Camille, finally setting out into the cold November rain for the Veteran's Day Service. I wanted to explore his range of ambiguous reactions and feelings to the service and his own situation. I got bogged down.

Some months later, 4,000 miles from home, as I was sitting alone in a restaurant in Victoria, British Columbia, the real beginning came to me. I lopped off about two pages—all the preliminaries—and started right in. Ace was arguing with himself.

> "Not *exile*. Too pretentious a word." This he says in his mel-
> lower moments.
> "By God, it's exile."
> This in his harsher moments, usually to himself. Because

Camille—blessed with that softer rounder temperament, that way of deflecting, of demurring, that throws into relief his claims as just so much show-off—Camille would understand and she wouldn't. Mostly wouldn't.

This is a harsher moment, right now, as he pushes along beside Pops in the freezing rain, down the hill, cheeks stung by November wind, holding Jimmie's hand.

Yes, definitely. Harsher.

Lead on, Ace, toward the Cenotaph. New word, Cenotaph. New ceremony: eleventh hour of the eleventh day of the eleventh month. . . . New and not new. When was it new to remember the war dead?

I'd found my beginning. I hoped that now it would dramatize Ace's dilemma and interest the reader from the start.

Some writers shoot you right into the story, such as Nobel prize-winning novelist Toni Morrison in the beginning of *Jazz*.

Sth, I know that woman. She used to live with a flock of birds on Lenox Avenue. Know her husband, too. He fell for an eighteen-year-old girl with one of those deepdown, spooky loves that made him so sad and happy he shot her just to keep the feeling going. When the woman, her name is Violet, went to the funeral to see the girl and cut her dead face they threw her to the floor and out of the church. She ran, then, through all that snow, and when she got back to her apartment she took the birds from their cages and set them out the windows to freeze or fly, including the parrot that said, "I love you."

Others take a much more leisurely approach. With every story you begin all over again, because it's never the same twice. How a story begins influences everything that comes after. See *A Way In*.

BELIEF

Believe that what you have to say matters. This may require "a willing suspension of disbelief"—a phrase coined by Romantic poet Samuel Taylor Coleridge to refer to the reader's peculiar state of mind as he reads. I apply it here to the writer's state of mind in undertaking a story. You may have to push aside, ignore, fight against niggling doubts, failures of belief in your own talent. If you don't believe in yourself as a writer, no one else will.

BODY LANGUAGE

When you're in a room full of people, watch their body language. Consider what it conceals, reveals, suggests. You can sometimes intensify a scene by opposing a character's body language to her words. For example:

> "You know you're free to come and go as you wish," she said. But he saw that she leaned against the door frame, her careless posture blocking his only possible exit. While she spoke, she tapped her brightly manicured nails against the frame.

See *Adverbs; Dialogue; Gestures.*

BOOKS

Modernist writer Franz Kafka, in a letter to his friend Oskar Pollak, said, "A book should be an axe to the frozen sea within us." I love that quotation. It suggests both the power of books and our own need to be invaded by their strange magic. Do you love the feel of a book, its cover, binding, paper, smell, weight in the hand? See *Promise; Read.*

BRAINSTORMING

Brainstorming can be a useful technique for coming unstuck. Keep a colored sheet of paper by you as you work and jot down all your questions, your odd ideas. Let the list grow without worrying about it as you write. Practice clustering. Sit in a chair, relax, close your eyes, let your characters on to the quiet stage of your mind. Watch them move about, engage with each other. Don't push them. Listen. See what they do and say. See *Alternatives; Clustering; Grandma.*

BREATHE

"Let the music breathe!" urges the piano teacher to the tense back of his student. It's a subtle skill that comes partly from feeling, and being, in control of the material and partly from relaxing. Letting inner tension go. Then you can become a bit playful and that cramped feeling drops away. In writing, this combination of security and playfulness usually comes after numerous drafts. It makes all the difference to the voice coming from the page. See *Tone; Voice*.

BRIDGES

Your fiction is a bridge. It spans the abyss, chaos. It leads your reader to another place where chaos is controlled and shaped. It is made of words, only words. It could collapse. Watch it! As the Italian novelist Italo Calvino put it in his book of writing theory titled *Six Memos for the Next Millennium*:

> The word connects the visible trace with the invisible thing, the absent thing, the thing that is desired or feared, like a frail emergency bridge flung over the abyss.

Actually, your bridge-building is double: to the reader, and to hidden parts of yourself, past and present. To build these bridges requires refined engineering skills. Any number of things may impede that process. The power of your fiction will rest partly on internal bridge-building: forging connections with feelings and incidents, long past, deeply buried. See *Anxiety; Buried*.

BRIEFING

How tempting (and how much easier!) to tell a reader something than to show him. In his *The Screenwriters' Workbook*, Syd Field describes how he and his colleagues who wrote and produced television documentaries in the sixties had one rule: "Never tell people what they're seeing." Their motto was "Don't say what you show."

"Why it's a sea gull," she exclaimed in recognition.

See how insulting that sentence is to a reader? See *Scene; Showing (vs. Telling)*.

BURIED

The most powerful sources of fiction are deeply buried in our own experience. Handle your excavating tools gently but firmly. Dig deep. Seek out the Carthage of your soul. Don't avoid a straight look at pain. The strange. The inexplicable. The incongruous. The coincidental. Explore the area around the bits you uncover. What feelings—

contradictory, baffling—are attached? No incident arises alone, unencumbered. Look at the stuff it drags along with it—that bit of dirt, that odd-shaped half-image, that shard of pain. What can you do with that? Are you willing to use it? If not, why not? If so, how? See *Association; Exposure.*

CARE

Care about your characters. If you don't, no one else will. Let their motives, hang-ups, choices, and omissions haunt you waking and sleeping. It will show in your fiction. Since fiction dramatizes a pattern of character change, something is always at stake for your characters. The level of caring you develop toward your fictional characters will depend on several things: (1) how *you* assess the value of what's at stake for your character; (2) how deeply you understand what motivates your characters' choices; (3) how much room you leave them in your musing imagination to work out their roles in your fiction. To care about your characters, you need to connect with them at a fairly deep level. This does not mean you necessarily approve of their actions. It means, rather, that you can find a significant point of connection with them. If, for example, you are developing the character of a serial killer as William Trevor does in his novel of an innocent Irish girl's fate, *Felicia's Journey*, you find some angle that will illumine, at least partially, the mystery of that being, the dimensions of his need.

CHANGE

Change is essential to narrative. You draw a picture through concrete details, but in the course of the telling some part of the picture has to change. Your character, therefore, must be capable of change. And those changes must seem plausible to your most critical reader. Change does not necessarily involve physical movement. I can sit absolutely still and change my way of seeing. Nor does it mean rearranging the scenery. I can attend a meeting where the wallpaper is new and potted plants have been brought in, but the characters at the meeting remain, in their essences, more fixed than the potted plants. Change means a shift in the way characters see and respond to their situation.

What are the sources of a capacity to change? You need to know this about your character. What makes us inflexible on some points and willing to change on others? Think about background.

Don't be fooled by the glamour of external events. They may signal the consequences of change, but mere events or incidents will feel hollow to your reader if they are not connected to the character by a circuit of understanding you have developed and conveyed. In her book *Writing Fiction: A Guide to Narrative Craft*, author and teacher Janet Burroway offers this helpful analysis of the difference between change, movement, event, and action.

> When a wife picks up a cup of coffee, this is mere event. If she finds that the lipstick on the cup is not her shade, that is a dramatic event, a *discovery*; it makes a difference. She makes a *decision* to fling it at the woman wearing the Cherry Ice mouth. Flinging it is a *deed*, but this changes nothing of itself until the second character's realization that she has been hit. Or suppose instead the first woman has an *accident*, hitting her wrist against the mantelpiece as she raises the cup to fling it. No change has been made in the character until her *discovery* that the coffee is spreading across her white skirt—and so on.

As you read fiction, isolate moments of decision and discovery. As you write, try to find the crucial moment of character change. What precedes it? What results from it? Identify a significant moment of change in your own life. Analyze the preparation that led up to it, enabling you to change.

When you come to the end of your story or novel in first draft, ask how all the major characters have changed. Can you name the change in a single sentence? What is its significance? What triggered it? Is he or she aware of it? How does he or she view it? How would actions your character might initiate now, at the end of the story, differ from those at the beginning? See *Action; Character(s); Choice; Questions.*

CHAOS

How on earth do we make "sense" out of life's randomness and seeming chaos? Henry James compares the novelist's task to that of a needleworker choosing which holes to push the threaded needle through in order to yield the desired design. Making such choices can be excruciating.

Are you feeling overwhelmed by the sheer multiplicity of options implicit in your material? Try this exercise: Take a small unit of time, the time it takes, say, to iron a shirt, to change a bicycle tire, to pump a tank of gas, and show your character changing significantly in the course of that very limited unit of time. Working with a small unit of time can be an antidote to the sense of flux, infinite possibility, randomness, chaos, that besets and paralyzes any writer at times. See *Constraints; Limits.*

CHARACTER(S)

History is peopled with memorable fictional characters: Emma Bovary, Gustave Flaubert's frustrated housewife who chooses adultery as escape from tedium in the provinces in the novel *Madame Bovary*; Heathcliff, Emily Brontë's vengeful lover-figure in *Wuthering Heights*, whose passion destroys lives and loves around him; James Joyce's hero in *Ulysses*, Leopold Bloom, who moves through the streets of Dublin absorbing its smells and sights, longing for confirmation as father and lover. Great characters stay with us, perhaps because we recognize in them some part of ourselves, even a deeply buried part, just a sliver. The place to start thinking about character, in general and in particular, is in your own experience: What do you, as an adult people-watcher, already know about human beings? *Lots.* (1) There is always more to the other person than you can see. (2) A person's words may conceal or reveal what he feels—or a little of both. (3) His actions spring from motives that are complex, often unfathomable, sometimes disguised even from himself. (4) No two people will agree in every detail in their view of a third party. (5) Though at times it may seem doubtful, given the right situation, most people are capable of astonishing changes. (6) A person's reading of others and of situations is conditioned by experience, education, background, genetic inheritance. No one else sees images, events, or people exactly as you do. All this will play into your treatment of character in fiction.

What are your basic tools to render characters alive, whole, believable, and interesting?

1. *Naming.* Decide names sooner rather than later. Names help stimulate writerly imaginations.

2. *Appearance.* In describing your characters, aim to be specific and concrete. Appeal to the senses. Bear in mind, as well, that in presenting a character's appearance, the narrator may be barely felt or rather strongly felt.

Compare the following. In the first, I offer only external description.

> Her coffee-colored hair, neatly braided and pinned up to circle her head, framed a round, pale face, its light blue eyes set deep above a prim-looking mouth whose thin lips usually remained unsmiling.

In this example, I modify the picture, nudge the reader to interpret appearances, and throw in an allusion for good measure:

> She kept her coffee-colored hair in one long braid wound tightly round her head like the badge of an old-fashioned woman, someone of Puritan ancestry. Light blue eyes could change suddenly from sad to secretive to accusing, and left one confused. Her set-looking mouth, with its tightly sealed lips drawn now in a straight line, seemed to say that behind those sealed lips lay a secret she would reveal only at the Apocalypse, and perhaps not then.

Finally, a skillful writer can fuse a character's present appearance with an interpretation of his past. Let's infuse just a bit of history into the description above and deliver it from the point of view of her oldest son, now twenty.

> He had never been sure where he stood with her—an odd way to feel about your mother. Looking at her now, standing behind the pitted pine table he had sweated to strip and varnish when he was twelve, he felt himself twelve again—trying vainly to read his mother's eyes. Behind her, in the room whose door was closed, lay the body of his father, that stolid, savagely

stubborn man whose criticisms and put-downs she had borne with stoic manner and set lips these past how many years. Was she grieving? Or did those set lips hide relief, a sense of release—joy even, that she was still alive, and he wasn't?

3. *Movements, gestures, and body language.* Think of your character not only visually and in terms of her past, but imagine how she might act and react in the present moment.

She stood behind that table as if cast in stone. He saw that her left eyelid flickered a bit, but she held her head with its familiar pinned-up braids perfectly steady. Her hands, which she held clasped before her as if in prayer, looked old. Worn.

He saw from the wrinkles in the front of her dress that she was leaning slightly against the table. And the thumb of one hand began suddenly to rub back and forth against the other, as if she were readying herself to speak.

4. *Allusion.* It can play into conveying the essence of a character. For example, in the second description, under Appearance (number two above), I might have added that the woman described reminded her son of Hester Prynne from Nathaniel Hawthorne's novel *The Scarlet Letter*, thus associating the figure with sin, adultery, punishment, and the whole Puritan world Hawthorne depicts.

5. *Words, dialogue.* In addition to the conventional patterns of dialogue, you can illuminate one character by presenting two characters talking about a third. Imagine, for example, three women. They've been discussing whether or not Louisa should try to get pregnant. Louisa leaves the table in the restaurant to go to the ladies' room. Joanne and Roxy, both tired mothers of toddlers—Roxy pregnant again and suffering from morning sickness—look at each other:

"Think she'd make it?"

"She hasn't a clue, really," says Roxy, suppressing a burp. "But how can she?"

"She's got more support than you or I ever had."

"That might change when she's green in the morning and exhausted at night. Besides, she couldn't stand to lose her figure. Louisa's always been inordinately proud of her Scarlett O'Hara waistline. . . ."

"So has Robert."

"Shh. Here she comes."

Here, the reader gains double insight: into how Louisa's friends view her and how their minds work.

6. *Thoughts.* The point of view you choose will determine how, and whether, you present your character's thoughts. If point of view allows your narrator access to a character's thoughts, try to heighten tension by dramatizing the gap between his behavior and his thoughts. In the example above, we can imagine that when Louisa returns to her friends, the words they direct to her will not reveal their thoughts.

The discrepancy between what a character says and does, or between what he thinks and says, is an area rich with implication. Exploit it to build tension and intensify character revelation.

A few questions that may plague you in developing your characters:

1. *Whose story is it?* You may discover, as you write, or when you read your novel or story, that while you made it one person's story, you were actually drawn to develop another figure. Pay attention to that hint.

2. *How do you keep characters straight in your reader's mind* when they are only a passing part of a story and remain nameless? Give them a tag line, as great Southern storyteller Flannery O'Connor does in her "Everything that Rises Must Converge." Two nameless bus passengers are important to the developing action. She reminds us of them as "the woman with the protruding teeth" and "the woman with the canvas sandals."

3. *How much do you need to know about your characters?* You can't know too much. You can, however, get too involved at the beginning in figuring it all out. As you write, your characters make choices, move forward, react, speak, reveal themselves to you. Developing characters seems to involve two major stages, sometimes overlapping: (1) You invent their past and present: birth, home circumstances, parents, social setting, schooling, friends, hobbies, friends' views of them, work, boss, love life, basic attitudes, loves, hates, tensions—hidden and manifest, and so on. (2) You become intimately acquainted. Walk around with them. Imagine them doing little things—having a meal, brushing teeth, taking a shower, flirting, hanging out the laundry. Talk to them. Let them come to life for you. Relax. You've

got the facts down. Now the trick is to move beyond facts. This is the only way you'll reach the point where a character will move for you, and sometimes independently of you.

A few cautions: Leave room for your reader to interpret what he sees and draw his own conclusions. Don't feel you have to reveal everything about your character in the beginning. Withholding information can be important. Be alert to chances for side characters to comment on the main character's action or lack of it. Don't be afraid to create contradictions in your characters. We're all a bundle of contradictions.

Use your journal. Avoid having a character look in the mirror to convey to us what he looks like. It's a tired gimmick. Finally: if your character is based on you or someone you know, *alter* him. If he's strictly from observation, dig around to find an inner point of connection that will free you to be inside that character. See *Dialogue; Gap; Irony; Journal.*

CHOICE

Choice lies at the heart of action—to act or not to act. Do not unwittingly deny your characters that power. In reflecting on your characters' choices, however, weigh how deep and how real is the freedom that underlies those choices. Do you aim to represent actual freedom or to qualify it ironically in context? You might tell the story of a jockey's stressful rise to fortune, for example, his strenuous training, personal sacrifices, and ultimate success in a breath-stopping race. You might also place that narrative action within a larger context illustrating how invisible (to him) powers in the horse business world actually manipulated his victories. His individual acts of choice might be real enough, but context qualifies all. See *Action; Attitude; Irony.*

CLICHÉ

A cliché means a stereotype, a slug of type which holds an entire phrase. A writer thinking in clichés is just assembling such slugs, and is therefore sluggish of mind.

> Ladies and gentlemen
> in this day and age
> the bottom line is
> life is no bed of roses.

Sometimes we use phrases because they are handy and fill a need. Native speakers of every language learn expressions, or idioms, that do not make sense literally and may puzzle a child or foreign visitor:

> You're losing your figure.
> The trees are turning beautifully this fall.

Some of these phrases are metaphors that have become dull with time: the leaves of the trees are turning (changing color). The writer may think the phrase adds flavor but in fact its imagery does not affect anyone. To "toe the line" means to stand in a row and measure up to discipline, but it is often written "tow the line" because it seems vaguely to mean to share in a hard, common task. What is the temperature range of a cool cucumber?

Many story situations can seem clichés in a larger sense: strangers when we met, the barefoot boy and his trusty spaniel, victimized by my parents, whitecoated scientist asks, "Will it work?" Nonetheless, skillful writers do make fascinating, lively variations on well-worn materials: young lovers discover themselves as they discover each other; a forbidding stranger rides into town.

You may choose to exploit clichés for character revelation. For example, a figure parroting clichés shows both her mental limitations and her snobbishness, as in Flannery O'Connor's "Everything That Rises Must Converge," where the mother repeats "Rome wasn't built in a day," and reassures her son (who's seething with antipathy toward her) "Of course, . . . if you know who you are you can go anywhere. . . ." See *Character(s); Metaphor.*

CLIMAX

At some point, probably not in your earlier drafts, you may find it useful to identify the climax of your story, the place where tensions tighten and the action turns to critically affect your main character. At this point, you need to be clear about what is at stake for your characters. It's easy to muffle a climax, especially if it is subtle. Place your climax or turning point close to the end of a short story. No matter how subtle or quiet it may be, as is sometimes the case in a contemporary short story, the reader needs to feel the shift of tensions that signals an ending soon to come. Otherwise, he will feel shortchanged. See *Closure; Ending; Tension.*

CLOSURE

At least some elements of a story have to come together in an important way for a reader to be satisfied at the end. You need not, in the manner of some nineteenth-century novels, project into what happened "ever after." You do need to bring together enough story elements in the ending to generate a sense of "Oh yes, I see" in your reader. Readers' tastes differ, of course, but the desire for some sense of closure is justified and, perhaps, universal. This demand might spring from our unconscious protest at the openness of life itself. Please, writer, at least for a brief while, enclose me in your magic circle.

Beware of the tendency in early drafts to make the ending too abrupt. Here is an example of closure from "Easy in the Islands," the title story of the National Book Award-winning collection by Bob Shacochis. The protagonist, Rillman, living in a foreign country, has faced numerous perplexities over how to dispose of his mother's dead body. Beleaguered by bureaucratic tangles and suspicions, he finally takes the body up in a plane with a friend, a pilot. Shacochis might simply have written, "I saw it drop, part the waves, disappear." Instead, he chose to pull together meanings and metaphors from earlier in the story and thereby rounds off our sense of the narrator while providing a strong sense of closure.

> He looked down at the endless water, waves struggling and receding, the small carnation of foam marking his mother's entrance into the sea, saw her, through the medium of refraction, unwrapped from her shroud, naked and washed, crawling with pure, unlabored motion down the shafts of light and beyond their farthest reach, thawed into suppleness, small glass bubbles, the cold air of her last breath, expelled past her white lips, nuzzled by unnamed fish. . . . Now she was a perfect swimmer, free of the air and the boundaries of the living, darkness passing through darkness, down, down, to kiss the silt of the ocean floor, to touch the bottom of the world with dead fingers.

CLUES

As you manage the narrative and move characters through a plausible action toward the ending, plant clues strategically. Dialogue, imagery, situations, and choices all work to suggest, implicitly, what is to come. You withhold some information, deliver other. For the ending to be convincing, you must select your clues carefully, bury them with care. See *Arranging; Foreshadowing; Suspense.*

CLUSTERING

This is a useful creativity technique, especially if you're stuck. Take a sheet of paper. In the center of the sheet write a word that answers this question: "What feeling am I trying to get at in this scene?" Be quiet and honest. Suppose the feeling is anger. Write that in the center of the page and circle it. Now let your mind, memory, imagination go. Write quickly, jotting down randomly around the central word all your associations: for example, an image—"dark frown"; a remembered epithet—"You rat!"; a scene from the past—Mt. St. Helens erupting; anything. Circle those words and connect them by lines to the central emotion you are mining. These lines and circles will quickly grow into a spider web of associations connected with *anger*: bits of talk, scenes, people, images, moments long buried from your past. Stare at this web. Walk around. Come back to it. Add more. Walk around again. Some idea or image in this web may be useful.

Now go back to your story. You may be surprised by the turn it takes. Something important may have been triggered from below the level of your conscious control, the source of real power in fiction. Welcome it. Free association has long been a friend to the fiction writer.

For more detailed treatment of clustering see Gabriele Rico's book *Writing the Natural Way.* See *Association; Design.*

COINCIDENCE

Your heroine is having a crisis. Her husband needs a lung transplant, her daughter has been caught shoplifting, and the money for groceries has run out. Suddenly, in the nick of time, someone's lung arrives, the police call to say the daughter is innocent (mistaken identity), and the heroine's mother drops dead leaving scads of money to put bread on the table. It won't wash. However, as Canadian poet John V. Hicks points out in his instructive book *Side Glances, Notes on the Writer's Craft,* if you begin your story with a coincidence, it then simply becomes the premise of the story and you are suddenly launched.

> That the day grandma left us a million coincided with dad's operation and my discovery of a lookalike in town seems to me now just one of those incredible coincidences that occasionally happen and change your life forever. . . .

Charles Dickens and other Victorian novelists frequently exploited coincidence. Shakespeare's tragedies move toward inevitable ends through means that are often accidental or coincidental. How often in fiction a figure just "happens" to overhear a crucial remark which changes the course of the narrative. Early in Jane Austen's novel *Pride and Prejudice*, Elizabeth Bennet, the heroine, just "happens" to overhear Mr. Darcy's comment that he finds Elizabeth "tolerable; but not handsome enough to tempt *me*." Elizabeth's feelings toward him thereafter, we are told, were not very "cordial." Without that coincidence, that seemingly accidental conjunction of person, time, place, and incident, Austen would have had to dream up some other coincidence of sufficient significance to delay the ultimate union of Darcy and Elizabeth.

The challenge is to make the chance meeting, the crucial overheard remark, work in some important way for the meaning of the story, not just to get you through a tough spot when you couldn't think of anything else to do. Why is this coincidence important to your character's development? If your story is comic, you can heighten humor by playing up coincidence. Many a hero rides through his narrative on a structure of ingeniously wrought coincidences. See Henry Fielding's eighteenth-century novel *Tom Jones* for an extended example.

Coincidence in life and fiction provide an antidote to life's randomness. See *Convincing; Surprise; Truth*.

COMMENTARY

Commentary, a favored technique of nineteenth-century fiction writers, is today often considered an indulgence. Commentary refers to the intrusion of the author's or narrator's voice, from outside a character or scene, making a general observation often only tenuously linked to the matter at hand.

In the following excerpt, nineteenth-century British novelist William Makepeace Thackeray comments on Becky Sharp, the wily heroine of his classic *Vanity Fair*. A young woman of sharp wit and shrewd soul, she has at last left Chiswick Mall, the hated school where she has spent six miserable years. Of Becky, the narrator says:

> All the world used her ill, said this young misanthropist . . . and we may be pretty certain that the persons of either sex whom all this world treats ill, deserve entirely the treatment they get. The world is a looking-glass, and gives back to every man the reflection of his own face. Frown at it, and it will in turn look sourly upon you; laugh at it and with it, and it is a jolly companion; and so let all young persons take their choice.

Contemporary readers tend to be impatient with such moralizing, pseudo-philosophical comments. Asides like this interrupt narrative propulsion and prompt the questions: Whose voice is making the comment? Where does that voice come from? Outside the story or novel? Inside? See *Narrator; Point of View; Voice.*

COMPETENCE
Do you know if "it's" or "its" "all right" or "alright" to use "a lot" or "alot" of apostrophes? Do you "lie down" or "lay down" a book? Have you mastered the structures of English? Be honest. If your underpinnings are shaky, take steps to strengthen them. Get a good basic handbook of English and do the exercises. You have to learn to manage your hands and the basic scales before you can play the piano. As a writer, you have to know the resources of the language and be able to play with them. See *Background.*

COMPETITION
Competitiveness spurs some writers to produce. Other writers find it paralyzing. Since competition is a reality, you must deal with it effectively. Consider the following questions: How much does the opinion of others matter to you? How important is a sense of power?

If your driving desire is to produce a better story than so-and-so, you will only begin to grow when you forget so-and-so and focus on your story. A spirit of competitiveness will not sustain motivation, will not see you through the tough slog of getting good words onto paper. Only one kind of competition works: competing with yourself. See *Ambition; Self-Knowledge.*

COMPOST

Your accumulated experience is your own rich compost pile. Something organic is working there all the time. If a glimmer for a story comes upon you, note it, throw it in your compost box. Most writers carry a small pad or notebook with them all the time. If you later read that note, its vitality may surprise you, along with its power to draw to itself other glimmers that have grown in your imagination (and your journal) in the meantime. Although there's a lot of deliberate work ahead, real power resides in the original glimmer. Don't leave it too far behind as you work. Return to the original notion to plumb its significance.

COMPRESS

You cannot compress until you know what you're doing in a story.

Choosing what to omit is always tough. A good question to ask, later rather than earlier, is: How much can I make happen in this scene, this chapter, and still maintain narrative drive? Compression creates density in a story that is ripe. If it is not yet ripe—ready for cutting—compressing can result in a thin, unsatisfying story. See *Density; Enough; Knowing Your Subject.*

CONFLICT

Conflict springs from two opposing forces. Two dogs want the same bone. Elementary. These forces can be outer or inner, or both. Conflict is related to significance of outcome. Do not confuse it with adversity. Adversity is bad luck. Conflict develops when a character pushes back against something, within or without, that is pushing against him as he tries to move from point A to point B. If nothing inside or outside is pushing him back: no story. If he's ground down by adversity, circumstances, if the reader sees he has *no chance*: no story. Two elements must be present in his initial situation: the possibility of success in moving toward his goal and a certain instability in his basic situation.

Do not make achieving this goal too easy for your character. If you are hesitant to exploit possibilities for conflict in a scene, you may "suffer" from a background problem. You may have been too well trained to value harmonious social interaction, to softpedal possibilities of conflict.

Invariably, I have to go back and see in each scene what the potential for dramatizing conflict is, try to bring it out in the light, heighten and intensify it. Make opposites nastier, sharper, clearer. Study newspaper stories for those that contain interesting seeds of conflict. Observe indications of submerged or open conflict in the people around you. See *Scene; Showing (vs. Telling)*.

CONSEQUENCES

Decisions, made or unmade, carry consequences. Children dread them; adults live with them. The anticipation of consequences can paralyze or inhibit a character from action. I've known fine writers who can never bring themselves to send something out, so fearful are they of one consequence: rejection.

CONSISTENCY

Does your character need to be consistent? Most of us are quite consistent about our contradictions. See *Contradictions*.

CONSOLATIONS

Every author seeks consolation—a comfort to offset the pain—in the face of hard work followed by rejection or poor sales or harsh reviews. It's an old story. Samuel Johnson knew it well as a hack writer always aspiring for better in the middle of the eighteenth century. His *Rambler* essays, which appeared periodically in the newspaper, often return to the theme of disappointment and the mind's effort to find a way around it. He speaks eloquently to this point in Rambler No. 146 which appeared August 10, 1751.

> Many are the consolations with which the unhappy author endeavours to allay his vexation and fortify his patience. He has written with too little indulgence to the understanding of common readers. He has fallen upon an age in which solid knowledge and delicate refinement have given way to low merriment and idle buffoonery, and therefore no writer can hope for distinction who has any higher purpose than to raise laughter. He finds that his enemies, such as superiority will always raise, have been industrious, while his performance was in the press, to vilify and blast it, and that the bookseller whom he had resolved to enrich has rivals that obstruct the circulation of his copies. He at last reposes upon the consideration that the

noblest works of learning and genius have always made their way slowly against ignorance and prejudice, and that reputation which is never to be lost must be gradually obtained, as animals of longest life are observed not soon to attain their full stature and strength.

By such arts of voluntary delusion does every man endeavour to conceal his own unimportance from himself.

Some things never change.

CONSTRAINTS

No adult lives free of constraints. Identify the constraints that impede your character's freedom to act. Interior. Exterior. The reader must feel the pull of possibility and frustration as your characters move forward. As prolific story writer Damon Knight points out in his instructional book *Creating Short Fiction*, a character with no constraints, no limits on his possibilities for action is an impossible subject for fiction. On the other hand, a character who is totally constrained, as Knight illustrates it, at the bottom of a well with rocks piled high above him, cannot *move*. For a fiction, the constraints that operate technically are setting, character, and situation. For the character himself, of course, the constraints may be subtle, interior, complex. See *Background; Change; Character(s); Choice.*

CONTEMPT

Tacked to the wall in front of my desk is a small card yellow with age, that says:

> Contempt poisons.
> Sentimentality weakens.

I came to work one morning and found, in different handwriting and different color ink (whose hand is this, I think I know), written beneath the above:

> God forgives.

CONTINUITIES

A reader may observe continuities in your work that you're not aware of. Don't worry about it; they're probably there. Our subjects wear many disguises, but usually, over time, a thread of continuity runs through them. After a reading in Oregon, a man in the audience who had read other stories of mine said he'd noticed "leavetaking" as a repeated motif. Did I think that would be a thread woven through the narrative of my life? I had never thought of it. He was right.

What are the deepest continuities you can identify in your characters' lives? In your own? Is there an intriguing connection?

CONTRACT

In composing a story or novel you make a contract with your reader: "If you pay attention to these words I put before you, I will not bore or insult you. On the contrary, I'll lead you, pleasurably, through the eyes of another, to a deeper way of seeing life, your own life and that of others. You may laugh, cry, sympathize, judge, but whatever your response, it will carry with it an element of satisfaction that cannot be exactly duplicated in any other way." See *Promise; You.*

CONTRADICTIONS

Contradictions are the stuff of a fiction writer's life. Our working habits encompass contrary "oughts": we need to be passive, yet alert and active; involved, yet detached; receptive, yet critical; disciplined, yet relaxed; open-minded, yet focused. We need to honor the irrational as we seek a logical or plausible narrative line. We need to dramatize fragmentariness, yet discover connections. We need to listen to our characters; we need to manage them.

Consider your loves and hates, your continuities and contradictions. Then think about these in connection with your characters. See *A Way In; Consistency.*

CONTRIVED

A story feels contrived when the mechanics you're managing show through, or make themselves felt so the reader is more aware of them than of the pleasure of story. If you heap up so many images that they clot on the surface of the narrative, your reader may lose the sense of story. If shifts in point of view, discontinuities in chronology, or arrangements of coincidence outweigh the pleasure that straightforward storytelling can achieve, be careful.

On the other hand, you may be exploiting artifice. Your purpose may be precisely to expose the glass with its bubbles and shine, to illumine the artifice by revealing structural hijinks. If so, be sure you're smart enough and do not expect a large audience. See *Artifice; Innovation.*

CONVINCING

Why do some characters in their development and choices convince us as readers and others not? What enables a reader to believe what we tell him happened? The arrangement of words on a page. That's what.

My formula for this is: "the latent becomes manifest." By that I mean that the seeds of what gradually emerges in a character or a situation were there all along, cunningly planted by you. The flamboyant actress who seems incapable of living without the stage, suddenly—for reasons you've invented—demonstrates a "new" capacity to leave it forever and head for a new life. When you look back, you see hints of such a capacity, or a need for new self-definition. "The latent becomes manifest" applies to situation or character. What your reader sees by the end of the story was implicit in the material.

Look around. Do you see couples whose traumatic break-ups or unexpected choices reveal, viewed over the long haul, the emergence of what was actually there (though hidden) now coming to light?

COUNT

Count words and pages every writing day—which should be every day. It will give you a sense of progress and enable you to meet deadlines.

CUT

How painful it can be to cut a passage we have labored over. The discipline of cutting calls for a certain ruthlessness, as Gustave Flaubert, that merciless reviser, expressed in a letter to his beloved Louise, March 26, 1854.

> One must turn all the words over, on all their sides, and do like the fathers of Sparta, pitilessly cast those with crippled feet or narrow chests into the void.

This requires detachment, a developed critical sense, flexibility of mind, and genuine dedication to the possibilities of our art. See *Delete; Revising.*

DANGERS

Subtle dangers threaten a fiction writer's exercise of craft today. Anton Chekhov, in a letter to his brother, advises writers to avoid stereotypes and write with compassion. In his introduction to *The Collected Stories of Isaac Bashevis Singer*, the Nobel-Prize-winning fiction writer reminds us that our subject is "the basic and ever-changing nature of human relations." He warns writers against "pretentious rhetoric ... greed for money and quick recognition."

I would add a few other dangers that can deaden, derail, or diffuse the efforts of today's fiction writers: loss of faith that in a world of instant communication and quick fixes audiences can sustain interest in patiently examining "the basic and ever-changing nature of human relations"; reluctance to cut one's own verbiage; lack of objectivity about one's own talent; willingness to settle for easy answers rather than frame difficult questions. Stopping too soon can also be a major error—stopping, that is, before you have plumbed the depths of your material. If you stop too soon, neither you nor your reader will be satisfied by your fiction. It will feel, and be, superficial and incomplete. Sometimes the small touches of the final revision make all the difference to a story. See *Art*.

DEADLINES

Meet them.

DEFINING PLACE

Where do you find yourself at this moment? Look around. When you find yourself in a new place, it's a good idea, before the scales of familiarity render you half-seeing or blind, to jot down what you see. Here, for example, are my random journal notes made in 1987 in Bemidji, Minnesota, as I tried to define the feel of a new place and reflected on a new teaching experience.

> I am in the world of tow heads and Nordic cheekbones, wall-eyed pike and Chippewa pride, the world of Paul Bunyan, Lutheran piety. There are 7 Lutheran churches in this town. These are merely impressions. This is the North Country, 5 hours south of Winnipeg, 5 hours north of Minneapolis (where the action is), smack dab between Grand Forks and Grand Rapids (what's this need to name them "Grand"?). Here the waitress brings you coffee sans cream or milk, unless you specify. Submarines are hoagies. All parts of the university are linked by tunnels to protect students against bitter Minnesota winter. Cars can still drive on the Lake, though from shore it looks perilous. The season of legal ice fishing is here. Dressing up means fresh jeans. Occasionally I see a tie. Jackpines abound.
>
> Students arrive. Begin to knock. "I live 20 miles out of town in a one room house with 2 kids." "When I try to get time for myself my 6-year-old comes and sits outside the bedroom door and bangs against it. I'm tempted to get on the horse, fill the saddlebags, and ride away." New variations on a room of one's own. In the student Rendez-Vous room the walls show, in garish colors, Indians, early settlers, buffalo herds. Downtown, a cafe has a stagecoach painted on one wall. I'm told Minot, N.D., is where the hats change—from baseball caps to cowboy hats. Here they use sacks instead of bags, and everyone seems to say *git*.

Now, seven years later and two thousand or so miles distant, I catch glimmers of possible story material there, just peeping through. See *Journal*.

DELAY

The greater the tension you create by delay, the deeper your challenge to make the outcome of the narrative significant. You have to justify that delay to your reader. To manage delay efficiently, you need to know where the narrative is headed. You need, as well, to combine delay with complication. Delay alone is not enough to generate significant tension in a story. See *Arranging; Plotting; Suspense.*

DELETE

James Boswell, the biographer of Samuel Johnson, tells us in his *Life of Samuel Johnson* that he once asked Johnson's opinion of the writing of their contemporary Scottish historian, Dr. William Robertson. Johnson replied:

> I would say to Robertson what an old tutor of a college said to one of his pupils: "Read over your compositions, and where ever you meet with a passage which you think is particularly fine, strike it out."

This is painful advice, but to the point and useful.

DENSITY

Density consists of the maximum number of things going on at one time in any given sequence or scene. To create density, ask yourself the following questions: Is there more than one idea being developed in my story? Is there something at stake for more than one character? Is that "something" easily evaluated, or have I given my reader room to exercise his moral imagination? Have I limited myself to one sequential story line, or have I crossed two or more lines that resonate with each other in interesting ways?

Some like 'em fat, some like 'em thin, but everyone likes a story with more than one thing going on in it. See *Sausage; Two.*

DESCRIPTION

Description can pull the reader into a scene and deepen his insight into character, situation, relationships. Concreteness is the very breath of lively description, as you can see in this brief excerpt from "The Fisherman from Chihuahua," by the versatile Evan S. Connell. The narrator describes a new, mysterious customer arriving at a little Mexican restaurant in Santa Cruz.

> ... This new man was tall, very tall, six feet or more, and ... almost black in the manner of a sweat-stained saddle. He was handsome, silent, and perhaps forty years of age. Also he was

something of a dandy; his trousers, which were long and quite tight, revealed the fact that he was bowlegged, as befits certain types of men, and made one think of him easily riding a large fast horse, not necessarily toward a woman but in the direction of something more remote and mysterious. . . . Exceedingly short black boots of finest leather took in the cuffs of his narrow trousers. For a shirt he wore long-sleeved white silk unbuttoned to below the level of his nipples which themselves were vaguely visible. The hair of his chest was so luxuriant that an enameled crucifix there did not even rest on the skin.

Don't forget the other senses when you select concrete detail for description. In James Joyce's *Ulysses*, Buck Mulligan sees the "snot green" and "scrotum-tightening" sea as he looks at Dublin Bay and his buddy, Stephen Dedalus, remembers his mother coming to him in a dream after her death, "her wasted body within its loose brown graveclothes giving off an odour of wax and rosewood. . . ."

Details of place can suggest character and situation. Here is part of the description of a teenager's room from Canadian writer Alice Munro's "Circle of Prayer."

All the clothes she owned, it seemed, old and new, and clean and dirty, were scattered on the floor, on the chair, the desk, the dresser, even on the bed itself. . . . Dirty glasses, empty yogurt containers, school notes, a Tampax still in its wrapper, the stuffed snake and tiger Robin had had since before she went to school, a collage of pictures of her cat Sausage, who had been run over two years ago. Red and blue ribbons that she had won for jumping, or running, or throwing basketballs.

A useful exercise: describe a place inhabited by a person, and let the specific details of the place implicitly describe the inhabitant. Test this on a listener and challenge her to identify the inhabitant.

Descriptive detail, held within a specific point of view, can suggest both the situation and the sensibility of the character speaking. Below, Eleanor, a young mother in Hortense Calisher's story "The Rabbi's Daughter," tries to explain to her judgmental family why, for her trip to join her husband in a new town, she's put on her wedding dress.

"Oh, I don't know," she said. "It just felt gala. New Yorkish. Some people dress down for a trip. Others dress up—like me."

Staring at her own lap, though, at the bronze velveteen which had been her wedding dress, sensing the fur blob of hat insecure on her unprofessionally waved hair, shifting the shoes, faintly scuffed, which had been serving her for best for two years, she felt the sickening qualm, the frightful inner flush of the inappropriately dressed.

If you describe a landscape, be careful to follow the movement of an eye. In his celebrated novel *Swimming in the Volcano*, Bob Shacochis renders the view of an active volcano on the Caribbean island of St. Catherine as seen by his central perceiver, Mitchell Wilson, a view that is changing moment by moment. Notice how carefully Shacochis works to get the sequence right.

In time the light around them came from candles surging with a fresh draft, the gloom brightened and the nimbostratus that was on the mountain began to drag off the far rim and tear into pieces, first a white edge of sunlight, then a distant patch of milky blue that was both sea and sky, next the circling shape of the burnt crown, and then, as though a lid had been pried and removed, the immense bore of the volcano's crater, shattering any sense of human proportion.

When you revise, look critically at descriptive passages and ask: (1) Are they merely holding up forward movement of narrative? (2) Do they show us something besides themselves, i.e., are they connecting two or more elements of the fiction—character, setting, plot line, narrative voice, subject? (3) Does the choice of descriptive words dramatize some aspect of the narrator who voices them? See *Density; Foreshadowing; Narrator.*

DESIGN

E.L. Doctorow compared writing a novel to driving a car in the dark. You can see only so far ahead, but it's enough to get you to the end of your journey. (At least in first draft.) You may start with a plan or your design may emerge only after you've pushed through one or more rough drafts of your story or novel. Only when the overall design has begun to emerge can you start to shift parts around and shape the story. See *Beanbag Chair; Revising.*

DESIRE

We all inhabit the land of desire.

If you cannot understand a character from the inside, if you sense that your grasp of that character is too superficial, ask yourself *what does she want?* I've found it helpful to write out, *in first person*, what I desire *as that character*. What's keeping me from it—in myself, in others? What are my secrets? Who's in my way? How do I see myself? How does my desire connect with how other characters—friends, family, enemies, associates—see me. What do I allow them to see? Why?

Desire is a powerful motivator. It generates fantasy and sometimes launches action. If it does not, why not? The sources of inaction can become a story. See *Action; Character(s)*.

DETAIL

Writing teachers sometimes stress the awakening of the senses through exercises in concrete descriptive detail appealing to sight, touch, taste, hearing, smell. When you set about composing your own fictive worlds, however, the question will bedevil you: How much detail is enough? What makes a detail "apt"? In a letter to his brother Alexander, Anton Chekhov advises the writer to "seize upon the little particulars, grouping them in such a way that, in reading, when you shut your eyes, you get a picture."

William Faulkner does just that in the excerpt below, which introduces Miss Emily Grierson, the proud, uncompromisingly dated heroine of his short story "A Rose for Emily." Here, she enters a room to meet emissaries from her town's Board of Aldermen who have come to serve notice that she owes back taxes.

> They rose when she entered—a small, fat woman in black with a thin gold chain descending to her waist and vanishing into her belt, leaning on an ebony cane with a tarnished gold head. Her skeleton was small and spare; perhaps that was why what would have been merely plumpness in another was obesity in her. She looked bloated, like a body long submerged in motionless water, and of that pallid hue. Her eyes, lost in the fatty ridges of her face, looked like two small pieces of coal pressed into a lump of dough as they moved from one face to another while the visitors stated their errand.

Test yourself this way after you've written a descriptive passage. Can you "see" it? If you can put your descriptive detail in motion, so much the better. Notice that Faulkner's description begins and ends with movement. In the excerpt below, contemporary Australian novelist David Malouf uses motion to good effect. His novel about the gulf between aborigines and "civilization"—*Remembering Babylon*— opens with three children frightened by the approach of a mysterious, moving object, dazzling in the glare of a sweltering Australian afternoon.

> In the intense heat that made everything you looked at warp and glare, a fragment of ti-tree swamp, some bit of the land over there that was forbidden to them, had detached itself from the grey that made up the far side of the swamp, and in the shape more like a watery, heat-struck mirage than a thing of substance, elongated and airily indistinct, was bowling, leaping, flying towards them.

Both Malouf and Faulkner imbed details in a moment that implies someone *seeing* those details—a useful hint for energizing descriptive detail.

Despite what your high school English teacher may have told you in a well-intentioned effort to make your writing richer, less is often more. Leave something in the picture for your reader to supply.

If you are writing about a world unfamiliar to most readers (I have written stories, for example, about a convent, a penitentiary, and the world of the deaf), your judgment about how much detail is enough becomes trickier. You must give your reader enough to enable him to feel "inside" that world, but not so much that he feels overwhelmed. An editor's dispassionate eye can help here. See *Adjectives; Description*.

DETERMINATION

Lewis and Clark, the great American explorers who discovered a route to the Pacific Ocean, wrote every single day a record of where they were, what they saw and did—and maintained this schedule as they faced floods, accidents, storms, and illness. You, too, are on a journey of discovery. Staying at your desk, facing the blank page, finding first one word and then another requires great tenacity. Taming the wilderness of your own imagination and getting through the Rockies of fiction-making requires an explorer's determination. See *Inspiration; Serendipity; Will.*

DEVELOPMENT

For many writers the middle, or development, of their story is the most troublesome part. A few tricks may help you. Play the "what if" game with your characters. Make lists—of things in a room, of their hates and loves at the moment, of possible choices they face. Practice clustering. Visualize. See *Clustering; Plotting; Sequence; Structure.*

DIALOGUE

Dialogue looks easy to write—and isn't. Don't be fooled by all that white on the page. Some of Beethoven's most difficult piano passages exist on pages with a lot of white, not clotted with notes. Playing them involves mastering rhythm shifts, pauses, crescendos, diminuendos, rests, and more—with little to obscure your goofs. If you are playing with a partner, as I do, it means listening, as well, for the notes coming from the other side.

So it is with writing dialogue. You have to listen to what's not said as well as to what's said. Hear it in your head. When we talk to others, we dramatize ourselves. How we choose to do this varies greatly. Instinctively, we consider audience when we speak. Otherwise, we're boring. "Do you have new sunglasses?" asks my mother. "Cool shades, Mom," says my son.

Dialogue is a carefully structured exchange of words between characters. It accomplishes many goals, all important. It (1) moves the story forward; (2) dramatizes character; (3) communicates information about the past to the reader (expository material); (4) foreshadows; (5) establishes relationships between characters; (6) comments on the action of the story: "Never thought Joanne would make it as a body-builder, did you?" "Nope, but she says she's goin' on to compete in the Miss Nebraska competition next week."; (7) describes setting: "Can you believe the combination of junk in her room?" (8) connects scenes (by references to what has passed, what is to come); (9) develops conflict or suggests submerged conflict; (10) effects transitions; and (11) exposes or suggests motivation.

Points to remember about dialogue:

1. It is not conversation. It must be shaped to an end which is not simply "talk." Ordinary conversations often go nowhere, are merely an exchange of monologues, full of *um, uh,* and other space fillers. Some of this can be used only *if* it dramatizes character and advances action.

2. Dialogue often progresses by missed cues, speakers interacting, as Milan Kundera puts it in his *The Book of Laughter and Forgetting,* "in the perfect solidarity of perfect mutual misunderstanding." Two monologues beside one another, supposedly connecting with one another, actually just bouncing off one another.

3. Dialogue works best when loaded with implication. It is not necessary to say everything. As a story progresses, a reader gathers a sense of each character's inner life and therefore can fill in much that is not said.

4. Don't overdo dialect in dialogue. A little goes a long way. A few tag expressions or pronunciations suffice to create for your reader the basic impression of regional speech. Read Mark Twain's *The Adventures of Huckleberry Finn* for a deft use of dialect and Southern rural speech. In his explanatory note to the book, Twain says he uses eight different dialects, each studied and written with great care. Huck begins his story in this manner:

> You don't know about me, without you have read a book by the name of *The Adventures of Tom Sawyer,* but that ain't no matter. That book was made by Mr. Mark Twain, and he told the truth, mainly. . . . I never seen anybody but lied, one time or another, without it was Aunt Polly, or the widow, or maybe Mary.

5. Using summarized dialogue, sometimes called indirect discourse, instead of direct dialogue, may move your story along and still convey the sense of people talking to one another. In the following excerpt from Elizabeth Spencer's stunning novella *The Light in the Piazza,* Signor Naccarelli, hoping his son Fabrizio may win the hand of the American Mrs. Johnson's beautiful daughter Clara (who has a mental age of ten), invites them to attend a local celebration in Florence the next day.

> . . . he by chance had extra tickets and the seats were good. She must excuse it if his signora did not come; she was in mourning.

"Oh, I'm very sorry," said Mrs. Johnson.

He waved his hand. No matter. Her family in Naples was a large one; somebody was always dying. He sometimes wore the black band, but then someone might ask him who was dead and if he could not really remember? *Che figura!* His humor and laugh came and were over as fast as something being broken. "And now—you will come?"

Choosing summarized dialogue or direct dialogue influences pacing in a scene. You may find, on reviewing a scene, that parts of the dialogue are better cast in indirect discourse, to break up the dialogue and speed up the scene. Casting the crucial part of a scene in direct dialogue intensifies drama.

6. Beginning a story with dialogue can draw the reader immediately in because the moment your characters start to speak, your reader begins to imagine them. You need to provide pointers of time, place, and basic situation for the reader, however, so the dialogue does not exist in a vacuum.

7. Visualize your characters as they're talking. Then you'll remember to intersperse dialogue with movement and gesture, both of which may reinforce or play against their words.

8. Finally, if point of view denies your narrator access to your characters' thoughts, dialogue becomes your main vehicle for revealing or suggesting inner stress. See Ernest Hemingway's classic short story, "Hills Like White Elephants," where the reader is left to infer the situation—a young couple discussing an abortion—simply from dialogue.

9. We carry many voices in our heads—arguing, observing, commenting, judging, denying, imagining. Making clear to your reader the interplay of those voices requires careful attention and lots of revision.

Pitfalls to avoid in writing dialogue:

1. shapeless dialogue that oozes like a stunned jellyfish on the sand of the story:

"What're you gonna order?" asked Jocelyn.
"Dunno. Lemme see the menu."
"I've already made up my mind. Garlic fingers."

"My, they've garlic fingers with every order today. Do you really like garlic fingers?"

"Hi," said a young woman arriving at their table.

"Oh, Sue. Didn't know you were coming. This is Rob."

"Hi. Garlic fingers special today, Sue. Do you like them?"

Sue looked around at the crowded restaurant. Rob looked at the menu.

"Well, it's crowded." She hesitated. "Okay. I like garlic fingers."

No hype for garlic fingers can redeem rambling dialogue. There is nothing *at issue* here. Compare the following brief dialogue between Cajun cop Dave Robicheaux and a gangster Julie (Baby Feet) Balboni from James Lee Burke's *In the Electric Mist With Confederate Dead.* Years before, Robicheaux and Balboni knew each other as schoolkids. Now they meet while Robicheaux is on a case. Baby Feet and his entourage are staying at the Holiday Inn. Behind the encounter between Balboni and Robicheaux lies suspicion on both sides. We know this seemingly pointless dialogue is leading toward an ultimate showdown between the two men.

"What you up to, Dave? Somebody knock a pop fly over the swimming-pool wall?"

"I was just in the neighborhood. I heard you were back in town for a short visit."

"No kidding?"

"That's a fact."

"You were probably in the barbershop and somebody said, 'The Bone's in town,' and you thought, 'Boy, that's great news. I'll just go say hello to ole Feet.' "

"You're a famous man, Julie. Word gets around."

"And I'm just here for a short visit right?"

"Yeah, that's the word."

His eyes moved up and down my body. He smiled to himself and took a sip from a tall glass wrapped in a napkin, with shaved ice, fruit, and a tiny paper umbrella in it.

"You're a sheriff's detective now, I hear."

"On and off."

2. telegraphic, rushed dialogue:

Mike banged on the door and came in.
"You've gone bankrupt," he announced.
Marianne collapsed on the sofa. "When?"
"Just got the word. And you'll have to leave."
"I'll leave tomorrow."
"I've got the tickets."

3. unnatural, stilted, or stagey dialogue unless, of course, your purpose is to parody a character who's always on stage:

"I recollect reflecting that of a summer's eve an occasional auditory pleasure deriving from birdsong nearly undercut my melancholy."
"Oh, Richard, I comprehend your meaning."

4. inert dialogue—containing only expository information that you could better convey in straightforward exposition or summary:

"You remember Mary Jane who lived at 9 Milton Street and used to walk to school at age seven and then at age 10 her mother let her ride her bike and then she moved to Cincinnati."

5. a dazzling variety of adverbs modifying "said":

He said laughingly. (Impossible)
She whispered gleefully.
He murmured longingly.

OR

"He cried." "She sobbed." "He declared." "She argued."

As a rule, the simple word "said"—or no word, if the identity of the speaker is clear—suffices. See *A Way In; Voice.*

DIRECTION

The appearance of casualness and spontaneity in prose writing deceives. Behind that seemingly improvisational air lie hours of concentration; hard-won skill at turning out a sentence, a paragraph, a developed sense of narrative drive; a sensitivity to the possibilities of material at hand.

In a radio interview in Buenos Aires, that master of relaxed improvisation, jazz composer Duke Ellington, made a comment on this subject that applies to writers "playing" the language as well as to musicians playing their instruments.

Anyone who plays anything worth hearing knows what he's going to play, no matter whether he prepares a day ahead or a beat ahead. It has to be played with intent.

What Ellington calls "intent" may be compared to the writer's evolving sense of where a narrative is headed and how best to get there. Sustaining one's sense of "intent" through the necessary distractions of managing all the elements of fiction constitutes a major challenge. It is so easy to get lost. I find no substitute for leaving aside the manuscript and then returning to it again and again with a fresher eye and the following questions: Where is this going? What is this character growing toward? How does this scene or description suggest or foreshadow what is coming? Is this scene necessary or merely repetitive? Such questions can only be answered bit by bit as you compose a narrative. Your answers to them will change as you work, but it's important to keep asking them. See *Beanbag Chair; Questions; Revising.*

DISCONTINUITY

Contemporary readers can sustain a considerable degree of discontinuity in a narrative so long as you make your links or clues abundant enough and clear. Linear discontinuity can excite interest and heighten tension. If a body is discovered in chapter one, chapter two may go on to something else entirely, provided we eventually learn' about that body. Once you understand the basic line of your story, fool around with discontinuity for maximum surprise and effect. In the end you may decide to tell the story straightforwardly, but your writing of it will be improved by having explored and tested alternatives. See *Time.*

DISCOVERY

Moments of discovery are important. You can place them anywhere, even in the first line, as the premise from which the story flows. "Once I grasped that Josephine would never be what they call 'normal,' I knew I had a life task cut out for me." Stories that echo in the mind long afterward often close with a moment of discovery. It may cast a subtle or striking new light on all that has preceded and also a beam into the future, leaving the reader with a sense of what a character will be like "from now on."

In life itself, moments of real discovery come about through a process of thought-reflection-recognition about what has happened.

We all know the hours of only dim "seeing" that precede a moment when light strikes and suddenly we "get the real point" of what we've been struggling to say. Throughout the dimness, something besides pure grit keeps us going: an intuition of something yet to be found, waiting to be discovered. In his collection of essays *The Poetics of Music*, Igor Stravinsky, the great twentieth-century composer, makes a point which applies to the creative act of writing as well as to music-making.

> All creation presupposes at its origin a sort of appetite that is brought on by the foretaste of discovery. This foretaste of the creative act accompanies the intuitive grasp of an unknown entity already possessed but not yet intelligible, an entity that will not take definite shape except by the action of a constantly vigilant technique. For the true creator, possibilities of discovery lie all about him within his reach.

That "foretaste of discovery" drives a writer to continue when the going gets hard. Surely there's great possibility in this idea, he thinks, and pushes on, because he senses that form waiting to be discovered and realized, made beautifully intelligible, by his tools: words. See *Beanbag Chair; Exploration; Journal.*

DISPOSSESSION
Writing fiction is a process of dispossession. While it enables you to possess your own experience—an accomplishment not to be sniffed at—it frees you, as well, from attachment to that experience. When a story or novel is finally finished, its parting from you is akin to the parting of a grown child whom you now see as separate, different, warts and all. An adult. No longer tied to you, ready to make his way and claim his life in the wider world. See *Autobiography.*

DISTORTION
If you start your novel or story with ready-made material—a hunk of your past, remote or recent, that you wish to explore—beware of the

resistance you may feel when faced by the need to alter that material. You might think, "But that's the way it really was." We are all attached to our own experience and may feel deeply reluctant to distort it for the sake of "mere" fiction. This reluctance has sabotaged many a promising story by persuading a writer to suppress her sense of what shape the material requires.

Ask yourself: What is the emotional center in this scene, this chapter, this character? If you can identify this center, seek ways to manifest and illumine it through word and action. You may bypass the "but this is how it was" hurdle. See *Beanbag Chair; Memory.*

DISTRACTIONS

Ah, how insidious the human mind. You've just gotten into your writing project and you're bugged by a persistent distraction—another story, better than this one, another book, the next, and better, yet to come. Take a double attitude toward such distractions: (1) recognize that they may be important, that the playful, uncensored, freely imaginative part of your mind may be offering a promising germ for later on; or (2) realize it may just be human nature discouraged at the prospect of work. Jot distractions down, throw them into a box or put them in your journal, and get on with your present work.

This book, by the way, began as one huge ongoing distraction that persisted over years. See *Journal.*

DRAMA

Frank O'Connor, in his study of the modern short story, *The Lonely Voice*, offers the following summary of what constitutes drama in fiction:

> There are three necessary elements in a story—exposition, development, and drama. Exposition we may illustrate as "John Fortescue was a solicitor in the little town of X"; development as "One day Mrs. Fortescue told him she was about to leave him for another man"; and drama as "You will do nothing of the kind," he said.

Scenes are the most dramatic elements in fiction. Exposition and narrative links, though necessary, are not in themselves dramatic. See *Narrative; Narrator; Scene.*

DREAM

Identify your characters' dreams. And heed your own. Some writers claim they keep a notebook by the side of their bed. (I don't.)

Within a fiction, dreaming or fantasizing can be an important aspect of character presentation. In the excerpt below from William Trevor's short story "Access to the Children," Malcolmson, a divorced man, separated from the warmth and comforts of domesticity, is spending a boring, lonely Sunday with his two daughters. As he watches TV with them and drinks, he dreams about what will happen later, when he brings them back to their mother.

> He had a definite feeling that today she'd ask him in, both of them pretending a worry over Susie's obsession with death. They'd sit together while the children splashed about in the bathroom; she'd offer him gin and lime-juice, their favourite drink, a drink known as a Gimlet, as once he'd told her. They'd drink it out of the green glasses they'd bought, years ago, in Italy. The girls would dry themselves and come to say good-night. They'd go to bed. He might tell them a story, or she would. 'Stay to supper,' she would say, and while she made risotto he would go to her and kiss her hair . . .

By showing this fantasy midway in the story, Trevor accomplishes several goals. He enlarges our understanding of Malcolmson—his desires, his need to fantasize—and deepens the sadness of the end, when Malcolmson's wife tells him she'll marry another. By a kind of shorthand available to the fiction maker—cutting into the dreams and fantasies of a character and framing that by the literal action of the story—the reader is left with a sense of the ongoing, not to be re-solved, loneliness of the man and the end of his marriage.

Handle the writing of dreams with caution. Waking up from a dream, discovering "it was all a dream," never makes a satisfying ending for a contemporary realistic fiction. Inserting a dream into a narrative to avoid devising the next logical narrative step will merely dilute narrative power. Dreams are not simple to construct in fiction. They follow their own internal logic and to succeed in fiction they must resonate with the other elements of the story. Otherwise, a dream becomes a mere contrivance or a way to duck hard work. See *As If (As Though)*.

EAR

Listen to the voices in your head. When you think your manuscript is ready, read it aloud. Unintended clots of sound or rhythm may emerge. This is one benefit of giving public readings. Invariably, as I prepare for or give a reading, I catch some glaring infelicity in my prose.

Recently, in going over a copyedited story of mine, I came across: "From her ear dangled a tangle of silver." It's easy to miss such internal rhymes. Or to bestow names whose similarity will confuse the reader: *Ava and Ada and Albert live together. Ava loves Albert but Albert loves Ada.* Or to indulge in too many sentences of one kind. *He stopped. He saw it. He wondered. He went to the window. He wanted it.* As you work for economy and clarity, keep listening. Is your prose muddy? Tangled? Too simple? One step removed from *See Spot Run?*

Writers who achieve a conversational tone that speaks directly to the reader have learned not to trust the eye alone. They have cultivated an ear sensitive to the rhythms of prose. Writers who focus on too many questions at once—where are my characters? what time is it? what happens next?—often fail to listen for the narrative voice their words are creating.

All great instrumentalists develop the habit of listening to the music they're making *as they make it.* Nineteenth-century composer Frédéric Chopin advised his students to practice in the dark so they could hear their own music, undistracted. You have the advantage of time to revise, hear, and weigh each word on the scale of your ear-in-training. What looks good may sound bad.

Once you know what you're talking about and have found the voice that feels right, deciding which words will best carry it is largely a matter of ear. See *Economy; Listening; Voice.*

ECHO

Our heads are echo chambers. Half-recognized, a niggling shadow at the edge of memory can drive us daft. Recognized, it offers peculiar satisfaction.

Writers count on the echo effect in constructing narrative. We offer the reader the pleasure of hearing echoes as she reads. Figures, gestures, images, situations, scenes, characters, and single words all participate in the symphony of echoes we orchestrate.

Not only can echoes vibrate throughout a story or novel to reinforce internal meanings, skillful fiction awakens echoes in the reader's own experience. This play of echoes creates a major bridge into the reader. *Oh yes, I've felt something like that, harbored a similar thought in a dark corner of my mind.* Such an echo to "real life" may be glancing, oblique, or overwhelmingly familiar and intimate. Echo, both within fiction and within the reader, becomes a powerful tool, and a subtle one.

For a virtuoso performance of echoes—figures, images, and situations that play off against each other in mysterious ways—you might look at renowned German writer Thomas Mann's classic novella *Death in Venice*, which traces the gradual decline and surrender of a rigidly self-controlled artist to the seduction of youthful beauty.

Early on, Aschenbach, the famous writer, is described as one who always lived like a closed fist, never in the relaxed manner of an open hand hanging loosely down from the back of a chair. After his return from an abortive attempt to leave Venice, he sits by his hotel window watching the object of his passion, the boy Tadzio, on the beach below:

> . . . he raised his head, and with both hands, hanging limp over the chair-arms, he described a slow motion, palms outward, a lifting and turning movement, as though to indicate a wider embrace. It was a gesture of welcome, a calm and deliberate acceptance of what might come.

That slow simple gesture acquires weight because it echoes earlier images of Aschenbach. The reader knows now that he has given in, that his physical and moral disintegration is inevitable.

Physical position holds rich possibilities for echo effects. We follow Aschenbach in his many positions—from sitting rigidly at his writing desk in the beginning, to sitting in the deck chair on the ship to Venice, to the black-upholstered gondola chair, to the reclining chair on the sand by the sea, to his chair by the window, to his final placement on the sand when he rests his head against the beach chair and dies in the presence of his obsession.

Check your compositions. Have you placed characters in physical positions that carry metaphorical implications? Do you have a character frequently raising windows, opening doors? Could that have significance? Does another character habitually hurry past others, ignoring them? If you can lift to consciousness such repeated motifs you may uncover a buried strand of meaning in your story—or even in the overall design of several stories or novels.

Take a break and listen, quietly, to a favorite piece of music. Listen only for echoes—instrumental, harmonic, melodic, whatever you can hear. The opening of Beethoven's Fifth Symphony. Or his Piano Concerto Number 4, the First Movement. Can you make something like that happen in your prose?

ECONOMY

To suggest more with less, that is the great challenge. Economy comes with craft, a sense of design. Some writers produce a lot of copy and whittle it down to size. I have sent forests to my wastebasket. Some writers revise mentally before the pen strikes the page. You will find your own method. As you revise, these questions may help.

(1) Could you devise a brief scene that would say more than lengthy exposition of background material? Instead of several paragraphs describing the feelings of Simon for his employer, for example, show them in a scene with submerged, or exposed, tensions. (2) Could you shift from third- to first-person point of view and pull the reader deeper into the fiction with no loss of substance and a significant gain of intensity? (3) Could you take your reader deeply and directly into the twistings of a character's mind as she remembers, considers, associates, moves through time and place? (4) Could you feed in important expository material unobtrusively throughout the fiction, rather than leaving it in clumps? Recently, I shortened a story by seven pages

largely through this strategy. Before I could do this, however, I had to understand two basic points: (a) the most important subject of the story and (b) the arrangement of scenes in the story.

Using metaphors and allusions may help you suggest more with less. Metaphor aids economy by suggesting more than is actually said. Allusions imply another dimension of reference that often resonates ironically, or playfully, with larger thematic meanings in a story. Consider the following use of allusion by Robert Stone in his novel *Outerbridge Reach*.

Owen Browne, the hero of the novel, is sailing alone in a race around the world. His boat and the winds have failed him. He decides to record a fake log of his trip, leave behind a false record.

> Three weeks of that would have borne him most of the way to Australia. He marked his imaginary daily positions on the chart, the road not taken.

For allusions to work effectively, however, they must connect with a range of knowledge in the reader. If a reader doesn't know Robert Frost's "The Road Not Taken," the allusion above adds nothing.

Finally, sentence structure critically affects compression and economy in prose. Look at the compressed, rich implications of feeling and situation Robert Stone conveys in the simple sentence below, which depicts Owen Browne walking through Penn Station:

> Confident and watchful, he passed unthreatened among the hovering poor.

Economy is not always the highest good in fiction-making. We enjoy hearing patterns of sound and meaning play against one another in interesting ways. In his essay "An Approach to Style," in William Strunk Jr. and E.B. White's *The Elements of Style*, essayist and editor E.B. White remarks that Lincoln could have saved words and spared his listeners some work if he had simply said "Eighty-seven years ago" at the beginning of the Gettysburg Address. Obviously, he was guided by considerations other than mere economy: the sound of his words, their weight in the minds of his hearers, how that would reinforce the solemnity of the occasion.

In your mania to cut, do not fail to consider other goals, above all, what are you trying to achieve? See *Delete; Ear; Revising*.

ELEMENTS

Characters, setting, dialogue, plot, narrative, exposition. These are the elements of fiction. We've heard of them many times, seen them analyzed in how-to-write books. You can buy outlines of the one hundred basic plots—your bouillon cube to start your own fictional stew.

These visible, obvious elements matter. But other, less obvious elements that are less easy to analyze and describe are equally important to fiction-making: identifying your story's real subject, moving the story forward, resolving its tensions in some significant way, talking to your reader as to an intelligent being, believing that your story matters. Always, in good fiction, the whole is more than the sum of its parts. This is why you need, again and again, to stand back from the large elements of craft, look at the fiction you've made, and see what you think it adds up to *as a whole*. See *Organic*.

ELSEWHERE

Milan Kundera titled his novelistic study of a young poet *Life Is Elsewhere*. This witty title touches a fiction writer's anxiety. I live in a town so small that cars slow down to see who you are as you walk along the street. If I walk one block away from home, I might encounter munching cows. Surely real life is elsewhere. The anxious writer might be tempted to say, "If only I could get away from all this, be stimulated, see something more exciting, and write."

On the other hand, I've lived in Chicago, Washington, D.C., and New York. The sheer pressure of all those lives out there—so smart, so connected, so "with it," so competitive, so achieving—can work its own kind of "elsewhere" disease. The anxious writer cries out, "If only I could get away from all this, be alone, free of stimulating distractions, hole up, and write."

I'm convinced no "elsewhere" is the perfect place for writing fiction. Needs vary. Temperaments vary. The essential "here" for a writer is the quiet space of the imagination, an inner space where you can sift through and transform what you have experienced and observed, whether munching cows or munching humans.

Once, sitting in a Boston restaurant, relieved to be surrounded however briefly by urban noise, energy, sophistication, and a menu blessedly devoid of canned peas and gravy, I overheard a chic young woman say earnestly across the table to her female companion: "You don't know how I long to live away from all this, just a quiet place, far away, a little house, a picket fence." I almost choked.

EMERGING

The word "emerging" can refer to the way you gradually discover your story—its plot, its theme, its characters, its ultimate meaning. As the story emerges, it's a bit like watching a building slowly appear through fog. "Emerging" can apply, as well, to the way the story reveals itself to your reader, but I am concerned here with how the word relates to the writer's experience.

Some writers encourage their stories to "grow" over a period of time before attempting to order them into a defined structure. If you work best this way, you may profit from author and teacher Dorothy Bryant's instructional book *Writing a Novel*. She describes in detail her method of writing ideas, thoughts and images, on three-by-five index cards, letting them accumulate over time, often as she's working on other projects. She reads and rereads them until latent connections and possibilities grow clearer. She then sorts her cards into piles, shuffling them again and again to keep the developing material in a fluid state, to stop it from rigidifying too early. Her scheme allows time for a subject to show itself, to gather weight.

After the piles have been established and shuffled enough, the narrative line will emerge and she then begins to organize the novel's structure. British novelist Hilary Mantel describes a similar method in her essay "Growing a Tale." "Little words breed," she claims. That statement rings true for me. It is, in fact, an underlying premise of this book. Sometimes it takes only a word to unlock the imagination.

Some writers would find such a process trying and unhelpful. It boils down to figuring out which way works best to uncork the writer in you, which method will help you elicit the most from your developing materials. See *Journal; Self-Knowledge*.

EMOTION

"I was moved by your story." A high compliment.

Think about anger, grief, fear, love, lust, betrayal, hurt: the big emotions we work through in the course of life. Don't hesitate to press the situations you are writing about. Bleed from them depths of emotion hidden there. Instead of saying, or thinking "she was angry," seek the exact cutting edge of that anger. Is it a knife threatening to slice her in two? Or is it heavy, leaden, a weight that diffuses through her daily, that she feels the moment she wakes but can't name? Seek out new metaphors for deep emotions.

Ask yourself, again and again, what is the emotional center of this scene, this chapter, this encounter? What metaphors would convey that? See *Association; Feelings; Metaphor.*

EMPHASIS

Find ways to italicize without italics.

The following paragraph from chapter one of Leo Tolstoy's classic novel *Anna Karenina* describes Stepan Arkadyevitch as he confronts his wife's anger the morning after she's learned of his infidelities. Notice how carefully Tolstoy uses delay, lists alternatives, holds the reader in suspense until the final two words.

> There happened to him at that instant what does happen to people when they are unexpectedly caught in something very disgraceful. He did not succeed in adapting his face to the position in which he was placed towards his wife by the discovery of his fault. Instead of being hurt, denying, defending himself, begging forgiveness, instead of remaining indifferent even— anything would have been better than what he did do—his face utterly involuntarily (reflex spinal action, reflected Stepan Arkadyevitch, who was fond of physiology)—utterly involuntarily assumed its habitual, good-humored, and therefore idiotic smile.

No need to italicize "idiotic." The positioning of word in sentence, sentence in paragraph, scene in narrative creates emphasis. Play around with your arrangement of elements, once you know what you are doing. Figuring out what you wish to emphasize will focus your subject, your design, and the individual weighting of your characters, problems of pacing, and even your own beliefs. Misplaced emphasis easily throws a reader off track.

Consider spacing on a page when you're thinking about emphasis. Sometimes you may want to set off a sentence on a line by itself, although technically it could remain as part of the paragraph above it. Asking where you want the strongest light to fall may help you decide what to emphasize.

In this example from my story "Mother Love," Hamp Spitsky, past sixty, widowed young and newly married for one year to a flighty, lovable woman, has driven home an attractive young woman from a course in investments they've taken together. They park for a moment in front of her apartment, exchanging comments about the course. She asks if he has ever been married.

> "Just briefly, when I was younger. My wife died very suddenly." She would have been, he wanted to add but didn't, about your age.
>
> The girl's face softened. "I think I'd better go in," she murmured, as if they'd crossed some invisible line and she wished to go no further. "But thanks a lot, Hamp." She turned her full face toward him and reached out one hand to touch his, lying beside him on the seat. "It's been a pleasure meeting you. Good luck."
>
> So old fashioned, those words. So gentle. It pained him. He wanted to know everything about her—who she lived with, on what terms. Was she lonely? With those ankles? Did she weep in the middle of the night? Did she see him as foolish? Interesting?
>
> It was like guessing about the dark side of the moon.

Setting off the last line emphasizes Hamp's sense of the unbridgeable distance between him and the young girl. See *Arranging; Spacing.*

ENCHANTMENT

Fiction weaves its own enchantment. Great fiction stops time, compels belief, and opens avenues to other worlds and lives. It breaks apart the prison of self. The absorbed reader begrudges interruption, wants and doesn't want an ending. This is enchantment.

Even writers who aim to break the spell must first cast it. See *Artifice; Promise.*

ENDING

To make an ending satisfying, *something* has to come together. Endings can easily be overdone or too abrupt. Some stories narrow toward the end so their meaning becomes clearly focused. Others open out to suggest multiple meanings. Still others execute a surprising turn that forces the reader to reinterpret all that has gone before.

When you are searching for the ending to your story or novel, reread it slowly, letting its cumulative meanings sink in. Make yourself that attentive reader you long for. Then write your ending. If it's too abrupt your reader will feel cheated. If it's too long drawn out, too detailed, your reader may feel insulted.

The tendency to spell out endings, nail down their meanings, may spring from two occupational hazards of fiction writers who also teach: (1) distrust of the reader's intelligence and (2) a habit of making a point in several different ways in hopes of penetrating comatose bodies and minds.

Essentially, as writers, our task is to understand our materials so deeply that the ending "comes." Easier said than done. Read stories whose endings have satisfied you and try to analyze what has come together and how, and what's left open.

You are lucky if the ending just comes with a kind of click your instinct tells you is right. Sometimes a simple image that gathers and echoes strands of meaning in the story is enough. Sometimes a snip of dialogue can recast a whole story into a new and complex design of ironies. A few other points to consider:

There is no need to tie up every detail with a bow and knot.

Decide if you can end a story one or two paragraphs short of where you intended to, just past the middle. Often, you can.

Sometimes a brief image, a short scene plus a narrator's reflection, can effectively conclude the action of the preceding narrative, shut the door on it, so to speak. Emily Brontë achieves this at the end of her passionate, complexly structured *Wuthering Heights*. The narrator, Lockwood, visits the graveyard where peace of a kind has at last closed over the tortured lives of Edgar, Catherine, and Heathcliff.

> I sought, and soon discovered the three head-stones on the slope next to the moor—the middle one, grey, and half buried in heath—Edgar Linton's only harmonized by the turf, and moss creeping up its foot—and Heathcliff's still bare.
>
> I lingered round them, under that benign sky; watched the moths fluttering among the heath and hare-bells; listened to

the soft wind breathing through the grass; and wondered how any one could ever imagine unquiet slumbers for the sleepers in that quiet earth.

Sometimes a writer creates a sudden turn at the end of a story, surprises the reader, and challenges her to understand more deeply the hidden depths of a character. American short story writer Tobias Wolff accomplishes this in his story "In the Garden of the North American Martyrs." Mary, a mousey, job-seeking, mid-career academic in history is invited, through her old friend Louise, to seek a tenure-track job interview at a northeastern college. In the midst of her required lecture to the department, Mary realizes that she is engaged in a charade. The department is using her merely to meet their affirmative action requirements. Suddenly she veers from her improvised talk on the North American Jesuit martyrs and stares down the learned professors' attempts to silence her:

> "Mend your lives," she said. "You have deceived yourselves in the pride of your years, and the strength of your arms. Though you soar aloft like the eagle, though your nest is set among the stars, thence I will bring you down, says the Lord. Turn from power to love. Be kind. Do justice. Walk humbly."
> Louise was waving her arms. "Mary!" she shouted.
> But Mary had more to say, much more; she waved back at Louise, then turned off her hearing aid so she would not be distracted again.

Because Wolff has carefully developed character and situation, Mary's sudden explosion at the end of the ordeal is not only believable but, in terms of the whole story, illuminates buried strands of meanings.

Beginnings focus tensions. Endings require just the right number of cadences to release those tensions. See *Beginnings; Closure; Contract; Promise.*

ENERGY

British novelist John Braine divides novels into the quick and the dead. Dead prose lies inert on the page. Quick prose vibrates with energy. What imparts energy to fiction writing?

Consider the following two examples. In the first, I offer an alternative to the quoted excerpt from the short story "Man with the Axe" by Canadian Terry Griggs:

> *Mine:* Elaine was the restless child, always discontent. She left home early and was destined, they thought, to be a disappointment.
>
> *Griggs:* In family lore Elaine was the restless one, the one with *ants in her pants.* She twitched and itched, unsettled as a wild bird on a bobbing branch. In pictures she was the disruptive blur, the streak of light cutting through their tight embrace. No one could hold her. *I'm not marrying this rock pile,* she said at eighteen, and left. She wrote home occasionally—short, energetic messages, the words themselves seeming to spring and tumble like acrobats off the page. Slow suspicious readers, the family had trouble catching even these.

What imparts energy to prose? A combination of factors, weighted differently in every passage. In the passage above, it's word choice (verbs!), syntax, and holding it all, the cadence.

Often, you can inject energy into a static scene by two techniques: (1) delivering it from a slightly skewed point of view and (2) connecting it with time passing—ticking clock, sun moving overhead, that sort of thing. In the following opening by contemporary author Thomas Keneally from his novel *Woman of the Inner Sea,* we meet Kate, a woman running, momentarily stopped.

> A woman in her early thirties, our traveler, the handsome but slightly frowning Kate Gaffney-Kozinski, running across the rain-glossed pavement in Potts Point, saw from a poster in front of the closed newsagents's that her defrocked uncle had given another interview to one of those smooth-paged magazines.
>
> She stopped in front of this poster. As an artifact she found it hard and sad to believe in. Her hand sought—beneath the neck of her dress—the scar tissue behind her left shoulder. She had no time—the delicatessen was about to close and she had no coffee for Murray—but she stopped, shuddered, let her breath go in large gasps of steam and began to weep.

A less skilled writer than Keneally might have opened his novel with Kate standing before the poster, weeping. Instead, he catches her on the run with a time deadline, breathless.

Here are few other energizing strategies of fiction writing.

1. A sense of threat, or menace, will inject verbal adrenalin into your fiction. This does not mean a murderer in the closet; menace may arise from something as small as a significant secret on the verge of being found out, or time ticking away its deadline.

2. The anticipation of closure, ending, will heighten energy in fiction. It creates a pressure. Is this story about to end? Isn't it? But some crucial elements haven't yet been resolved. Which woman will he choose? It's clear that now he *must*. Tightening that mix of inevitability and possibility energizes prose.

3. Directness of tone of voice, that is, the felt pressure upon the reader that he is being implicated. "I stand here ironing, and what you asked me moves tormented back and forth with the iron," are the opening words of the narrator in Tillie Olsen's classic story "I Stand Here Ironing."

In considering the energy (or lack of it) in your prose, begin by scrutinizing your verbs. Where possible, eliminate passive voice. Change "The floor was swept by Marilyn" to "Marilyn swept the floor." Change "He was angry and she felt sad" (a copulative and an intransitive verb) to a gesture or an action: "He shouted and as his voice rose, she cringed." Then look at your nouns. Study the variety in your sentences. Go easy on adverbs and adjectives. And decide if you are directly addressing a reader. See *Rhythm; Syntax; Verbs*.

ENOUGH

How much is enough? I think this is one of the toughest questions in fiction writing. There is no hard-and-fast answer. It depends on many variables: the intelligence of writer and reader, the writer's trust in the reader, the writer's understanding of where his story is going and what it is actually saying, and the writer's own temperament.

One useful question when you're trying to decide if you've given the reader enough to go on, particularly if you're paring metaphors and imagery: "Does this image/metaphor help my reader's imagination move forward or does it distract him, make him stop to admire the writer?" Many a brilliant conceit or thrilling analogy in a draft is better *cut* because it stops the flow of the story. It seems to be asking for attention to itself, rather than directing attention to the story. Have you ever come away from a film feeling "Yes, the photography was beautiful but I didn't want a slide show. Where was the story?"

You must offer enough information, plant enough clues for your reader (how intelligent do you assume him to be?) to gather meaning as he progresses, to delight in his partial understanding. Too much information means a loss of interest because not enough has been withheld. You do not need, in the manner of the nineteenth-century novel, to provide your reader with large clumps of character description early on. The contemporary reader creates his version of your characters as he reads. This is why seeing a movie after you've read the book it's based on can be such a let-down. You'd already created your version of Jay Gatsby. He was more dashing, more sinister.

Therefore, less rather than more detail often suffices to deliver a character to your reader's imagination. You need to know your character to his depths, but you do not need to state it all in detail. Leave something for your reader's imagination to do. See *Delete; Detail; Pacing; Questions.*

EROTIC

If you are trying to write an erotic scene, I offer one caution: less is often more. The more detailed and explicit your description of the sexual act, the more risk you run of becoming parodic, sentimental, tiresome, just plain boring. Adults are generally familiar with the geography and the mechanics.

The route you choose into a scene of lovemaking or sexual satisfaction, the way you place it in your narrative, can charge it with tenderness, sadness, comedy, pathos, excitement, pleasure, irony, or delight. Here are three examples. Note how in each the perspective is skewed by context, that is, the way each scene is framed contributes to the feeling it conveys: tenderness, talkative ecstasy, a more callous lust.

In the first, from Don DeLillo's novel *White Noise*, the sexual encounter is framed by domestic details: the porch light, the tricycle, a child doing homework, a messy bed.

> We walked home under a marigold moon. Our house looked
> old and wan at the end of the street, the porch light shining on
> a molded plastic tricycle, a stack of three-hour colored-flame

sawdust and wax logs. Denise was doing her homework in the kitchen, keeping an eye on Wilder, who had wandered downstairs to sit on the floor and stare through the oven window. Silence in the halls, shadows on the sloping lawn. We closed the door and disrobed. The bed was a mess. Magazines, curtain rods, a child's sooty sock. Babette hummed something from a Broadway show, putting the rods in a corner. We embraced, fell sideways to the bed in a controlled way, then repositioned ourselves, bathing in each other's flesh, trying to kick the sheets off our ankles. Her body had a number of long hollows, places the hand might stop to solve in the dark, tempo-slowing places.

The syntax here suggests a ritual repeated often within a context of home and habit. "We embraced, fell sideways to the bed in a controlled way, then repositioned ourselves. . . ." contributes to the sense of an intimacy that is mutual, tender, practiced, and ongoing.

The next excerpt comes from Jeanette Winterson's exploration of sexual passion in *Written on the Body.*

She kissed me and in her kiss lay the complexity of passion. Lover and child, virgin and roué. Had I ever been kissed before? I was as shy as an unbroken colt. I had Mercutio's swagger. This was the woman I had made love with yesterday, her taste was fresh on my mouth, but would she stay? I quivered like a schoolgirl.

"You're shaking," she said.

"I must be cold."

"Let me warm you."

We lay down on my floor, our backs to the day. I needed no more light than was in her touch, her fingers brushing my skin, bringing up the nerve ends. Eyes closed I began a voyage down her spine, the cobbled road of hers that brought me to a cleft and a damp valley then a deep pit to drown in. What other places are there in the world than those discovered on a lover's body?

Winterson's scene is delivered in terms more abstract—"the complexity of passion" and more literary—"virgin and roué," "Mercutio's swagger." Both DeLillo and Winterson move into metaphor, one way to avoid literal bodily geography.

In the example below from Bob Shacochis' short story "The Heart's Advantage," a man returns to his lover after a month away and finds her different: permed, the bedroom rearranged, all her responses somehow altered.

> "My dear Sims," she said, her eyes inspecting the ceiling, bored with my accusation, "I haven't slept with anybody but you, believe it or not."
> I slouched into bed on all fours and hovered above her, sniffing like a bear for the scent of a stranger on the body beneath me, eyeing the sheets for the stains of carnal labor. She held out her arms for me to collapse into and then, thank God, she smiled, cracking the hard red candy of her lips.
> "What'd you bring me from Africa?"
> "Disease," I answered, colliding with her bones.

The scene implies an ironic relationship, limited mutual trust, a certain objectifying of "the body beneath me," perhaps a more callous lust. It implies, as well, not the ritualized quasi-permanence of DeLillo's excerpt, but an understood transitoriness in the world of sexual encounters.

There is simply no recipe for writing about the erotic. Study your characters, their needs, desires, and sensibilities. *Go* with them.

ESCAPE

Fiction offers escape for reader and writer. Imagining other lives, other ways of seeing and feeling, other routes through life's mayhem, can break the locks of what Romantic poet William Blake called "mind-forged manacles." Think of it: here's your chance at the lives you never had.

EVASION

It may be a universal temptation of fiction writers: the secret effort to circumvent having to do that difficult scene. I've certainly succumbed to it. Your instinct tells you a scene should be included, but it seems just too *complicated* to try. Reduce it to exposition, summary. Find a way around it. Turn to coincidence as a way out. Or say it was all a dream.

If you feel you're evading, most often the fact is that you simply do not know enough about a character. You may not be letting him breathe, giving him enough space on the stage of your imagination. Sit back. Study him. Stare. Close your eyes. Throw him forward on the stage of your mind. Let him indicate the solution. All action springs from character. Forward movement in fiction is organic, not mechanical.

Listen if your sixth sense tells you another scene, a demanding scene, is required. Walk into it, not around it. See *Scene*.

EVENTS

In conventional fiction, something happens. Yet no happening holds meaning unless it connects with a person and awakens feeling. Reported events bombard us daily, hourly, in the "real world." So far away. Terrible, terrible, but what can you do? So disconnected from us.

Fiction consists of reported events, but what gives fiction more power than the evening news? Its shape, its implication of meaning, its defining point of view, the attitude (judgment) it develops toward its narrated incidents, the connection it forges between event and character. Even contemporary fictions that are anti-event are grounded in an awareness of the hollowness of event alone.

Every happening has consequences for your characters. Your reader reads to discover what these are. Connect event and complication and feeling in your writing mind. Include no event in your fiction if you cannot demonstrate its connection with your character. Sometimes, small characters play out their destinies against horrific backgrounds of war, famine, brutality. OK. Still, you must answer two crucial questions about the events you include: How do they connect with your characters? How can you make their meaning reach your reader?

EXCITING INTEREST

Failure to excite interest soon enough affects the pacing of a story. Your challenge is to engage the reader's interest from the opening paragraph. Everything in your story is in some way implicit in its beginning: mood, character, direction. Fear not a bold beginning.

Consider the following opening of Canadian Timothy Findley's long novel, *Headhunter*.

On a winter's day, while a blizzard raged through the streets of Toronto, Lilah Kemp inadvertently set Kurtz free from page 92 of *Heart of Darkness*. Horror-stricken, she tried to force him back between the covers. The escape took place at the Metropolitan Toronto Reference Library, where Lilah Kemp sat reading beside the rock pool. She had not even said *come forth*, but there Kurtz stood before her, framed by the woven jungle of cotton trees and vines that passed for botanic atmosphere.

"Get in," Lilah pleaded—whispering and holding out the book. But Kurtz ignored her and stepped away.

Lilah Kemp was a spiritualist of intense but undisciplined powers. She had once brought Teresa of Avila back into being and lost her on Yonge Street.

As readers, we are launched. A problem has been unleashed. Setting, character, mood, angle of vision: all are established.

For a short story, begin as near the middle as possible. Avoid too much windup.

In a novel, you're persuading your reader to cross the threshold into your book. He'll grant you a few pages before he decides whether to retreat. If the beginning is overlong, however, you may well lose today's impatient reader. See *A Way In; Beginnings*.

EXERCISES

Are writing exercises useful? Debatable. Some writers feel they are a waste of time, making a would-be writer into an exercise junkie without developing a real sense of how a story works. Others—popular writing teacher and novelist John Gardner, for example—feel exercises help a writer get a handle on the elements of fiction while sparing him confusing considerations of the whole, which can be daunting.

Some pianists swear by their daily warm-up exercises; others integrate exercises into the actual piece they're trying to master, working with trouble spots *in context*, as if they were exercises. Try both with your fiction writing. If you're feeling overwhelmed, an isolated exercise may free you to return to the larger task—story, novel, chapter, scene—with renewed vigor. How-to books with writing exercises abound.

Students seem to benefit from exercise writing, at least in the short term. Except for clustering when I'm really stuck, or writing out a monologue as from within a character, I avoid isolated exercises. They do not seem to help me because the problem I'm facing is always embedded in a specific fiction.

Patiently staring at your materials may be the most useful exercise of all.

Physical exercises are important if you're writing with a keyboard most of the day. Do exercises to prevent body problems. Neck, shoulder, wrists. Change your position every half hour. Stretch. Move your eyes away from the screen. This is important.

EXILE

Separation from home can have salutary consequences for a writer. James Joyce wrote obsessively about his native Ireland while living in Trieste, Zurich, and Paris; Bernard Malamud holed up in a Quonset hut in Corvallis, Oregon, to write about immigrant Jews in Manhattan and Brooklyn, where he grew up.

For some writers, exile becomes a catalyst to intense imaginative activity. It generates a desire to build a bridge to an audience beyond the place of exile. I speak from experience. At this writing I have lived in Canada since 1971. I came here from Chicago and felt, almost immediately, the need to reach out from this small town in a foreign country to make contact, I hoped, with other minds in more familiar places. The subject I chose, convent life, had absolutely nothing to do with the foreign country in which I found myself. For me, writing fiction has been grounded in an effort to reconnect.

As William Goyen, in his panegyric novel about his childhood home in Charity, Texas, *The House of Breath*, puts it:

> . . . And to find out what we are, we must enter back into the ideas and the dreams of worlds that bore and dreamt us and there find, waiting within worn mouths, the speech that is ours. . . . For all that is lost yearns to be found again, remade and given back through the finder to itself, speech found for what is not spoken.

EXPECTATION

Composers of music and of fiction work to generate expectations in their listeners and readers. Movement forward comes about as we make those expectations grow, frustrate them, turn them in new and unexpected directions, achieve surprise. Just as a musical line makes beauty *while it moves* toward resolution, a narrative builds with a sense of direction. The minute your reader expects nothing, he'll stop reading.

Therefore, at some point, you must know what you're writing *toward*. See *Discovery*.

EXPLAINING

Readers are bright. (They've picked up your book!) It's easy to explain too much. Trained by film as well as by the tradition of reading novels and stories, contemporary readers quickly catch implication, absorb jumps in narrative time. Consider how much you can convey in this dialogue, this scene, without explanation. Think about it, lest you insult your reader. See *Implication*.

EXPLORATION

We are explorers in unmapped territory.

Every explorer sets out with a general plan, subject to revision as he proceeds. And every explorer knows risk. It's better not to know what lies ahead—miles of ocean, snowcovered mountains, or yards of prose yet to be written.

Do not write only what you know. How boring. You know far more than you think. Write to find that out. Every explorer ventures forward hoping for surprise.

John Meares (1756-1804), an explorer hoping to profit from the Northwest fur trade, sailed down the coast of Washington on July 6, 1788. He sought a harbor, steered for a promising spot, met instead the treacherous sandbar near what is now Ilwaco. Unable to navigate the bar and judging the entrance to the Columbia River to be just a little bay, he named the treacherous spot Cape Disappointment and sailed on. Had he judged differently, he might have discovered a new route into the continent and our history would have been very different.

Writing fiction involves risks, navigational skills, acts of judgment. What you estimate to be a puddle may be a river leading you to discover a new world. See *Discovery*.

EXPOSITION

Exposition is important narrative material that does not merit treatment in a full-scale scene. It may describe a place or person, convey background information, give necessary data on a situation. Your choice not to put it in a scene arises from your overall design, your sense of pacing, your grasp of the most important moments in the story. These you will dramatize in scenes. Your sense of what belongs in exposition, what belongs in scene, may shift, however, as you work on a story and come to understand its subject more deeply. See *Summary; Tension.*

EXPOSURE

All writing is an act of exposure. This may be why some writers fear rejection. They feel it is a rejection of themselves.

Instinctively, also, we know reading to be an act of intimacy. Therefore, the process of writing involves getting past that fear of exposure and coming to trust our reader. Fear can make us hold back as writers from mining the deepest sources of our power.

Respect your readers. Imagine them as intelligent, responsive, open to your point of view, ready to listen. Imagine them as having felt grief, love, passion, betrayal, confusion, joy. Speak to those feelings. See *Family; Privacy.*

EXPRESSION

If you've something to express—and you'd better—the challenge is to make out of that a design that pleases, entertains, mystifies, challenges, accomplishes whatever your dominant goals are. Inevitably, even if you start in a burst of self-expression, the task and pleasure of making something, of design, arrangement, fitting parts together, taking some out, reviewing, revising: all this will distance you— sometimes a far distance—from that initial urge to self-expression. In his *Autobiography,* the prolific nineteenth-century British novelist Anthony Trollope makes an essential distinction between the writer who has to tell a story, and the writer who has a story to tell. In the second case, he says, the story will succeed. In the first, eventually the emphasis on self-importance will show through. See *Finger Proud.*

FABRIC OF ILLUSION

In his instructional book *The Craft of Writing*, former editor and publisher William Sloane cautions the writer against rupturing fiction's "fabric of illusion."

"Come, Jane, it's time to wash your hands for supper." Recall how, as a child, that parental interruption jarred when you were reading.

Any tiny slip can tear the fabric. Consider the following example:

> Lurilee thought she'd have a quick coffee on her way home from work, delay feeling again the newly-empty house. The dripping faucet. The empty closet. The almost bare fridge. The silence.
>
> Though the day had been cold and rainy, in McDonald's the air conditioning was on. She pulled her light sweater tighter, hugging herself.
>
> "Sam left after all, did he?" asked Marie, as she poured Lurilee's coffee, double-double, into the Styrofoam cup.
>
> Marie had that knowing look. Trust her to pick up the news before anyone else in town.
>
> "Last Saturday," murmured Lurilee. She took the cup, set sixty cents on the counter, and turned away quickly.
>
> "Sorry, Lu," said Marie.
>
> Lurilee pretended not to hear. She'd find the farthest table, over in the corner. Sit facing the window, her back to the counter. Did she have a cigarette left in her purse? The hell

with Marie, she thought. Might as well get used to it. This was just the beginning.

Unconsciously, Lurilee kept her eyes focused on the coffee as she headed past crowded tables.

The word "unconsciously" makes a tiny rip here. It suddenly pulls the reader outside Lurilee because the voice saying that word can only be the voice of someone outside the situation. In a flash, the reader becomes a spectator watching Lurilee, rather than a participant, moving along with her, inside her thoughts.

At times you may wish to pull the reader back outside. Just be sure you know when you're doing it. See *Point of View*.

FACTS

Get your facts straight.

In *One Writer's Beginnings*, great Southern storyteller Eudora Welty's engaging little book about her origins as a writer, the author describes how for years she held a mistaken notion about the course of the moon traversing the sky. After she had misplaced the moon in a published story, a critic counselled her: "Always be sure you get your moon in the right part of the sky."

A good motto for any fiction writer.

On the other hand, once you have them straight, don't let facts terrorize you. You're writing *fiction*. You have your purposes. Putting a moon in the wrong part of the sky may serve your design.

Recently, a copyeditor objected to an element in a story of mine she was preparing for a collection. In this scene from "Leaving the World," two children return with their mother to a chapel where the mother, in an earlier life, spent hours as a monastic cloistered nun. I quote this rather lengthy passage because my decision to *violate fact* was connected with the larger context of the story, with such concerns as pacing, perspective, and the narrator's tone of voice.

> We picked our way over debris, stepped through the hint of a doorway. Inside—nothing. No altar. No windows. No communion railing. No choir stalls. No organ. Had the chapel died on a grander scale, had there been time for moss to grow and sparrows to nest, had my children been more attuned to invisible angelic hosts—we might have stood within that

transformed temple and imagined monks chanting, our spirits refreshed by the echoes of their strenuous piety. Bare ruined choirs. But no. Nothing like that. No sweet birds sang. A few bats swooped. The iron sun beat upon our uncovered heads. Weary from hours of travel in a hot car, the children were thirsty and irritable.

The copyeditor crossed out "monks" and wrote "nuns" above it, underlined "a few bats" and wrote in the margin, "in the day?"

Her points, both well taken, came down on the side of accuracy. I thought about context. The whole episode ends a few paragraphs later with mother and children finding a new cinderblock convent down the road, stopping there for a glass of water, receiving one lukewarm Styrofoam cup full of tepid water from a begrudging nun.

The passage concludes:

> I could have quoted her chapter and verse: "Whatsoever you do unto the least of these. . . ." Instead, we drove away.
>
> That abortive trip begot in me only the urge to get on with life, leave the past where it belonged, to the bats in that particular belfry.

I wanted those bats, or at least one bat, for many reasons. To change them to robins or sparrows wouldn't do. I wanted the contrast with "sweet birds." I wanted the spookiness of bats. Simultaneously, though I did it instinctively as I recall, I wanted the Shakespearean echo. And monks worked better for the suggested picture. Finally, I wanted the metaphoric "bats in the belfry" to become an ironic echo of the earlier, literal bats. I compromised with the copyeditor and held onto one bat.

Conveying factual information without becoming boring can be a challenge. Rather than narrating lots of straight exposition, it often works better if you can devise a scene where one character is *doing* what you want explained and in the process explains the steps to another character. This passage, from award-winning novelist E. Annie Proulx's *The Shipping News*, aims to convey to the reader something of the process of boat-making. Quoyle, the character for whom the boat is being made, visits York, the old man who is making it. Quoyle watches and helps. They work together and talk.

... With his scraped and worn tape he [York] calculated the midpoint of the hull length and marked the keel a second time a few inches forward of the midpoint mark. ...

"Leave me take that saw, boy," said the man. ...

Quoyle handed the saw, the chisel, the saw, the chisel, leaned over the work watching York notch the timberline to take the timber pacers. At last he could help set in the timbers, holding them while the old man fastened them to the floor with stout braces he called spur shares.

"Now we notches the sternpost, my son."

What might have been only exposition here becomes tied to action and character revelation as they work.

FAITH

In his essay "An Approach to Style," E.B. White, well-known essayist for *The New Yorker*, says that finally "what a man is, rather than what he knows, will at last determine his style. If one is to write, one must believe—in the truth and worth of the scrawl, in the ability of the reader to receive and decode the message."

I've never met a fiction writer who didn't struggle at times to sustain faith in his or her identity *as a writer*. So much of this effort is exploratory, tentative, reflective, revisionary. It requires throwing away, wasting paper, pushing past mental blocks, picking away at sentences. Houdinis of the word—trapped, we devise escape routes. The disproportion between effort and effect: five years to write, five hours to read! The long wait to hear from publishers. The dawning awareness that you can never write like the authors you most admire. The certainty that the end product will always stop short of its initial impulse. Facing down prophets of doom about the future of the written word itself, you slog away at your story or book, you call yourself a writer but *what have you to show*? It takes a strong faith. Sheer nerve. A kind of pigheadedness. A rare form of nuttiness, perhaps.

FAME

Our town paper comes out on Wednesday afternoon. It specializes in such information as who grew the largest zucchini this year, whose beef cattle won first prize, whose son in British Columbia has telephoned recently, who was married or buried.

One Saturday morning the daily paper in a town thirty miles distant carried my picture and an article overstating my developing fame. That very afternoon, it said, at one o'clock, two stories of mine would be read on national radio, CBC. This was July, 1984.

Had anyone in town seen the article? Which friends should I alert? An odd shyness beset me. (A shyness I now know goes with having those too "close" to you hear your fiction. They'll make wrong—and sometimes disturbing—connections.) Finally, I called an old friend who was already out at her cottage for the summer. Her husband is the local coroner.

The following Monday, five people who had read that article approached me at different times. Maureen: "I was out buying groceries." Geraldine: "I had just tuned in the radio to listen and a call came for the coroner. We get poor reception out there at the beach. I couldn't hear the story above Tom's voice on the phone. I got about the first five minutes." Sue: "Saw your picture in the paper and planned to listen. I noted it on the kitchen calendar. We got our side of beef for the winter that morning. Had to get it all cut that afternoon. Had the radio on but couldn't hear you over the power saw." Shirley: "I feel so bad. I had two notes to myself and I forgot." Peter: "I must confess, I fell asleep."

A few years before that, just after my first book of stories had come out and I'd held it in my hand admiringly, I was on my way to the States with my family. Just over the border we stopped at a homestyle restaurant for lunch. My five-year-old son grew thoughtful. He looked around the restaurant and finally whispered: "Just think, Mom: no one in this whole place knows they're sitting in the same room with a famous author."

In a world seduced by the possibility of instant fame, don't count on it to come your way. Though the passing accident of fame may happen to you, at heart, committed fiction writers seek something else: to shine a light, through words alone, on some corner of this mysterious human life we are all living out; to illumine at least a tiny part of its meaning; to give voice and shape to stories that would otherwise forever remain unspoken.

FAMILY

You love 'em; you'd leave 'em. You find them endearing; they drive you out of your mind. You've just caught the wisp of an idea and the baby bawls. You've nailed the elusive verb and the doorbell rings. If only, if only, you could have solid, unbroken time away from them you could connect with your Muse, the one they thwart unawares, or even perhaps deliberately. You could *become a real writer*. If it weren't for them, you'd be more productive. If it weren't for . . . , etc.

From the age of nineteen, Anton Chekhov supported through his writing a family—a tyrannical father, an anxious mother, a collection of hangers-on and disagreeable relatives who just wouldn't go away. Listen to him in a letter to his brother Alexander, written in April 26, 1888:

> You know my place has a multitude of adults living under one roof only because we cannot separate, in view of certain incomprehensible circumstances. With me are Mother, Sister, Mishka (who won't leave until he is graduated), Nikolai, drunk and half undressed, who does nothing whatever and has been abandoned by his *objet*, Auntie, and Alyosha. . . . Add to this that Ivan is around from three in the afternoon until late at night and on all holidays, and that Papa comes evenings. They are all nice people, jolly but egoistic, pretentious, unusually talkative, prone to stamping their feet, impecunious. My head is in a whirl. . . .

Despite ill health from adolescence onward, Chekhov wrote over 4,000 letters, hundreds of stories and sketches, plays. He researched the convict island of Sakhalin, worked tirelessly as a doctor, managed a small estate, and travelled Russia, Europe, and Asia, through it all sustaining humor, curiosity, alert observation, and the habit of writing. See *Time*.

FEEDING-IN

The nineteenth-century novel, typically, delivered character descriptions and exposition in chunks of prose. It's more customary today— and readers expect it—to feed in exposition and description in the midst of other fictional goings-on: action, dialogue, scene. Deliver your characters to the reader in bits and pieces. This way you don't slow the pace of the narrative. You also break up those intimidating blocks of solid print. Finally, feeding-in will reduce the need for flashback, usually a poor way of dealing with important past information.

Here is a series of homemade examples which demonstrate various stages and kinds of feeding-in.

Meet Marlene alone, straight description, no feeding-in.

> Marlene was a tall woman, chunky about the hips, given to throwing back the length of her straight black hair when she felt annoyed or uneasy. She wore dark glasses as a rule, to conceal her rather startling blue eyes, and a ring on every finger of both hands. Expensive rings. Cheap rings. It didn't matter. She spoke slowly, as if weighing every word, and let long heavy pauses fall between statements.

In the example below, Marlene arrives in the midst of a narrative moment. Notice that the point of view from which she's seen belongs to someone else—the mysterious "he."

> Running down the stairs, she stopped suddenly at the bottom and looked him straight in the eye. He was surprised again to discover that her eyes were blue. Always hidden behind opaque lenses, he somehow thought of them as dark.
>
> "Sorry if I've upset you," he said, grabbing hold of the banister for support. Those eyes—unnerving.
>
> She threw back the length of her dark hair, planted both hands on her substantial hips.
>
> "Upset . . ." she said. "Upset." She raised her hands, rings gleaming on every finger, and clasped them in front of her waist, as if about to pray. The rings shone. "You think you have the power to upset me?" And then she began to turn the diamond on her pinkie. "You . . . actually supposed . . . that? Still?"

If you want to sneak in the *time of day*, you might insert after "pray":

> The slice of late afternoon sun filtered through the skylight made her rings glitter.

If *locale* is important to some dimension of the story, you could elaborate the staircase, wallpaper, curved banister, etc.

Running down the curved length of staircase, she paused for an instant on the landing to peer below. Seeing him there, she slowed her pace on the last turn of the stairs. She trailed her hand along the polished banister.

He watched her black dress slowly pass the pale cream flocked wallpaper, watched her small bare foot land neatly on each carpeted step.

A month earlier, this staircase had been a point of pride. Now, she descended as if she were in a movie, Scarlett O'Hara coming down to tell off Rhett.

He didn't feel like any Rhett.

Emphasize what you need to for the purposes of the moment in the narrative. Decide where lights and shadows should fall. If the underlying theme is social climbing, for example, you might wish to make more of the staircase here, or bring it in again later. Perhaps one ring on her fingers holds special significance for him: he pawned something precious to obtain it. Now he regrets it. That ring, flashing on her hand even in their most intimate moments, is a constant reminder.

In other words, weigh not only *how* you feed in but *where* you feed in detail, description, background information, interpretive comment.

It is sometimes easier to see how things go together if you look at second-rate prose such as mine above, where the seams show. It will not inspire you, but it may teach you. See *Flashback*.

FEELINGS

Consider feelings from at least three angles. First, which of your feelings are you willing, and able, to plumb for your current fiction? (This changes over time.) Second, what is the feeling most central to the scene you're creating? Feelings are tied to characters. Which of your characters' feelings are you seeking to dramatize here? Third, what feelings do you hope to evoke in your reader at this point in the narrative?

Point three is accomplished by skill in dealing with one and two. Consider it in a general way as you are making up your story or novel, but realize readers differ. Eroticism to one is comedy to another; thrilling adventure to one may be boredom to another. You cannot second-guess your reader's feelings.

Concentrate, therefore, on exploring your own range of emotional response to your fiction-at-present, and work at managing words skill-fully, aware of all their associations, their connotations, to dramatize feeling. Words and only words are your tools. Beware of relying on adverbs.

A caution: though introducing a character's emotions with "She felt" may be necessary as a transition, it can easily be overdone, killing immediacy, and distancing the reader.

When I'm trying to dig down deep inside a character's responses, move with him, so to speak, I find it useful and stimulating to play with metaphors. Search out comparisons, however weird or far-fetched. Cluster. Doodle. I also sometimes write monologues from within that character, secrets he will share with no one. While trying any of these strategies, I keep my awareness loosely centered on the feeling I'm trying to express. See *Emotion; Metaphor.*

FIGURATIVE

Figurative language achieves special effects, exploits the power of suggestion, and builds bridges to your reader's feelings through com-parison and association. If I say "She had various complicated desires" the words feel general, abstract, vague. If I speak of "the latticework of her desires" I suggest something about the tangle of her inner life. In her novel *Housekeeping*, Marilynne Robinson describes a train sliding from a bridge "into the water, like a weasel sliding off a rock," and a freezing lake becomes "dull and opaque, like cooling wax." Such comparisons can link with the reader's imagination, his range of experience. In the nineteenth-century novel *Middlemarch* by George Eliot, a remark lies in Mr. Brooke's mind "as lightly as the broken wing of an insect among all the fragments there." Instantly we know this character and sense something of how he moves through life.

Figurative language—similes, metaphors, analogies, and compari-sons stated or implied—is an effective way of connecting your feelings to those of your character and those of your reader. Compare "She was dull" with "Her mind was as blank and smooth as a folded sheet."

Don't get carried away, though. If analogies and comparisons come too easily for you, your figurative forest may grow so dense that your reader loses the trail. Avoid sending your reader's associations off-track. "He loved her smell, the perfume she wore, like the odor of dying gardenias." And be wary of tired comparisons. "Her face was like faded roses. Her eyes twinkled." You can do better. See *Cliché; Metaphor; Symbols.*

FINDING YOUR SUBJECT

In both the large and the small sense, finding your true subject is crucial.

Large: What is the subject *you* can deal with best, with your native talent, your way of seeing and feeling, your life experience, your instinctive interests, your conditioning? What do you feel drawn to write about? After some time, you will probably discover certain thematic concerns, subjects you return to, often in different guises. Plot lines change; the essential subjects remain. Try to see what's there and make the most of it.

Small: In a given story it may take several drafts before you come to understand the real (as opposed to the ostensible) subject of your story. Years ago a student of mine in southern Idaho wanted to write about her experience traveling in Canada with her new husband who was a member of a small circus. In Quebec, the entire lion act was taken sick. Somehow the directions for the prescription were mistranslated from English to French, and all the lions died.

The student tried several versions in synopsis form with bits of dialogue, focusing largely on the colorful circus ambiance—costumes, animals, trapeze artists, clowns, all that. Suddenly, after the sixth synopsis, she ran into my office one day. "I know what my story is about," she cried. "I've found it!" It had dawned on her that the *real subject* she was after was her acute loneliness as a new bride of seventeen traveling for the first time away from her Idaho home, with a circus, in Canada, and being part of this bizarre incident, in a place where she didn't even share a language.

When you can state in one sentence the real subject, your other tasks may grow clearer, if not easier. Our real subjects find us, if we're lucky. See *Exposure; Self-Knowledge; You.*

FINGER PROUD

Describing why he felt a performance in Carnegie Hall was technically superb but lacking in real musicality, a critic remarked that the pianist was "finger proud." Wanted to show *what she could do*. In writing, that will also make itself felt. If you try to show what you can do—create superior images, plot intricately, perform verbal wizardry—instead of making the story as clear and compelling as possible, your reader will know it. Watch out.

FINISHED

How do you know when your story or novel is finished? You've revised again and again, rethought, cut, put it away, brought it out, been as critical as you can. You've checked for bloopers and read it aloud. You've listened. You've stated your subject, as you understand it. You've answered "What happens?" You've thought about the underlying action. You're sick of it. Now what?

Send it out. The worst that can happen is rejection. The best is that you'll be able to see it fresh when it returns. You'll have broken the umbilical cord. If it's accepted, congratulations. Move on. See *Enough; Rejection.*

FLASHBACK

Some writers lean too heavily on flashback. This comes, I think, from being puzzled about how to control fictional time. Flashback interrupts the forward movement of the narrative, a dangerous gamble if you're embarked on a predominantly linear realistic tale. Try to figure out another way to feed in essential background information.

A couple of questions: (1) Are you starting in the right place? Should you go back and begin earlier, so the narrative can move steadily forward and not be substantially interrupted? (2) Can you find ways, here and there, to feed in material you would have put in the flashback? (3) Is that material part "backstory" or is it part of "hidden story?"

Backstory refers to what happened before the main action of the fiction begins. It may or may not be important. Hidden story refers to what's going on offstage, in the narrative present, while you're conducting the up-front action. In a mystery, getting all the details of offstage events accurate may be crucial to the plot.

If you need to feed in bits of backstory which are minor, important but not crucial to know in detail, consider the examples under *Feeding-in.* Now, let's add a bit of backstory, just a bit:

> As she planted each small foot with its scarlet toenails on the cream-colored carpet, he thought of how happily they'd

shopped for that very carpet, how she'd run naked up and down the stairs their first night here, teasing him, thrilled at last to have left the third floor walk-up where they'd spent two penny-pinching years. It had seemed to him in that moment—she was coming closer now—that all happiness lay in having at last bought his wife a winding staircase.

And here she came, like a disenchanted goddess, tense, angry (he felt it), challenging.

If you decide it's important to spend a lot of time on backstory—the whole episode of buying the carpet, arguing over it, what featured in their argument—then go back, tell the story, think of it as *present* while you write it. Do not keep saying "had." One "had," in the introductory paragraph, will usually clue in the reader.

Finally, you may be attempting to dramatize a highly complex perspective on time so that swatches of material from the past overlap with the present. In his novel *Absalom, Absalom!*, for example, William Faulkner does just this.

Consider: Is your flashback taking place within a character's mind, as often in Faulkner, or is it held within the narrator's controlling voice? Or can you distinguish? Though discontinuity in narrative can interrupt, it can also stimulate interest, and today's readers seem particularly attuned to the fragmentary nature of life itself. The whole question of proportion in your overall design comes into play here, so your narrative doesn't just stand still. We cannot all hope—or even desire—to achieve that kind of trancelike immobility that is the final effect of some flashback-full Faulkner narratives. See *Had; Time.*

FOCUS

How maddening to be told by an editor: "You write well, your story is fascinating, but I found it somewhat unfocused." Hear such comments with an open mind before you feel too misunderstood. Some tiny misplacement of emphasis may be all you need to fix. You may need to ask yourself a few questions. Imagine your story as a play, with acts, the characters on stage. On what do you want the spotlight to shine? Where do the major shifts occur? A sense of focus becomes clear only after you see what the story is really about and where it is headed. You need to weigh the implications of every scene, every transition, every word to see how they all feed into the movement of the story toward its ending. Unlike the cheese, in fiction nothing stands alone.

Consider what you go through to focus one picture with your camera: the frame, the light, the foreground, the background. Achieving focus takes thought, concentration—and a certain distance.

Intensity of focus in fiction is influenced by the dimensions of the world you write about. The larger the social dimensions of your story, the more challenging will be decisions about focus. For example the novel *Wildlife*, by contemporary American writer Richard Ford, is slender beside Leo Tolstoy's massive nineteenth-century novel *War and Peace*. Ford examines the relationships within a small family while Tolstoy covers the social and political concerns of entire countries. Consider the dimensions of your subject. Limits and constraints bear directly on focus, as does the question of frame. See *Constraints; Limits*.

FORESHADOWING

This is an important means of deepening your reader's sense of anticipation as you move the story forward. You can foreshadow through word, thought, dream, scene, dialogue, comment, action, incident— through just about any element of fiction, small or large. As you write, you may accomplish much of this instinctively. Later, though, when the story is clearer in your mind, go back and take a hard look at possibilities for foreshadowing you may have missed.

Word: In the scene in George Eliot's *Middlemarch* where Dorothea Brooke first meets her husband-to-be, Casaubon, he is asked how he arranges his documents. He replies "In pigeon-holes, partly." How neatly this foreshadows what the narrative will reveal about his character.

Metaphor: In Gustave Flaubert's *Madame Bovary*, as Leon and Emma pass through the streets of Rouen enclosed in their coach, "bourgeois stared in wonder at this thing unheard of in the provinces: a cab with all blinds drawn that reappeared incessantly, more tightly sealed than a tomb and tossed around like a ship on the waves." "Tomb" foreshadows the end of their love, the end of Emma herself.

Allusion: As Leon, Emma's lover-to-be, is hurrying her away from the cathedral to their tryst in the coach, the verger cries after them, dismayed by Leon's obvious lack of interest in the history of the Cathedral, "At least you should go out by the northern gate . . . and look at the Resurrection, the Last Judgment, Paradise, King David, and the damned burning in the flames of Hell!"

Premonition: A character can express or feel a premonition that something is about to happen, thus casting forward the imagination of the reader. "She felt a sense that before a week had passed, his words might come true." In Leo Tolstoy's *Anna Karenina*, in the restaurant where Stepan, Anna Karenina's brother-in-law, talks with Levin, he describes Vronsky, the man who will become Anna's passionate attachment. Not only does this prepare the reader, set the stage, but Tolstoy does it so that his words will come true, ironically, by the end of the book.

> "Fearfully rich, handsome, great connections, an aide-de-camp, and with all that a very nice, good-natured fellow. But he's more than simply a good-natured fellow, as I've found out here—he's a cultivated man, too, and very intelligent; and he's a man who'll make his mark."

Situation: One situation can foreshadow another, as the discovery of adultery, the family upheaval, and Stepan's inability to face the depths of his own being in the opening of *Anna Karenina* foreshadow, in a different key, what is to come with Anna and Vronsky.

Action plus comment: In the novel *Mao II*, by Don DeLillo, when the father trains his binoculars on the mass marriages taking place in the stadium below, he asks: "Who the hell thought it up? What does it mean?" We come to see that looking through lens—camera, binoculars—and trying to fathom exactly that question, lies at the heart of DeLillo's book.

A character's thought: Here is Anna, near the end of her story in *Anna Karenina*:

> ... death rose clearly and vividly before her mind as the sole means of bringing back love for her in his heart, of punishing him and of gaining the victory in that strife which the evil spirit in possession of her heart was waging with him.

An action or gesture can foreshadow. Moments later she will cast herself beneath the wheels of a train.

Tune into the fantasies, the hallucinations, the visions of your characters. Perhaps they can reveal elements of foreshadowing for your story. In Thomas Mann's *Death in Venice*, just as Aschenbach, the protagonist, is stirred with longing to travel—a travel that will lead to his spiritual and physical death—the narrator tells us:

> Desire projected itself visually: his fancy, not quite yet lulled since morning, imaged the marvels and terrors of the manifold earth. He saw. He beheld a landscape, a tropical marshland, beneath a reeking sky, steaming, monstrous, rank—a kind of primeval wilderness-world of islands, morasses, and alluvial channels. Hairy palm-trunks rose near and far out of lush brakes of fern, out of bottoms of crass vegetation, fat, swollen, thick with incredible bloom. There were trees, misshapen as a dream, that dropped their naked roots straight through the air into the ground or into water that was stagnant and shadowy and glassy-green, where mammoth milk-white blossoms floated, and strange high-shouldered birds with curious bills stood gazing sidewise without sound or stir. Among the knotted joints of a bamboo thicket the eyes of a crouching tiger gleamed—and he felt his heart throb with terror, yet with a longing inexplicable. Then the vision vanished.

Dream, fantasy, vision, hallucination: any of these can help move your reader forward in a narrative, heighten a sense of expectation. When that something hinted at does happen, if you've planted clues well, foreshadowing will evoke in your reader an echo. "Oh yes." He's been prepared for this moment, could feel it coming, even though he didn't know just what it would be. See *Echo*.

FORGIVENESS

Forgive yourself your mistakes and move on. I've made a sixty-one-year-old woman pregnant and called a two hundred-bed hospital "small." Yesterday, I found a message on my answering machine from my editor: "I want to talk to you about pitchforks," her voice said. "Think of the picture *American Gothic*. Call me tomorrow." When I called, her first question was: "How old is that child?" "Ten." "Then she's too small to manage a pitchfork." (A ten-year-old child is trying to dig into hard ground to bury her dead dog.) A discussion about pitchforks ensued—size, shape, weight. It turned out that what I'd imagined right along was, as she suggested gently, a garden fork. Flat tines. Different handle. OK for this child to manage.

These literary sins are venial, easy to forgive. More challenging to forgive is our failure as writers to produce a story that matches the vision it sprang from. What we imagined as compelling sits limp on the page; what we hoped would stir hearts seems now more like a block of ice. The only solution I know for this ongoing problem is to push on to the next story. Though it's important to be tough on yourself as a writer, it's counterproductive to harbor a grudge against yourself. Words are an infinitely renewable resource. And the next story may come closer. There is only one way to find out. See *Ambition*.

FRAME

You can sometimes deepen complexity in a story by placing it within another story, as in a frame. In Joseph Conrad's classic novella *Heart of Darkness*, Marlow, the narrator, tells his assembled audience of his encounter with the corrupted ivory-trader, Kurtz. Is *Heart of Darkness* the story of Kurtz or of Marlow? Need we choose? The frame is integral to the wonderful complexity of the story.

I have found, however, that using a frame can dilute a story. Unconsciously, I have used frame as a warm-up tool, a way to get me into the writing. In these cases I've come to realize that the framing device has provided me a comforting path over the writing threshold rather than adding a significant dimension to the story itself. Editors have saved me from such dilution by questioning whether the frame was integral to my story. When I dropped the frame, the story stood forth clear and compelling.

As a narrative strategy, therefore, use the device of framing with care. One you've finished the story, stand back from it and ask: How does the frame I've used contribute to the framed story? Make yourself analyze just what it adds: Thematic echoes that are not merely repetitive, but deepen the story's meanings? Contrasts in character development? Metaphoric strands that resonate against one another and lead to a deeper understanding of both inner story and frame? Does the frame serve the distance you're aiming to establish in your story? Do you want the reader pulled in close or distanced from the narrative?

One odd note about narrative frames: The frame you cast off from the beginning of one story may serve another. This has happened to me. Stuck for closure, suddenly I remembered a cast-off frame that felt intrinsically connected to the story at hand. When I added the frame it seemed to work wonderfully, to pick up and deepen themes in the second story as though it had been waiting to do just that. Life's mysterious interconnectedness was at work here: one of the little gifts in a writer's working life.

Think a bit about framing in the larger sense. Each of us views life through a unique frame, our personal vision. The *way* we see both focuses and limits *what* we see. Ideally, as we grow personally and artistically, our capacities to see deepen. Ideally also, we develop a sense of our own vision, we learn to recognize certain peculiarities about the way we see and interpret the world. It can be both humbling and exhilarating to realize that no one else frames the world in quite the same way. We grow sensitive to the frames we put on experience as we move through a week, a day, an hour.

In her book *One Writer's Beginnings*, Eudora Welty speaks of this development in her own extensive writing life. During the Depression, her first job as a junior publicity agent in the Mississippi office of the Works Progress Administration (WPA) required her to travel through the state taking pictures, writing news stories. She learned to seize the moment. This meant learning first to recognize it, then how to frame it.

Welty takes the idea of a photographer's frame and applies it to the way a writer comes to frame experience. In the course of her development as a writer, the frame through which she viewed the world changed, she says. "Greater than scene, I came to see, is situation. Greater than situation is implication. Greater than all of these is a single, entire human being, who will never be confined in any frame." See *Focus; Point of View*.

FREEDOM

To write fiction you need to feel free. Daily life weaves a web, a thousand threads of worries, responsibilities, distractions, suspicions, fears. And then there are those invisible judging presences watching over our shoulders as we write. It has been said that the biggest hindrance for some writers is their mother's chin on their shoulder.

Cultivating inner space where your imagination can range freely, and finding an actual place where you can write daily are important. You may find claiming your own spot in a crowded house or apartment hard to justify to others, and even to yourself, if your writing is not earning an income. Don't be dissuaded. Define boundaries of time and space that are yours *as a writer*. It will pay dividends. It may mean claiming a corner of a room, or a closet under the stairs. For some, it means getting up every day hours before others do, seizing in the early morning quiet time and space for their imagination to work freely. I started my first book working in a borrowed office from 5:00 A.M. until 9:00 A.M. throughout one summer. It may mean making your children knock on the door of your study when you're at work. When we put a small study in one end of our third floor, during my writing time I made my children ring a bell at the bottom of the stairs if they wanted to come up. Seek a way to hold unencumbered that outer and inner space where your writing work can freely flourish. See *Exposure; Family.*

FREEWRITING

Moving your hand across the page, keeping it moving, having no predetermined focus, writing to make yourself write: this is often espoused as an effective way to create. For certain temperaments it may be more useful to pick a word, an object, something concrete, and set yourself to write about it for ten minutes. I have seldom practiced these techniques myself, I must confess. Others, however, find them helpful. I know three or four writers who gather once a week, set something—a candle, an apple, a vase, anything—on the table before them and just write about it for ten minutes. Sometimes they open the dictionary and pick a word at random to write about. Wondrous things emerge, not fit for print, perhaps, but fit to be read aloud and enjoyed. Poems. Stories. Unfinished narratives. Reminiscences. Often they hold surprising power. They may also be a springboard to realized fictions. See *Improvising.*

FRESHNESS

No one sees the world quite the way you do. Keep looking, to tell about the world as you see it, feel it. It will change over time. If you can find words for that, they will carry freshness. See *You.*

GAP

Hold this tiny word in mind as you look critically at your story or novel. Where can you exploit gaps that will deepen implications, heighten tensions? The gap, for example, between what a character would say and what she actually does. The gap between what one character overhears another say and how the overheard character ordinarily speaks. Between expectation and realization. Between gesture and desire. Look for chinks, cracks, provocative and suggestive gaps. See if you can mine them in a scene. You may be surprised at how they deepen your story. See *Irony*.

GERMINATE

Growing a story or a novel is an organic process. It takes time, care, watchfulness—and sometimes long hours of weeding in the heat of the day. It requires the patience of a gardener. Often, the seed of an idea that has lain fallow for months, even years, can suddenly connect with another idea, image, memory. Life begins to stir. Be tender with such stirrings. Jot them in your journal. Don't begin to prune the growing plant too early. It may put out many stalks that droop, turn wayward, but all will become clearer to you once the basic outline of your growing plant emerges. The tiny seed, the merest inkling, may one day surprise you with the radiance of its blooms. See *Journal*.

GESTURES

If you are with a group of other writers, this exercise can be fun. Have each writer jot down a gesture or two. Then go around the circle trying to guess what state of mind or emotional condition each gesture suggests. You'll quickly discover that gesture divorced from context of character and situation is meaningless, a sheet flapping in the wind. This exercise can also help wean you from reliance on adverbs. Gestures bring your characters forward, alive and moving, on the stage of your mind.

> He raised his eyebrow, stared at her, and took a long deep breath.

> She began to pound the pillow on their bed, as if to flatten every last feather.

> He stood tall, sucked in his stomach, let his hands hang by his sides, and remembered to keep his eyes straight ahead.

Give yourself a list of adverbs. Write sentences that contain gestures and bodily movements a person feeling that way might make. Proudly. Wonderingly. Condescendingly. Frantically. Then throw out most of the *ly*'s in your writing.

GHOSTS

They stalk the hidden chambers of memory, flicker faintly at the edges of thought. Their shadows plague our daylight minds, their whispers tease us. Hear them. Honor them.

Fiction clothes ghosts, gives them bodies, movement, personalities, stories. Slays them. If you can find a way to create vividly imagined stories for your ghosts, for whatever haunts you, your fiction will carry power. This may involve pushing past your fears, your inhibitions, the very conditioning of your whole life. It may involve facing a *You* you'd rather not face. It certainly involves stretching language, seeking out metaphors, confronting strangeness, honoring lurking unease, learning how to be quiet inside. Strenuous work.

Ghosts of other writers may haunt you. It took Brahms twenty-two years to write his first symphony. He complained that the ghost of Beethoven did him in. Don't let James Joyce or Joseph Conrad or Saul Bellow or John Updike or Toni Morrison or any other favorite intimidate you. If you love fiction, the more you write, the more difficult you may find it to accept your own inadequacies as a writer. That can either motivate you or undermine your efforts. Let it motivate you to keep writing, rewriting. See *Exposure; Time.*

GIFTS

You're breaking your brain over what your character's next move will be. You face a wall, are tied in knots. Need help. You know better than to seek out a friend and discuss your dilemma. You go for a long walk, clear your head, look at the dandelions. You meet someone unexpectedly, stand on the streetcorner to chat. He tells you about his sixteen-year-old son's success in scuba diving. You nod, respond. You hope he can't read the preoccupation in your eyes. Eventually you leave, grateful in a way he couldn't suspect. You happen to be writing about a treasure recovered through deep-sea diving. One of his remarks, an aside, unlocked your brain, broke through the wall, revealed your next move. Now you can inch ahead. Such gifts will be dropped into your life as a writer; helpful things, unsought.

Little miracles occur. Miracles of memory: suddenly something you'd forgotten floats into your mind. Miracles of incident, passing visions that strike you as "just right." I stood at my kitchen sink a few years ago, having come down from my writing study to fortify myself with a cup of coffee. I was stuck. I had my character on the way to the laundry. She was at a crucial point in her development. Surprise was going to meet her in that laundry. As I stared out the window into my backyard, a large pheasant strode across the lawn. His proud beauty took possession of the yard, of my seeking mind.

A while later I returned to my desk. As my character makes her way across a little path toward the laundry where something momentous is about to happen to her, a large pheasant crosses her path. It's simply *there.* I knew that somehow it was right. That's where it belonged.

All unawares, people hand you bits of stories. Images. Beginnings of characters. Situations. Now and then you may sense, just beneath the opaque surfaces of this passing life, a ripple of connections that you have been gifted to touch. Be grateful.

GLIMPSE

Henry James, in *The Art of Fiction,* describes an English "woman novelist" who, while climbing a staircase in Paris, caught a glimpse, through a partially open door, of a group of young French Protestants sitting around a table. When praised for her experience and knowledge of French Protestant youth, she responded that one glimpse, gave her the image she needed to write about that world.

You do not need the whole story delivered to you on a silver platter. You need only the glimpse that stops you, catches you, sets you imagining, won't let you go. Plumb its implications and you'll find the beginnings of your subject.

GOAL-SETTING

It is so easy to let time slide by, to make excuses, to spend hours staring out the window. So easy *not* to count pages, words.

When I first started to teach myself how to write fiction, being already far past thirty and less than naive about the work I faced, I set myself a goal to produce a book within five years. A practical move. It paid off. I decided that if, in five years, I hadn't learned enough of the basics to construct a publishable narrative, I'd turn to something else. Deathless prose or a proseless death: I'd face it.

Goals for this day, this week, this month. So many words. So many pages. Keep to that discipline and you'll develop a sense of work mounting up, even when no one may yet be buying it. If you cannot set realistic goals for income, set them for output.

Years ago I heard Larry McMurtry, author of the popular western novel *Lonesome Dove*, say he decided as a young man that he could write three pages a day. He stuck to it. For me, the page count goal depends on whether I'm in a first, or second, or later draft. But I set myself a realistic goal—so many pages—and aim to meet it, daily. See *Routine*.

GRAMMAR

As you develop dialogue for your characters, pay attention to the level of competence in English grammar appropriate for each character. Remember: You are speaking in their voices, and therefore with their diction, not your own. For other considerations about your own grammatical competence, see *Competence*.

GRANDMA

She loves you dearly, uncritically, applauds your every accomplishment. A loving audience. Do *not* show grandma your story. That goes for your mother, your father, your spouse, your partner, your friends. Adulation from already predisposed parties won't help you a bit and you'll suffer, as well, from having let the cat out of the bag too early. A second point: Family and friends can unknowingly constrict your sense of inner freedom in writing. If you think too much about their opinions, you may hesitate to tackle certain subjects, or you may deal with them less honestly than you could.

My husband is a writer. Years ago we agreed that we would look at each other's work only after it was in final form, published. Though I'm aware of the symbiotic relationship some writers-as-partners sustain successfully, for maximum mutual respect as well as for freedom of the imagination, our pact has worked well for us. See *Exposure; Family; Kindness.*

GROWTH

James Joyce planned his complex novel *Ulysses* as a short story. George Eliot planned a novel about a town called Middlemarch and another to be called *Miss Brooke.* How happy the fusion! Be aware that making fiction involves honoring the organic development as it occurs. It may take longer than you imagine. Set goals. See *Goal-Setting.*

HAD

This innocent three-letter word is a villain, waiting to sap strength and vigor from your story by stopping the reader, thrusting his imagination backward. Consider this example:

> Marlene forced herself to listen to her daughter without interrupting. She had always wondered about Joanne's silences, about her sudden disappearances—for a day, a night, a week even. Often she had thought Joanne must be hiding something. Once she had considered asking outright. But she had resisted, gone on in silence. Wondering.

You may need to fill the reader in on background. See if you can pull the recollection from the past into the *present* by making it part of present action. Move into the remembering mind. Knock off "had" where possible. (You may need it once, as a transition word.)

> Marlene forced herself to listen without comment. Was Joanne, finally, after all these years, about to reveal the why of her silences? What was she hiding? At last it was about to come out. And without motherly prying.

Or you may incorporate a bit of the background into dialogue.

> Joanne took one last swallow of coffee, set the cup carefully back on its saucer. Her precise way of moving was unchanged, after all these years.
> Marlene stilled herself. Waiting.

"I've been thinking . . ." began Joanne, her pale hands set before her on the table, one finger rubbing a bit of moisture from the Formica top.

Wait. Don't ask. Let her talk. Let her see you're not going to pry anymore.

"Yes, I've wondered. What mother wouldn't?"

"Well . . ." Her voice sank to a near whisper. "I know you've . . . wondered why I've taken off so many times." Her finger continued rubbing, round and round, back and forth. She watched it as she spoke.

"Well, remember the time a year ago, the first time I disappeared?"

"How could I forget it?"

You get it. As a basic rule, study your copy for overuse of "had," and figure out ways to avoid jerking your reader's attention *back* rather than *forward*.

HEIGHTEN

Connect "heighten" and "intensify" in your writer's mind. You aim to heighten the effect of a sentence, a scene, a characterization. This may involve a lot of staring, reflecting, rearranging. Thinking about light and shadow may give you a clue about *what* effect to heighten, though not necessarily *how* to do it. Identifying what you want to heighten is a first step, at least. Exactly where do you want the bright light to fall in the scene? On which character? On which words? On which implication? Would the addition (or subtraction) of a gesture heighten the suggestion of what your character is feeling, but perhaps not saying? Would adding a third character who hears and sees but is not visible to those in the scene intensify its effect?

Heightening effects is the work of second, third, fourth, and other drafts. Gradually, as you see what your story is about, it will become clear to you that you've spent too much time on character X's appearance while character Y, actually much more significant as things are now working out, needs to be spruced up visually, needs to be explored more in his disguises and inhibitions—needs, that is, a brighter light on him. Your work is more like that of an oil painter than a water colorist. It may take many strokes, layering, and scraping. Heightening makes a work of fiction three dimensional. See *Intensify*.

HINDSIGHT

When you look back on past work—a novel, say, that never saw the light of print—you may feel, as I do about my first unpublished novel, that you never quite told the story that was there to tell. Somehow, it's unfocused, blurry. Something was muffled.

Every single story and novel presents its own unique problem. As a writer, you may learn the "tricks of the trade," but you are denied forever the certainty that "if I just apply this formula I'll have a satisfying finished product." If you can't live with that comfortless future, go into another line of work.

A writer lives between two tensions: recognition that the last story didn't quite do it, hope that the next one may. Fiction writing can be viewed as Samuel Johnson described a second marriage: "a triumph of hope over experience."

HOBBIES

How you relax away from writing can affect your writing. Writers specialize in solitude, sitting, and staring. We spend hours inside our heads, alone. Physical exercise becomes important to relieve tension. Go swimming, walk, run, play golf, ride horseback: something to get you out of yourself. You'd be surprised how it can unravel a knot in your writing.

Collaborating with another person can relieve writer's solitude, especially nonverbal collaboration: a sport, a game, dancing, music-making.

If your hobby involves talking with other people, however, you run the risk of discussing your work. When they say "How's your novel coming?" and you haven't been able to grind out two paragraphs in the past week, just say "It's coming," and switch to another subject.

HONESTY

This is a crucial quality: honesty in assessing your own work as critically as you are able, honesty about your own ignorance, honesty in responding to editors' comments, honesty, above all, in deciding again and again whether you are committed, really committed, to this ongoing task. Unless you are obsessive or driven, you may have to review your situation periodically and ask again: Is it worth it to me? Answer honestly.

HORIZONTAL THINKING

Some people think primarily in columns, outlines with *I, 1, A, a,* etc.; some think in ranges of association. Though we combine both much of the time, you probably have a sense of how you work most effectively.

Damon Knight offers a suggestion in his instructional book, *Creating Short Fiction.* We can get stuck while writing because we're trying to look at the story head-on, down the tunnel of narrative, looking from the beginning. Turn the story on its side. Look at it horizontally. Its shape and its difficulties may open up for you.

I do this by writing on separate slips of paper a brief summary of a scene, often just a couple of words, then setting them alongside each other on my desk, moving them around, letting them assume new configurations. This can help release anxiety's death grip on my imagination. Clustering can also encourage horizontal thinking.

For those academically trained, breaking the mold of vertical thinking may present a challenge. There's that long line of English literature—back to Beowulf and on down through the Romantics, the Victorians, the Moderns, the post-Moderns, until right at the end you stop at your tiny output, the small dimensions of your fiction. Don't let the weight of that vertical line destroy you. See *Association; Clustering.*

HUMOR

Very few subjects in the world do not allow for a crack of humor in their treatment. Something to let in air, help the material breathe. (Shakespeare certainly knew this.) In fiction, this release, or breath, can come from the voice of the narrator skewing the narration (which may be about something utterly serious) in such a way as to make it humorous. Or it may come in the depiction of a certain character with pronounced, eccentric habits. Even a story about death can hold humor. See, for example, Leo Tolstoy's classic study, *The Death of Ivan Ilych.* For contemporary gallows humor, sample a story from Sherman Alexie's short story collection about Native Americans on the Spokane Indian Reservation, *The Lone Ranger and Tonto Fistfight in Heaven.*

Review your fiction to see whether you have missed a chance, however subtle, for humor. Perhaps you never loosened up sufficiently to discover its humorous dimension. Don't fear that humor will destroy seriousness. It will allow your fiction to breathe.

On the other hand, humor that is inappropriately placed or attempts to be funny which are just plain gauche can destroy a scene and kill a story. Oh, how unconsciously boring a would-be wit can be. See *Breathe; Tone; Voice.*

IDENTITY

Your identity as a fiction writer may sometimes feel precarious, fragile, even phony—especially as rejection slips pile up. It's a common problem, with no easy solution. Until you see your work in print, how do you know you are a writer? Because you are steadily writing, that's how. You will save yourself some frustration if you do not talk a lot about being a writer, but simply keep your fingers to the keyboard and write. When you feel a manuscript is ready, send it out. Do not be hasty about this, though. Be sure you've revised, put the manuscript away, looked at it critically, distanced yourself from it. If, after all that, you collect rejection slips, as I have for years, consider them badges of the trade. They show that you are producing and are sufficiently serious to risk the judgment of a professional eye. If you are in love with the "idea" of being a writer, you're fooling yourself. Writers write. It's work. But as the work mounts up, pages written, stories sent out, gradually the identity grows firmer. The day your first story is published you will feel a rare thrill. It will help to confirm the identity you've worked to sustain perhaps for years. Relish that confirmation, and get back to work. Unfortunately, there's nothing static about a writer's sense of identity. You have to keep writing. See *Affirmation; Belief; You.*

IDLENESS

Idleness can be the Muse's workshop. Writers do a lot of staring. Sitting still. Letting the outside seep in. Letting the inside surface.

Letting the project you're laboring to put together begin to move about in your mind untended, so it becomes something more than a thing "assembled." A moment of creative idleness, if you're lucky, may generate a design you couldn't will to happen. If that occurs, run with it. Remember, though, the words of Louis Pasteur: "Chance favors the prepared mind." See *Mull*.

IMAGE

An image—that is, a word or expression that evokes an object of sensuous appeal—pushes your reader's mind away from the abstract toward the concrete. Instead of saying "the afternoon was peaceful," you create a picture of a lake with late-summer flowers around its edges, water placid, sky clear blue, the occasional bird winging past. Images lead straight to your reader's imagination by presenting something that can be imagined as seen, tasted, touched, heard, smelled. Images sometimes slide over into metaphor, as in the excerpt below from Minnesota writer Jon Hassler's novel *A Green Journey*, where the view of an Irish landscape moves the narrative toward metaphors of marriage and birth.

> The three Minnesotans beheld the sea. Lost it and beheld it again as the road lifted them into great rolling clouds of mist and dropped them down beside the crashing waves. . . . Rock and water. Water and rock. The marriage of sea and land seemed to have given birth to rock the color of the sea—dark gray with a tinge of blue.

Don't, however, overload your fictional page with images. This is sometimes the temptation of writers moving from poetry to fiction. Overloading a page with imagery can slow the pace of narrative and distract the reader from immersion in your story. See *Adjectives; Description; Detail; Enough; Figurative; Metaphor.*

IMAGINATION

It is a mysterious power, imagination. Joseph Conrad called it "the supreme master of art as of life."

Believe in the power of your imagination to transform something old, to create something new. Many things conspire against sustaining that belief: a dry period in writing, a sudden insight into the dullness of one's own prose, the inevitable gap between what you imagined you would produce and what you actually do. Imagined, it was riveting. Written, it seems flat and dull.

What develops your imagination, what releases it? A world event— the latest terrorist kidnapping, say—may leave your imagination untouched; on the other hand, a tiny happening, this morning's blossoming petunia, may awaken your imagination. It's important to recognize what kinds of accident, coincidence, juxtaposition, or even joke—however seemingly trivial or banal—spark your particular imagination.

As Canadian short story writer and novelist Jack Hodgins points out in his study of fiction writing, *A Passion For Narrative*, some writers are sparked by the perfect word—which points them toward the next perfect word, and then the next. For that kind of writer, the word carries a generating power. Other writers, less taken with the perfect word, are spurred on by what Hodgins calls the "unrolling sequence of events." What releases your imagination?

There's no formula—except, I believe, fostering the kind of inner space that allows imagination its freedom. Imagination needs room not guarded by an iron will.

You may juxtapose two events in a story. Only by ruminating, letting them knock together and roll around, only by walking away from them—literally or figuratively, then coming back—can transformation into something new occur. If you're lucky! See *Association; Freedom; Will.*

IMITATION

Choose a sentence or paragraph that strikes you. Make yourself duplicate everything in it except its subject matter. Duplicate rhythm, figurative language, syntax, tone of voice. If you do this occasionally, it may help free you from the tyranny of your own limitations with language.

Don't worry about influence. Language is our homeland. We are constantly resisting or internalizing the world of words that houses us. As readers dedicated to learning from the words of others, we are bound to be influenced to some degree. What mortal could claim immunity to influence? Worry more about mental poverty.

Narrowness. Inflexibility of mind. Being rigid. Closing down too early your sense of what you can do. See *Sentences; Words.*

IMPLICATION

Implication is the felt charge in a human encounter, its unspoken meaning. If we sense that any human moment holds more meaning than it reveals, that tweaks our curiosity. We attempt to "read" that moment. "He seemed cold to me. It was out of character. What did that imply?"

Henry James, in *The Art of Fiction*, calls reading implications "the power to guess the unseen from the seen." Modern Irish writer Sean O'Faolain, discussing compression in the modern short story in his essay "On Convention," considers implication one of the writer's "hieroglyphics of technique."

Fiction achieves implication both within its smaller parts (dialogue, scene, etc.) and through its total design. We are answering a question of implication when we attempt to say, at the end, what a fiction "added up to."

When a reader catches the implication of a scene or a new turn in your story, you've moved her an inch, or a mile, along the narrative trajectory and immersed her more deeply in its web of meanings. Therefore, do not spell everything out. Letting connections and consequences remain implied will *involve* your reader. After many revisions, you may be amazed at how much can be left out. However, *you* must know what you have left out.

The dialogue below, from Robert Stone's *Outerbridge Reach* is loaded with implications: for characterization, for theme, for the movement forward of plot.

Anne and her teenage daughter Maggie visit Annapolis, where Anne and Owen were married years before, during the Vietnam War, before Owen went to serve in Vietnam. The filmmaker, Strickland, middle-aged, politically cynical, experienced, unsympathetic to veterans, and his younger assistant, Hershey, accompany Anne and Maggie.

> "Jesus," Hershey said, looking around the grounds as they
> headed for the gate, "it's all so fascist!"
> "Think so?" Strickland asked.

"Certainly."

"I don't find this place particularly fascist," Strickland said. "I mean, resist the obvious. The Guggenheim Museum is fascist. This is about something else."

"Yes? What?"

Strickland eyed the athletic fields and the statue of Chief Tecumseh.

"Virtue. Republican virtue. Republican virtue in the water."

"I don't get it," Hershey said.

Hershey has not lived, as a thinking adult, through the Vietnam war.

In a book whose central thematic concerns are the dangers of innocence, the contradictory national impulses animating America, and the loss of faith in a meaningful future—and in the old high virtues of loyalty, truthfulness, and love—this little bit of dialogue resonates with implication. See *Clues; Density; Suggesting.*

IMPROVISING

Improvising in any field depends upon developed habits and skills. The improvising musician exploits, intuitively, habits of harmonic association, a knowledge of possibilities so refined and deep that he intuits, instantly, a musical possibility of this moment, "what would fit here." In a personality profile for *The New Yorker*, Whitney Balliet quotes the words of contemporary violinist, Stephan Grappelli, about his experience of improvising:

> Improvisation, it is a mystery. You can write a book about it, but by the end no one still knows what it is. When I improvise and I'm in good form, I'm like somebody half-sleeping. I even forget there are people in front of me. Great improvisers are like priests; they are thinking only of their god.

For writers, the exercise of improvising verbally can hone skills. As I've mentioned under *Freewriting*, I know of four writers who gather once a week for an hour of linguistic improvisation. They open the dictionary, pick a word, and write about it. Or they set an object before them and write. Poems, stories, narratives: surprises and wonders emerge. They limit themselves strictly to write for ten minutes or so. Such pressure, in a friendly competitive atmosphere, can call forth wonders. Think of the nineteenth-century wizard at the keyboard Franz Liszt asking his audiences to write on a piece of paper what they wished him to improvise. Responding to such suggestions as "an old boot" pushed him to new heights of inventiveness.

Improvisational sessions, it seems to me, offer some advantages: They may stimulate associations and generate delight, the sheer pleasure of writing and creating—without regard to publishability or profit. A sensitivity to the possibilities of language may grow through such sessions. Though I do it only at my desk, alone, when I'm stuck, I recommend improvisation to you. See *Competition; Freewriting.*

INADEQUACY

David Dubal, pianist, writer, and teacher at the Juilliard School, asked virtuoso pianist Vladimir Horowitz why he didn't devote more time to composing and getting his keyboard compositions published. Horowitz said he felt his background in theory and composition was inadequate.

Small wonder that we ordinary mortals often feel inadequate to the writing task. An inner voice may say to me: "This is yours to write. This subject is calling to you." Another voice may counter: "Don't be ridiculous. You don't know enough about that." Don't let a sense of inadequacy paralyze or undermine your writing efforts. The higher your ambition, the greater the threat. Practice affirmation. Set goals. Count pages. Bit by bit, the work mounts up. It may not be the work you originally envisioned, yet having produced it will go a long way to counter a sense of inadequacy as a writer, will go a long way to strengthen your identity as a writer. See *Affirmation; Identity.*

INCIDENT

Tying a shoelace is not usually matter for fiction. If, however, you are writing a story about a mentally impaired child, tying a shoelace may represent achievement. It may enter importantly into the stream of cause and effect you're orchestrating to show his development. Thus it becomes even more than incident, it becomes a major event.

You will spend a lot of time dreaming up incidents to move your story along. Good stories and novels, however, are much more than incidents strung together. For an incident to matter, you need to test the depth of its connection to your characters, to their development, to the outcome of the fiction. Incident alters character. You need to ask: What can I make it show? The important question is not how many incidents, but what you intend to make of them. Only when you know this can you judge the resonance an incident can carry, the dimensions of the treatment it deserves. Context is all. See *Events; Sausage; Stretch and Shrink.*

INCONGRUITY

We all have eyes for the incongruous detail. "Somehow, her gesture didn't fit her expressed feeling." "How odd that he turned out to be a trapeze artist after all his training in science." "Did you notice that although she's a clotheshorse, her outfits are always ten years behind the times?" "She seemed so affectionate, yet when we hugged to say good-bye, she was stiff as a board. I wonder what that meant?" That we notice something as incongruous means we have developed expectations about people's appearance and behavior, as well as about life itself. An incongruity is a blip that jostles that imagined harmony. It makes us question. Incongruous juxtaposition of detail can make us grin. A sign outside a small cabin near our town advertises for tourists every summer: "Fireworks, lawn ornaments, and lobster."

Similarly, in fiction. Tiny or large incongruities awaken your reader, keep him on his mental toes. They disrupt narrative smoothness, like a momentary discord or sudden modulation in music, and by that can offer your reader new perspective on the narrative. Incongruities derive their suggestiveness from the larger pattern of expectation you've generated through the narrative itself, the way you've developed character, the implied direction of the story. Against that background, the reader, with his sixth sense of what this story is about, is brought up short by an incongruity. What's going on here? Ah, now I see.

You've created a character, Ben, who is pointlessly garrulous, always interrupting, his words veering off in all directions. In a given scene, you keep Ben nearly wordless, letting his few remarks show unexpected coherence. How come? thinks the reader, and reads on. You've created Alice, a softie on animals, a die-hard animal-rights activist. Yet, in a minor scene, we catch sight of Alice pulling her three-year-old by the ear. Does it fit?

Incongruity is connected with surprise. Develop a keen sense of the incongruities that permeate daily life. It may improve your fiction. It may also breathe humor into it. See *Juxtaposition.*

INDIRECT DISCOURSE

Sometimes called summary dialogue, indirect discourse is simply stating the words of a dialogue indirectly instead of enclosing them in quotation marks. In place of *"It's raining out," he said,* you write *He said it was raining outside.* Sometimes it's useful to break up long chunks of dialogue with indirect discourse as a way of integrating background material quickly into a story.

> They spoke for a while about what it had been like on the tour to Kyoto. He reminded her of the shrines, the endless shrines, the crowds.
> How could she remember all that with such affection?
> "But the downtown at night," she said. "It was brighter than Times Square. So much neon!"
> He said he could happily find his neon elsewhere.

The proportion of direct and indirect dialogue affects the pacing of your story. You decide what goes into direct dialogue and what to summarize in indirect discourse partly from intuition and largely with a revising eye, once the material has cooled and you can judge design, proportion, and pacing. Often, a line of indirect discourse leads into a character's memory or some other detail of his invisible life which direct dialogue reveals less easily. In the example above, for instance, we can easily imagine the last sentence continuing "and since childhood had found the nightlights of Manhattan a fascination." See *Dialogue; Scene.*

INDIVIDUAL

Your story may deal with social issues, levels of society, but your real subject is the individual—in all his or her wonderful quirkiness, contrariness, complexity and depth. Ultimately, visible though our lives may be, we live the deepest parts in secret. Think about that secret space in your characters as you write. It will involve thinking about the secret space in yourself. See *Implication; Secrets.*

INEVITABILITY

Successful fictions integrate an evolving sense of inevitability with a sustained sense of openness and the possibility of surprise. It's a delicate dance. A sense of inevitability is bound up with the evolution of character and event. Moments of surprise—sometimes blips of delight, sometimes actual turns in a story—keep your reader going. Once you've finished composing a fiction, study its balance of inevitability and surprise. Otherwise, it may be boring.

INNER SPACE

You need a sense of inner spaciousness to write effectively. Your imagination requires room, a sense of amplitude, of wide-ranging possibilities to choose from. Give yourself wholehearted permission to rummage through memories, make outrageous connections, scramble words haphazardly on a page. Later you can sort out, put in order, cut and shape.

If you clamp down too soon on your imagination, box it in, so to speak, that premature limiting will make itself felt in two ways: you will feel mentally constricted as you write, and the very words on the page will mirror that crampedness, as if produced through clenched teeth rather than transformed by imaginative power.

Below are bits of advice offered in a music workshop on the Alexander Method, a method to help piano students release music from a composition. I saved these nuggets because they applied, I felt, in interesting ways, to the whole process of fiction writing. For the word "music" supply "fiction." For "notes" supply "words." For "keys, chords," substitute "words" and "phrases." For "keyboard" substitute "fiction."

Give yourself inner space to witness the unfolding of this phrase.

Allow mental breath.

You're too overprotective with your notes.

To make good music requires the whole of our attention rather than a lot of our reaction.

The music is found inside ourselves; not in the fingers.

117

Choose the keys, the chords. Don't just land on them. Make a tactile choice. Treat a chord not as a lump but as a single sound, a group of tones that happen to sound together. A chord is a *chorus of tones*, not a thing or a clot.

There is space in you that has to open to *enable* you to reach the four corners of the keyboard.

Do not *push* the key. Release the finger into the key to go to the very depth of the keyboard.

Open up interiorly to reach the four corners of your imagination. Don't underestimate its dimensions. See *Association; Breathe; Buried.*

INNOVATION

The urge to innovate comes naturally to any writer, especially in a time such as ours when old forms can feel inadequate to express, dramatize, or represent what we feel as "new realities." In addition to that, every artist engages in a tug-of-war with the limits of his medium. Since language cannot render experience, all writers are caught in that impossibility. It can be interesting to see what other artists do to innovate within the limits of their medium.

The well-known Acadian artist Guy Duguay, skilled as a painter but seeking experiment, worked for some years creating "paintless paintings" with varnished bones, stones, sticks, knitting needles. Now Duguay claims to yearn for color. In 1990 he created a sculpture of five hundred smoked fish fastened to narrow sticks stuck in the ground. Bouncing in the wind, the fish appear to be swimming.

We writers have only words. In a world drowning in words, it wouldn't work, however, to imagine the reader of a book of blank pages.

Still, there may come a time in your writing life when you long to be more daring with your fiction, stretch its elements in a new way. Some contemporary fictions operate from principles differing from those spelled out in this book. Stories deliberately lack climax (as does life), characters do not learn (do *we?*), readers are invited—or manipulated—to remain outside a story, both enjoying *and* criticizing it as they read, much as the experimental dramatist Bertolt Brecht required his actors on stage to "stand outside" the characters they were dramatizing; verisimilitude is inconsequential and undesirable;

a subject seems not to exist; plot disappears; cause and effect are irrelevant. Any one or all of the above render a fiction innovative.

You may wish to do the verbal equivalent of making fish dance in the wind like waves. In general, however, radical innovations are practiced successfully only by experienced writers who know what they are doing. See *Artifice*.

INSPIRATION

Thomas Edison's adage that genius is one percent inspiration and ninety-nine percent perspiration applies, certainly, to writing. However, don't despise moments of inspiration. The twentieth-century composer, Igor Stravinsky, remarks in his trenchant little book on the art of composing, *The Poetics of Music*, "An unexpected element strikes me. I make a note of it. At the proper time I put it to profitable use. . . . An accident is perhaps the only thing that really inspires us." How similar this sounds to the habitual practice of writers—open to creative accidents, they jot down the wayward gem that comes their way, hoping to turn it, at some point, to profitable use.

The work comes in making an inspiration your own to use, to place, to exploit in your fiction. That involves hard work. Some writers are overprotective about their inspirations, as if editors, publishers, and other writers are circling ravenously, shark-like, to devour them. Cherish inspiration, use it, but don't overrate it. The real question is what to do with it. See *Germinate*.

INTENSIFY

Great fictions rely on intense effects. An intense scene, or moment in a scene, pulls the reader in close. What makes for intensity? In a scene, it is the depth of connection between action—what is happening now—and character. Action of great consequence to the character will create intensity.

Implication also intensifies a scene. In a narrative passage, intensity arises from moving the reader into the character's mind as he thinks. For thinking to be felt intensely by a reader, its direction, its implications, again must carry weight within the whole story.

If you wish to intensify, therefore, consider the following moves: keep point of view carefully limited to one character, without swerving to the angle of vision held by others; consider whether you have directly appealed to more than one of the senses through specific, concrete images; in a conversation or scene between two people, consider having a third party, unknown to them, watching or overhearing. If the action of a given scene is something illicit or disturbing, latent violence, say, it will gain intensity if it is being watched or overheard. Mercutio under Romeo and Juliet's balcony charges that scene with intensity. Examine your fiction for ironic implications. Irony intensifies implication. Cut all "he saw's" and "he felt's" and move in close, following the action in the mind of the viewer. See *Heighten; Point of View; Scene; Stretch and Shrink.*

INTENTIONS

The road to effective fiction is paved with the play of your characters' intentions: miscalculated, misunderstood, mixed, betrayed, violated, or simply naive. Intentions are related to motivation. Study the gap between your characters' thoughts, speech and actions. Many a fine story arises from the disastrous, comic, or even tragic slip between the cup and the lip, between intention and outcome. See *Gap; Motivation; Tension.*

INTERIOR

Change is the heart of fiction. Real change originates within. Don't shortchange the interior lives of your characters. Let their inner lives show by what they do (or choose not to do), but don't forget the thread that connects the outer life with the interior one. The reader must feel that connection or the book will be all dead incident. See *Events.*

INTERRUPTION

Interruption functions in several useful ways. In dialogue, interruption can dramatize character. Rather than showing two people who hear and understand one another, you may wish to dramatize the distance between them:

> John: "Look, Mary, I've brought home Dungeness crab for a big feed tonight."
> Mary: "Lovely. Do you like the new wallpaper in the kitchen?"

John: "I thought we'd invite over the Joneses and maybe Harry and David, since they're new on the block."

Mary: "I tried to convince the paperhanger to put a border of red, John, but what do you think? Yes, we can call Harry and David, did you say? I think red would have added the final touch, don't you?"

John: "At least they're all cooked. What kind of salads do you want me to pick up?"

Mary: "I'm calling him first thing in the morning, John. We definitely need a red border. It's perfectly clear now that I stand back and look at it."

When structuring your story or novel, don't think only in terms of the straight linear arrangement: A-B-C-D. Contemporary readers are accustomed to jumps in time, in locale, in subject matter. What seems to be an interruption—for example, a new character takes over as narrator—may actually come as a welcome variation in pacing.

INTERVIEWING

If you can't figure out what to do with a character because you're unsure what's motivating her, pretend you're being interviewed. Ask a few obvious questions. "Now, Ann, what would you say is the driving force in your character's decision to leave her husband?" Answer just as if you were helping out the interviewer. You would be surprised how this can loosen up information you have, but can't get at, for any number of reasons. I owe this suggestion to a historian friend who used the interview technique effectively when he was writing a book.

You may also learn a lot by conducting a mock interview with your character. Listen to his or her answers.

INVENTION

Invention discovers; imagination transforms. Together they keep you going as a writer. Occasional odd occurences have made me believe that what writers call inventions may sometimes connect with the actual world in ways we don't know. For example, a man sat on my porch the other evening and said: "You invented me before you met me." I'd written about a Paul Delaney; his name is Paul Delaney. Mere coincidence, you say. Of course. Stranger yet is the experience of devising a detailed scene and then having it happen. Many years ago

I wrote a scene about a young man in quite specific circumstances urging his mother to buy him a leather jacket. A few years later I found myself in that exact scene, dialogue replicated almost word for word.

I mention these anecdotes only to suggest that as we invent worlds through fiction, we may be engaged in an activity whose actual depths and connection with life itself we scarcely fathom.

IRONY

Irony involves the reader. And since reader involvement is one of our greatest goals, the level and kinds of irony in our narratives are important to consider.

Irony is created by the gap between what is said and what the reader is to accept as truth. Here, for example, George Eliot describes Lord Brackenshaw, a figure in her nineteenth-century novel *Daniel Deronda*, after his dinner with a group of ladies:

> ... And every year the amiable Lord Brackenshaw, who was something of a *gourmet*, mentioned Byron's opinion that a woman should never be seen eating,—introducing it with a confidential "The fact is" as if he were for the first time admitting his concurrence in that sentiment of the refined poet.

Eliot expects her reader to understand that Lord Brackenshaw is anything but "amiable": he is absurd, and a supreme bore. The reader, in other words, is expected to grasp the gap between the words literally and the larger context in which they occur. Verbal irony.

On the other hand, irony may arise from the way you skew events in your narrative. An event, for example, can have the opposite effect from the one a character intends, expects or desires. Irony of action. The classic example of this is the dramatic irony in the ancient Greek play *Oedipus Rex* by Sophocles where we know—and Oedipus must gradually discover—that he is himself the murderer he pursues.

Or you may inject considerable irony into a dialogue so that one character's meaning is not grasped, or is misunderstood by the other, while the reader is expected to understand the total picture.

The important point about the several kinds of irony available to a fiction writer is that irony always involves the reader's participation in working out implications of the narrative. See *Implication*.

ISOLATION

In fiction, *nothing exists in isolation.* That's the underlying lie of a book like this. Flip back and forth. See how items connect. No single item can stand by itself, really. Let notions collide and combine in your mind. That's the way fiction itself works. Its meanings, for the reader, are cumulative, interpenetrating, and always add up to more than any one element.

You need to isolate the elements in order to criticize them: How clean is my dialogue here? Is it loaded with implications? Is it moving the story along? Simultaneously, you need always to hold in the back of your mind the larger picture, the total design. See *Beanbag Chair.*

JOURNAL

I use my journal like a laboratory. It's the place where I store materials that must wait for a later time to grow, to recombine, and produce— who knows what? I may not write in it for weeks, then I write for several days: bits and pieces, phrases, glimpses of characters that strike me, memorable details of a landscape, ideas for stories, new turns on old ideas. Here's a glimpse of a place:

> German Restaurant which serves French fries instead of German potato salad, frankfurters instead of German sausage, and has a waiter and waitress like lightfingered zombies. Beside it sits a small building set back from the road. In front, natural wood backyard swings, lawn ornaments—chiefly of little black boys with red vests, holding a fishing pole, and Tweety birds, legs racing. A fountain, waterless, in the middle.

or a character:

> Alcide from the North Shore. Had 7 children. "Had to do something through the long winter. Could only listen to so much Jack Benny." Lined face. Plays guitar, lap keyboard, mandolin, fiddle, piano—picks away at it. Banjo. Had 4 daughters who sang around the North Shore. Couldn't read a note if he tried, he says. His daughter who lives nearby now can read music. He kids her as she practices. "You call that music?" He can't figure it out, he says, "The big B with the little B."

I flip back and forth sometimes, notice what jottings seem to connect, what germs seem still alive. Journals enable us to recover former selves. For getting on with life, losing those selves can be a boon. For a writer, however, that loss can be major.

Surprising strands of continuity emerge over years of journal keeping. You begin to see what matters to you as subjects. I keep my journal in an ordinary lined spiral notebook. These now number twenty-two.

Unlike contemporary American essayist and poet Annie Dillard, who claims to have her journals all indexed by subject, I could achieve no such thing. When I flip back in them, however, I sometimes find a story idea that came to me five or ten years ago. If I've written it since, I make a note and date it. Sometimes I discover just what I need to inject interest or get me past a hard spot in the story I'm currently working on.

A journal can be anything you want: a laboratory, a record, a collected memory, a compost, a junk heap. It may contain more resonance and vibrations than you think. Some writers find journal-writing a pointless nuisance. For me it has had a point.

JUDGMENT

From the time you pick up your pen or start tapping the keyboard as a writer, you are involved in acts of judgment. This subject matters to me, this one does not. This character needs highlighting, this passage is boring, and so on.

We all see the experiences of others, as well as our own, from a certain point of view. This involves judgment. Similarly, when you choose the angle from which the action of your story will be told, you are selecting an angle of judgment. You are, as well, inviting your reader into an extended act of judgment. On what? On the actions and reactions of characters to their emerging destinies, the consequences of their choices.

When, for example, in *Angle of Repose*, Wallace Stegner's novel about settling the American West, Emma's husband tears up the rose bushes which have stood for his love and devotion to her, the reader must come to a judgment about him, about the act: Was it justified? The bushes have required enormous effort. They signify his labors to beautify and tame a portion of the rough American wilderness for his lovely, Eastern-born-and-bred wife. When he misreads clues, suspects her of infidelity, and blames her for the accidental death of their son, he tears up the bushes, painstakingly, then rides away. This action, described in careful detail, requires the reader to make a judgment. The more complex a character and a situation are, as demonstrated in Stegner's scene, the more difficult it is to make a judgment.

Really great fictions often leave us pondering, with no easy sense of judgment—even though we recognize the rightness of outcome. This is because, as Frank O'Connor puts it in *The Lonely Voice*, such fictions stimulate our "moral imagination" and not our "moral judgment." By this he means that a fine story or novel opens up our capacities to weigh moral dilemmas from several angles, angles we might not have previously imagined, rather than narrowing our capacity to simpleminded certitude.

Once your reader closes your book, there remains the final judgment: What did the book add up to? Can it withstand the final judgment?

JUXTAPOSITION

Deciding what goes next to what becomes an important question when you revise. It affects the whole picture, because placing something next to something else always implies a relationship between them. Juxtaposition of words, images, scenes, characters, dialogues, settings, of elements large or small, can suggest several things: the menace latent in the ordinary, the humor in the texture of everyday life, the constant irony of life, the surreal quality of life. As an example, consider the following paragraph from the short story, "Radiation" by David Leavitt. The story centers on two teenage children's reactions to their mother's cancer treatments. Early in the story, Leavitt shows the children watching TV and their mother, in another room, exercising as she too watches TV before leaving for her treatment.

> On the screen Monica and Lesley were arguing over Rick.
> An alarm went off, a commercial came on. The mother stepped off the Exercycle, sat down at the make-up vanity, and began combing her hair. She had it cut specially by a hairdresser who specialized in ladies undergoing the treatment. As

the comb went through, lifting each tuft from the scalp, it revealed the concealed bald patches.

Juxtaposing a woman's disciplined exercise, her bruised vanity, and her habit of watching afternoon TV soaps enables Leavitt to suggest menace, irony, and the faintly surreal quality of ordinary life.

The Irish writer Edna O'Brien often builds her stories, bit by bit, on small juxtapositions, as she does here in "Paradise."

> In the night she heard a guest sob. In the morning the same guest wore a flame dressing gown and praised the marmalade, which she ate sparingly.

Are we to infer that behind the luxurious facade of a millionaire's beach party, behind proprieties of dress and deferential speech lie unarticulated human pain and suffering?

In the example below, from Thomas Keneally's *Three Cheers for the Paraclete*, a modern priest opens a cupboard and is assailed by ironies which Keneally conveys by careful juxtapositions, leading up to the final ironic phrase.

> ... The cold fust of old books assailed him in the dark: devotional books, Dublin, 1913, a good year for unalloyed faith. Why couldn't he have been alive and priested then? Saving up indulgences, averting tumours of the throat with a St. Blaise candle, uttering arcane litanies; going off to the holocaust the following year to be outraged by the intemperate use of the Holy Name by the men in the trenches; dying in 1924 of dropsy, rosaries, and the certainty of Paradise.

In contemporary novels, juxtapositions function in subtle and complex ways to suggest or evoke a feeling rather than laying the feeling bare in straightforward prose. William Gaddis, for example, in his novel *Carpenter's Gothic*, exposes the absurd juxtapositions that penetrate our daily life through this description of a man turning off a radio in the kitchen:

> ... he turned to obliterate Haydn's Notturno number five in C nagging at his back with a twist of the dial that brought them words of hope for hemorrhoid sufferers everywhere.

As you revise, observe what you've put next to what. Have you exploited juxtaposition deliberately? Or have you unwittingly established your verbal neighbors? Look for effect of humor, of menace, of surprise, of irony. Your reader will not be unaware. See *Arranging; Incongruity.*

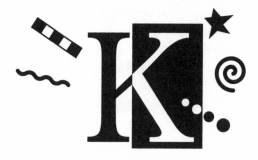

KINDNESS

Kind critiques from others will not carry you very far in learning how to write. Do not be eager to show your work to friends who you can bet will be generous. How many will ever tell you you're boring? You will learn more from a totally disinterested reader—if such can be found.

In the larger world of submissions and rejections, you need to cultivate a certain toughness. Kindness from those who are close to you will not arm you for that.

Kindness to yourself, however, is often well-placed. You know how perplexing and difficult, if rewarding, this task of writing is. Too heavy an imposition of will can crush or distort the gentle breath of inspiration. Therefore, toughness to the outer world but gentleness to your own inner world will pay off. Provided you keep working. See *Grandma*.

KNOWING YOUR SUBJECT

Until you have discovered what your subject actually is—as opposed to what you thought it was when you started out—until you've plumbed its depths and dimensions, you cannot choose where to begin, how to end, or how to best arrange the parts.

What if you want to write about something you know little or nothing about? It means research—books and people. No accumulation of notecards, however, will enable you to turn information into fiction. You need to forget some of what you've studied. Walk around with that material germinating, plant your garden, stare a lot, relax, until time and the alchemy of imagination transform data into something else, the beginnings of a fiction.

Do not be inhibited by directives to "write what you know." We all know more than we think we do. And there are many different ways of knowing. Write to discover not only what you already know but to discover what you're capable of knowing. Stretch yourself.

LANGUAGE

How odd that a medium so removed from matter, so disconnected from the tactile, sensible world, can be so intractable, baffling, frustrating, and seductive. As we work with language—teasing it, confronting it, sweet-talking it to suit our purposes—its fragility and many-sidedness become clear. Words cannot ever adequately communicate or translate our experience.

Yet, in moments of luck, or serendipity, or insight, a fresh turn of phrase can seem to arise from nowhere. We feel the possibility of reaching, through sheer language, into the mind and heart of another. And even when we later reread our words critically, we discover, with surprised pleasure, that this time we did say something worth saying.

One odd point: There seems little connection between the effectiveness of a passage and the effort or ease that went into producing it. You are swimming along strongly, the words are flowing. Or you feel blocked, stuck, you're wringing words out through sheer will, teeth gritted, fighting the sinking feeling in the pit of the stomach that this isn't saying it at all.

Later, when you look back over your efforts with a cool eye, you may discover that the rung-out session has produced something fine, the easy session has produced bathos or sentimentality.

Unless you are deliberately trying to draw attention to your linguistic strategies, your goal in writing narrative is to produce language transparent as glass, a medium for the reader to see through into the story it delivers. See *Finger Proud; Words.*

LENGTH

Don't get bogged down early in the question of length. While it can be argued that a novel's narrative drive tends toward *elaboration* while the short story's tends toward *limitation*, there are exceptions to every rule.

Your goal is to do justice to what is implicit in your materials. That can take a while to fathom. Moreover, in the process of writing, you may discover there's more or less of a story here than you originally thought. Adjust to that recognition.

LESS

Many contemporary writers feel that less is more, that a strategy of fewer words, simpler structures, less information about background and setting is more effective than the fully developed offerings of writers in the past. Is this true? Sometimes. Consider for example this simple opening of William Trevor's novella, *Reading Turgenev*.

> The mists of autumn came, clinging to the houses of Bridge Street, smudging the shop windows with drips and rivulets. The smell of the town was of turf smoke mainly, acrid in the damp air. The shortening days were caught between seasons until November arrived, claiming them for winter.

This looks so simple—until you realize how Trevor has invested a natural process with subtle action, a sense of change: "came," "clinging," "smudging," "shortening," "were caught," "arrived," "claiming." In three short lines summarizing time passing, he's conveyed an active sense of that passing, with its latent menace . . . appropriately placed in the development of the story itself.

Less, of course, can simply be less. Some writers, admonished to cut and compress, hesitate to cut an incident or event they consider "interesting" or "glamorous." But naked event does nothing in fiction unless organically connected to the reactions of characters.

More can also be too much. There can be too many adjectives, too many analogies to be absorbed, or simply too many elements in a description for the reader to follow with pleasure. Here is an example of overwriting which suffers from blurry focus. The reader is asked to take in too much.

The shining beams of bright midafternoon sun slanted through the lacy filigreed treetops and lay relentless like bars of molten gold against the ancient weatherbeaten porch whose posts were rotting and sagging like a weary ship, while freshly carved pumpkins lay heaped behind them, a pyramid of leering orange globes, and in the yard a tattered scarecrow waved fraying sleeves toward circling cawing blackbirds above a cluster of blooming magnolias and a pocket of sagging wilting daisies.

How do you know when less is less, less is more, and more is too much? Only by repeated revision, allowing yourself a cooling-off period, returning to the story and reading—aloud, preferably—alert to the overall rhythm of the piece. Tastes differ. Some readers like clotted, rich prose; some prefer a spare style. Develop your own sense of what you want to do and what you like. It may change. See *Enough.*

LETTING GO
The pursuit of the perfect word, the perfect sentence, can paralyze the imagination, especially when you are starting a story. Once you have the events in place, you know your characters well, sit back, relax, let them play on the stage of your mind, listen to them, watch them. Loosening up is essential. Only then will you achieve a tone likely to strike home for your reader. See *Revising; Voice.*

LIES
Several years ago I gave a reading at a college. At the end, I made a few remarks about the genesis of the story. I was filling time until someone asked a question. "Of course," I commented, "most of this is made up." Later, a member of the audience approached me looking disturbed. "You mean," he said, "it didn't actually happen?" I shook my head. "I'm *devastated*," he said.

He was the president of that college.

Why, one wonders, was he devastated? Fiction is, after all, an artful lie. Yet, when a story really works it carries the ring of "truth." It is convincing in a way that may suggest it "really happened." And of course it did. It happened in the imagination of the writer who both remembers and forgets, who observes and transforms what surrounds her, who may have taken some little nugget of experience and worked with it to make a new creation. Odd business this—of lying skillfully to arrive at truth. We need to study what's at the heart of our fictions, whether it rings true to what we know (hidden realities, seldom spoken of) about human beings in this, our strange world.

LIMITS

Writers live enclosed in a shifting web of limits—sometimes acutely felt, sometimes briefly ignored. Limits from all quarters: from the subjects we've chosen, from our materials (words, words, words), from ourselves. Limits of talent, insight, imagination, inventiveness, willingness to work, belief in ourselves.

Sometimes the difficulty is not in accepting limits but in setting limits. In the preface to his novel *Roderick Hudson*, Henry James describes this problem.

> Really, universally, relations stop nowhere, and the exquisite problem of the artist is eternally but to draw, by a geometry of his own, the circle within which they shall happily *appear* to do so.

Finding that geometry of the circle can be difficult. We live immersed in shifting relationships, perceptions, tensions that tighten, then ease, patterns of insight and thought that glow, then suddenly fade, as we grow. How, swimming in such flux, do we sufficiently stabilize language itself—to say nothing of thought and imagination—to structure a story or novel? We steel ourselves to work with elements, bit by bit: scene, dialogue, subject, chronology, character relationships, and all the rest, to shape out of that flux a circle that will define the limits of our story. At times the possibilities inherent in that material can feel so slippery, so complexly interconnected, so elusive and shifting that although we long to define it, we despair of doing so.

If you feel your story oozing away like unset jelly, try limiting it—in time, in characters, in incidents. The jelly may harden. Try telescoping the action into a week, a month, a year, instead of covering, chronologically, a lifetime. After the basic story is clear to you, perhaps in early draft form, figuring out how to compress that story into a limited time period will force you to devise ways to summarize, how to make a scene do double or triple duty, where to cut redundant dialogue.

Limitation and freedom are the Siamese twins any artist lives with in his contest with his materials. How do you make a body seem weightless? How do you make a percussive instrument sing? How do you make a flat surface appear three dimensional? How do you make fiction believable? See *Constraints*.

LISTENING

Perhaps every fiction writer is a snoop at heart, addicted to overhearing the conversations of the couple in the next booth. Useful and fun as this may be, the writer's essential act of listening to others involves more than the ear. It involves listening with the heart. What lies behind the spoken words of others? That's what we're after. The unseen. Implication. Unuttered speech. Eyes may reveal some of it: a subtle intake of breath, a pause, a slight gesture. Body language may suggest it: the sudden shift of position in a chair, a body that moves in too close as its owner addresses you, the leg swinging or fingers tapping as you seek another's attention. We listen for clues to the hidden drama that animates every life around us. Somehow, that secret life—intuited, listened for—will seep into the life of our fiction.

If you hear an inner voice telling you that you've neglected something, a point isn't quite right (you should have dealt with that difficult scene), listen to it. Experienced writers know when they've tried to duck a challenge. Don't tune out that voice.

LISTS

Books on writing often suggest making lists of alternative courses of action for your characters. Ask yourself what if X did this or that? Quickly list the possibilities that arise in your mind. It may loosen up your imagination, push you to see new possibilities for development.

Within the fiction itself, lists can serve another purpose. Use with caution, because list-making as a technique quickly becomes overdone and boring, a vehicle for displaying knowledge that neither advances action nor deepens characterization. Well used, though, a list can contribute specificity, density, and a sense of perspective. It needs to be organically tied to the actual subject of the fiction, however, not tacked on.

This example, from Jane Smiley's award-winning novel, *A Thousand Acres*, shows what a list can do:

For millenia water lay over the land. Untold generations of water plants, birds, animals, insects, lived, shed bits of themselves, and died. I used to like to imagine how it all drifted down, lazily, in the warm, soupy water—leaves, seeds, feathers, scales, flesh, bones, petals, pollen—then mixed with the saturated soil below and became itself, soil. I used to like to imagine the millions of birds darkening the sunset, setting the sloughs for a night, or a breeding season, the riot of their cries and chirps, the rushing *hough-shhh* of twice millions of wings, the swish of their twiglike legs or paddling feet in the water, sounds barely audible until amplified by millions. And the sloughs would be teeming with fish: shiners, suckers, pumpkinseeds, sunfish, minnows, nothing special, but millions or billions of them. I liked to imagine them because they were the soil, and the soil was the treasure, thicker, richer, more alive with a past and future abundance of life than any soil anywhere.

In a book centered on the treasure of land itself, its possession and disposition, its complex and profound connection to the lives lived on and off it, this passage serves many purposes. It offers insight into the narrator's sensibility; an enlargement of scale to help the reader grasp the dimensions of what's at issue; and specificity, density, and a sense of perspective.

LONGING

Longing breathes at the heart of fiction. Baffled longing, satisfied longing, frustrated longing.

Confront the longings of your own heart. It will help you understand and animate your characters. It will give you sympathy for them, even for the louses and the losers.

MATERIALS

How severely they limit us—*words*. Consider: The great violin maker Stradivarius is said to have fashioned some of his violins from broken oars he found on the Venice docks. From such humble origins came some of the finest musical instruments ever made, today worth a fortune.

What is less prepossessing than a single word? Despite their modest appearance, however, words carry power. They hold infinite possibilities for bridging chasms between writer and reader, for opening up distant and unknown worlds, for illuminating the strange. Grow word-sensitive. Listen to how others speak, read, and write. Read poetry—slowly and often, simply for the pleasure of noticing how words yoked in odd and interesting combinations can generate surprise, lead to insight, evoke feeling. Read prose slowly, listening to the way words go together. As you work with words, despite the inevitable frustrations all writers feel, their power will make itself felt. See *Language; Transformation*.

MEANING

The answers to two questions, at least, seem fundamental in working on a story. What is it about? What happens in it? These questions touch meaning. Although every good story carries multiple meanings and will add up to more than the sum of its parts, it matters to deliberately ask these two questions, to wrestle with them as you write. The first touches theme or subject, the second action. Your answer to these questions must have significance *for you*, or your work will not carry meaning for the reader.

Consider "meaning" also in connection with word choice, grammar, syntax. Except by tricks of structure—of plotting, that is—never aim to baffle your reader. The meaning of every sentence must be clear. Beware especially of faulty antecedent construction, for example, *John visited Gerard every day when he was in the penitentiary.* Who was in the penitentiary? Beware of cramming too much into a sentence, overloading the syntactic slots so the reader cannot find the trees for the woods. Take care to situate your reader clearly in narrative time.

To make sure your meanings are clear, consider connotations of words as well as their denotations. Otherwise you may send your reader a misleading signal. If, for example, you call your character "finicky" or "fussy" you may not mean to suggest something negative but it's there in the connotation.

Finally, your reader should never have to read a sentence twice to catch its basic meaning. See *Significance*.

MEMORY

Memory is an invaluable tool and resource—recent memory, deep memory, yesterday's incident, childhood's wound. Observation and memory form the wellspring from which stories and novels arise. At different times in your writing life you may be drawn to emphasize one or the other.

Forgetting is also part of the process. You can strive to remember too much, too accurately. Before you can transform what you remember and observe into something different and new, much must be forgotten. See *Buried; Compost*.

METAPHOR

A good metaphor moves your reader's imagination to a point of contact with your writing imagination. Metaphor implies a comparison between two things and actively involves your reader in a moment of imaginative sharing. It opens up a hidden ground of meaning which unites those separate things. In that shared moment, the meeting of two imaginations, the metaphor illumines in a new way something that might have remained unnoticed or barely seen. The momentary sharing may be fairly simple, as in this metaphor from

D.H. Lawrence's story "Love Among the Haystacks": "Heat came in wafts, in thick strands."

Or the implied comparison may involve your reader in more complex kinds of comparison and recognition, as this metaphor from Patrick White's *The Solid Mandala.*

Arthur was far from dishonest, but had the kind of buffalo mind which could not restrain itself from lumbering into other people's thoughts.

If the comparison is stated (something is "like" something else) it is a *simile.* Often you may find metaphor and simile combined, as in this opening sentence from Richard Ford's novel *Independence Day.*

In Haddam, summer floats over tree-softened streets like a sweet lotion balm from a careless, languorous god, and the world falls in tune with its own mysterious anthems.

When metaphors work, your reader and you are meeting at a point of abstraction. Consider the following example from Eric Larsen's contemporary novel about a midwestern family, *An American Memory.*

My grandfather was a man who went through life without grace of imagination. Stolid, purposeful, sternly comforting as he may have seemed on the outside, the wind blew through my grandfather's bones.

How much more effective than if Larsen had said "My grandfather was a lonely man" or "My grandfather was hollow inside" (also a metaphor).

Metaphors can be *dead* or *alive.* Writers unused to searching for live metaphors may fall into creating dead ones: "twinkling eyes," "the road of life." Dead metaphors provoke no mental activity in your reader, no involvement. They have been so overused there's no energy left in them. Seek out new ways to describe character, ways that will trigger and stretch your reader's range of association.

Some metaphors enable character description to do double duty: describe, plus carry implication about the deeper themes of a book. In *Flaubert's Parrot,* Julian Barnes' intricately conceived novel dramatizing the quest to uncover a writer's (Gustave Flaubert's) identity, the doctor-narrator offers this description of his insouciant, beloved, dead wife.

> She didn't ever search for that sliding panel which opens the secret chamber of the heart, the chamber where memory and corpses are kept. Sometimes you find the panel, but it doesn't open; sometimes it opens and your gaze meets nothing but a mouse skeleton. But at least you've looked.

The narrator is himself engaged in an ultimately impossible search for the sliding panel into the secret identity of Flaubert-as-writer.

Sometimes an action-turned-into-metaphor becomes critical to the understanding of a story. In Mark Helprin's story "The Schreuderspitze," for example, a young man transforms his weak body into that of a rugged mountain climber and readies himself to climb to the highest peak. As the story evolves, his ordeal of self-training becomes a metaphor for a deeper ordeal—finding his way through grief (the loss of wife and son) back to the affirmation of life.

Once you have completed a first draft, go back over it sleuthing for half-buried metaphors. A subterranean metaphoric strand may be partly hidden there, offering a clue to deeper meanings you may be trying to get at. Discovering it may help you write a more satisfying ending, one that does justice to the implications of the material.

In the process of writing, you may come to understand more deeply the metaphoric implications of an object or action you are describing. Literature is full of objects that seem to resonate with such meaning. Who knows how consciously the author endowed them with that resonance, when awareness struck? It can happen any time. A single action can suddenly turn metaphoric. In a story about strained mother/daughter relations, for example, as the daughter sees her own features in the mirror, she might want to smash the reflecting glass because she notices her mother's features emerging in her own face. Both object and action in this case could carry metaphoric resonance.

Places, objects, actions, gestures: all can take on metaphoric significance. You can develop your alertness to such possibilities by reading the work of other writers, and by revising your own fiction. Such alertness will add immeasurably to the quality of your fiction. See *Echo; Figurative; Objects; Symbols.*

MODELING

If you're temporarily stuck, take time out to practice modeling. Choose a passage you like from any author or poet. Choose a subject. Now imitate the passage in its sentence structure, syntax, grammar, rhythm, everything but the subject—which is your own. Occasionally I do this with a short poem. It's like having the musician's hand on yours as you find the notes. And you always learn something. See *Imitation*.

MOMENTUM

The advice to write a first draft at top speed makes sense: it sustains your momentum. Particularly for novel writing, which must be sustained over a long period of time, momentum becomes important. If you are writing a longer work, a big interruption in writing time will make itself felt in the manuscript. It's hard to reweave a seamless garment. The tone of voice slips, the character development is somehow off, and getting back "in" can be a major problem. Who were those characters? What were they doing? Why did I think it so important? The sense of overall structure grows blurry. Minor characters have faded.

Fight off the enemies that threaten momentum: your desire to escape work, your need for reassurance from others. Stick to your schedule, whether you are counting pages, hours, or words. See *Counting; Routine*.

MOTIVATION

What motivates a fiction writer to persist? Answers vary: desire for fame, money, satisfaction, release, the urge to make, the need for recognition, addiction to the pleasures of literature, belief in the importance of fiction itself, the driving sense that one has something to say. How often do we know why we persist at something? Later reflection may show deeper, more complicated motives than those we thought were at work.

Toward the end of his long life Joseph Haydn, prolific eighteenth-century composer and grandfather of modern classical music, wrote down what had sustained him through years of stressful work, the pressure to turn out composition after composition:

Often when I was wrestling with obstacles of every kind, when my physical and mental strength alike were running low and it was hard for me to persevere in the path on which I had set my feet, a secret feeling within me whispered: "There are so few happy and contented people here below, sorrow and anxiety pursue them everywhere; perhaps your work may, some day, become a spring from which the careworn may draw a few moments' rest and refreshment."

Such a motive may spur some writers more effectively than a movie contract.

What motivates your characters? This can be a troubling question. Although it is important to know your characters deeply and understand their complexities, do not feel obliged to pin down and name a *single, unambiguous* motive for a character's action. A look at major figures in literature shows that part of their enduring fascination springs from complexity of motive. In fiction, as in life, interesting characters always act from mixed motives. Question your characters' motives, as you create them.

MOVE IN CLOSE

You control your reader's attention and his reaction to a scene, an incident, an object, a place, by the distance from which you choose to tell parts of the story. If you seek intensity, let your narrator move in close to the scene and stretch it. Avoid exposition and summary. See *Point of View; Stretch and Shrink.*

MOVING CHARACTERS

Don't worry your characters out of every chair and through every doorway. It isn't necessary, unless such detail serves some larger purpose in your story. As a rule, cut the in-between movements and get your characters where they have to be for the next important event.

A simple example: Joanne is baking bread, a weekly ritual she loves. The telephone, in another room, rings. Her feeling of interruption matters to your story. You want the reader to understand that this ritual is important; getting her hands into dough and kneading it offers her relief after hours at the computer terminal.

She hears the phone, pauses, tries to clean her hands on her apron, heads for the phone, cursing the interruption. Picks up the receiver. As she listens to—her boss, her son, her lover, whomever—she stares at her floury fingers. Hangs up. Now what?

Quick transition: "Back in the kitchen . . ."

Quicker transition: "Her hands again immersed in dough . . ."

In narrating even this tiny incident, you face a host of decisions dependent on what you are trying to show about Joanne. Her decision to let the phone ring unanswered could be presented as momentous. Or you could cut out all the in-between, get her to the phone and back, minimum fuss. Always the question: How does this movement play in the larger design of the story you are trying to tell? See *Beanbag Chair; Design.*

MULL

Writers spend some of their time looking strangely unbusy. They are not producing words; they are mulling over what lies behind the words: their characters' motives, possible choices, the next turn in the story, the possible outcome, the deeper meanings—everything. I recommend a comfortable chair for mulling, away from your computer or typewriter. Also, a blank wall works best, no room with a view. As you mull, you're allowing your mind to play. This kind of free play is necessary for transforming raw materials into fiction.

MUSIC-MAKING

Learning to play an instrument bears many similarities to learning to write fiction. You must gradually build in *reflexes.* The fingers, the feet, the hands must function as independent, yet coordinated entities. You work and work at it, frustrated. One day you reach a threshold: your fingers have grown independent.

Similarly, in writing and rewriting you see how leaden your prose appears, how studied the scenes, how ungripping the narrative, how muffled the climax. If, however, you have a basic instinct for narrative, one day all the elements you've been struggling to master *merge.* You've reached a threshold. You are no longer simply playing notes, or words. You are beginning to make music, organic fiction.

Listeners and readers want a sense of moving forward: profluence, development, resolution. In music, you work to create the effect of melting bar lines, you think horizontally, you disguise units, create a continuum, a musical line. Even repetition carries you forward. For fiction, you select and organize, make summary or scene, feed in information, stretch or shrink, all to push the narrative forward. Even when you return to past events—through flashback, summary, exposition—you present them in such a way that your reader sustains a sense of forward movement.

Simultaneity is part of the challenge in learning any complex skill: too many things to think about at once. Constant decisions. Emphasize this scene? Elaborate this motif? Cut this repetition? So many choices. And always the question for both musician and writer: *where is this leading?* See *Direction*.

MYSTERY

I include the word "mystery" here because so much advice on how to write a fiction bypasses the fact that much about human beings and their activities defies rational analysis. Cause and effect are necessary considerations for every fiction writer. The ultimate sources of action, however, may lie deeper than simple cause and effect. The reasons why we do some things remain forever obscure to our analyzing minds. So too with characters in stories. That insoluble mystery, the elusive dimension of a human being, teases, perplexes, attracts, and finally remains with a reader, after the obvious questions of "will he—won't he" or "did he" have been settled.

NAMING

Names matter. Our initial response to a character named Percival Lancelot Shelley deMaurcy might differ from our expectations of a character named Burt Smith. Changes of name during a story can carry narrative implications, as acclaimed writer Margaret Atwood deftly suggests in her short story, "Hairball."

> ... During her childhood she was a romanticized Katherine, dressed by her misty-eyed, fussy mother in dresses that looked like ruffled pillowcases. By high school she'd shed the frills and emerged as a bouncy, round-faced Kathy, with gleaming freshly washed hair and enviable teeth, eager to please and no more interesting than a health-food ad. At university she was Kath, blunt and no-bullshit in her Take-Back-the-Night jeans and checked shirt and her bricklayer-style striped-denim peaked hat. When she ran away to England, she sliced herself down to Kat.

Writers find names in many ways. Kurt Vonnegut takes names from mailboxes. I sometimes raid local obituaries. The telephone book also can be useful. Take care not to give two closely related characters rhyming names that may confuse the reader, unless your purpose is calculated to provide comedy.

Although a quirky name is no substitute for developing a rounded character, it may help fix the character in your reader's mind. Consider Chizzle, Mizzle, and Drizzle, Mr. Guppy, Mrs. Jellyby, Mrs.

Pardiggle, old Mr. Turveydrop (father of Prince Turveydrop who was a Model of Deportment): to mention just a few of Charles Dickens' memorable names.

What's in a name? A lot. Handle with care.

NARRATIVE

Who has not stifled yawns through a ten-year-old's narration of a movie he's just seen? "... and then and then and then." Where is this going? Will it ever end? The impatient listener longs for a shape, a sense that one incident matters more than another, that all this is leading *somewhere*.

A reader, likewise, craves the sense of a shaping hand. He wants his interest awakened, his attention held. He's prepared to surrender these to you, if you earn them.

The grace period for earning that surrender is short. Any reader wants, early on, to feel some potential payoff. Mere events arranged in sequence are never enough to secure and hold a reader's interest. Event must be tied to character, characters must develop and change. Something must be at stake; the outcome must matter.

What, then, awakens and holds interest? What gives a narrative meaning? Many factors. A sense of emerging shape or design—not necessarily grounded in chronological or causal sequence; the drama of continuing challenge and change; the gradual revelation of inter-connectedness among what may at first have seemed discrete frag-ments; a compelling narrative voice; a sense of danger or menace—something to be avoided, fathomed, or conquered by the character(s); a question to be answered, a puzzle solved.

Who tells the story, from what angle, why, and to whom? The an-swers to these questions confer depth and focus upon narrative. *How* event and character connect, *why* that connection matters and where it leads: these considerations strengthen the fiber of your narrative.

Definitions of narrative vary, but all include, in some form: point of view, narrator, structure, audience, and the "so what" problem. Many, although not all, narratives contain conflict. All imply change of some kind.

Many changes occur in the course of a narrative. Characters and their relationships change. The connections between event and char-acters deepen and develop implications. Conflicts develop and lead to

deeper complications. Settings may take on more sinister or suggestive overtones as, for example, the place where a murder has been
committed. The place is now polluted by blood. A major narrative
action is accomplished. Objects gather to themselves metaphoric or
symbolic significance as the story is told. The narrator's perspective
on the events of the story may change.

Significant character *change* (action) and a *sense of structure* are
crucial. Something must happen. Someone, or someones, must
change as a result of it. See *Action; Change; Conflict; Plotting; Significance.*

NARRATOR

A tale must have a teller. Everything in a story—events, character
development, unfolding action, implied significance—comes to the
reader through a narrator. The narrator is a voice created by words,
separate from you. Grasping this basic point can free you. Self-
criticism becomes easier; rejection becomes less personal.

Pay attention to the voice you choose for a narrator. Or perhaps
you will choose to use a number of different voices, as William
Faulkner did in *As I Lay Dying*, where he uses the idiosyncratic voices
of various members of the Bundren family to explain the significance
of their mother's death.

The narrator who tells the story may be trustworthy or not. It's
up to you to arrange clues so that the reader can judge the level
of trustworthiness in the narrator. How reliable is that voice? How
unreliable? When an unreliable narrator tells a story, the reader's
interest derives partly from his ongoing effort to judge how much to
believe. He must judge the dimensions of the gap between what the
narrator says and his demonstrated reliability. Mark Twain's
Huckleberry Finn offers a standard example of a partially reliable narrator. Though Huck often misses the point, he tries to tell the truth,
and we are left to fill in those gaps.

If the narrator is completely unreliable, the story is infused with
dramatic irony. The reader, knowing more than the narrator, places
the narrator's words and readings of events in a larger context that
may contradict, render comical, darken or lighten the immediate
meaning of words as well as the larger meanings of the work. See
Gap; Point of View; Reader; Voice.

NEGATIVE CAPABILITY

English Romantic poet John Keats coined the term "negative capability" in a letter to his brothers. The term refers to the capacity to sustain doubt and uncertainty without undue restlessness—a capacity necessary to develop for the long haul of a writing career. We're often impatient to see the quick solution, the definite answer, the total picture. We see glimmers, small parts of a picture we sense may be there, we catch a little light shot through with shadow. Self-doubt, uncertainty about form and technique bedevil us at every turn. To hold one's inner self not only steady but even still, quiet, to maintain a kind of inner readiness to "see" in the face of that restlessness, is a constant challenge. In his letter of December 22, 1817, Keats described this quality:

> ... At once it struck me what quality went forth to form a Man of Achievement, especially in Literature, & which Shakespeare possessed so enormously—I mean *Negative Capability*, that is, when a man is capable of being in uncertainties, Mysteries, doubts, without any irritable reaching after fact & reason. ...

In a later letter to his friend, the lawyer Richard Woodhouse, Keats develops a second notion connected with "negative capability." He is writing about his sense of the poet's vocation.

> ... A poet is the most unpoetical of any thing in existence; because he has no Identity—he is continually in for—and filling some other Body—the Sun, the Moon, the Sea and Men and Women.

These words could well be applied to the capacity of a fiction writer to project into the lives of others, of his characters, and feel as from within them.

NONLINEAR

Today's reader neither expects nor hopes for a story that moves neatly from A to Z, hitting every in-between letter in sequence. Readers can sustain complicated jumps back and forth in time and space, so long as you provide enough clues to ground them, give them a sense of where they are at any moment in a narrative. No reader wants to feel totally lost. No serious reader wants to feel coddled. He appreciates an author's act of trust, enjoys the surprise of narrative risk. Strike a balance.

Perhaps you want to dramatize something of life's fragmentariness, the challenges presented by its discontinuities. Perhaps you wish to emphasize the puzzle of a character's life, the bits and pieces. Nonlinear form may serve your goals. As long as you're clear about the beginning and ending, you can mess a lot with Mr. Inbetween and your story may be richer for it. See *Discontinuity; Novelty; Order.*

NOVELTY

The person or object you notice from the corner of your eye as arresting, odd, somehow different, may be important. Don't discount the attraction. The uneasy feeling you experience in a moment that others seem to experience as serene may matter. The strong pull to deal with a subject that seems strange, "off the wall," or just plain unsuited to your background may be exactly the subject you should tackle. Do not be immediately suspicious of the eccentric idea, the odd association that suddenly springs into your mind. Finally, as you work with it, you may suspect there's a new, unorthodox way to tell this odd tale. Do you dare? Work on it. No single formula can contain the extravagances of life. See *Association; Freshness.*

NUGGET

Buried somewhere within or behind every story or novel is a nugget from "real life," some ever-so-tiny sliver of remembered or observed experience around which, by a mysterious process of accretion, a story, a scene, a situation, a character has grown. It may be that in the final version of your story that nugget will have all but vanished. Honor the power of nuggets. They matter not at all to the reader; they matter a great deal to you. See *Glimpse.*

OBJECTS

Objects surround us. We see them, touch them, smell them, cherish them. They carry power, hold us in thrall, stir memories and awaken hopes. The ghosts they harbor trigger associations that trouble, excite, tantalize.

While cleaning out her dresser drawers before leaving her home forever, my mother, an alert, unsentimental ninety-year-old, offers me a box.

"Do you want it?" Inside, carefully wrapped in tissue, a beautiful, delicate, wide-lace collar. "It's from my wedding dress. My sister Mary made it for me."

I never knew Mary. She died when I was a toddler. Mother was married in 1929.

The lace collar yellows. I don't throw it out. I don't wear it. I don't know what to do with it. It remains in its box, moved from place to place. What is its power over me? Is it the association it raises with the moment of my mother's bravely leaving so much behind? Is it some dim connection with a ghostly aunt? Is it the sheer lovely beauty of the thing, made by hands I never knew? It draws to itself a sense of time, place, character, and situation. All this from a handmade lace collar that stays in its box. Undoubtedly, the moment will come when I'll dispose of it, perhaps give it away. What connects us to, then frees us from, objects? Meanwhile, what enables us to manage them?

The narrator in Mary Gordon's story "Living at Home" reflects on an elderly woman's inability to cope with the accumulated objects of a day, a life.

> ... one day all of it is simply too defeating. The process of coping with leftover food. Of disposing with what's gone bad. Remembering to put the milk back in the fridge before it spoils. Understanding what to do with the clot of butter, the size of a penny, still left on a dish, not thrown away because of thrift but too disgusting to eat. ... To live a continuous life a person needs to be in relation to the world of objects. Why does everyone assume this is an easy thing, an accomplishment not worthy of praise? In the blink of an eye, we can be overtaken by or else abandoned by the things we live among.

Just such a blink could make a fine story.

Objects recurring throughout a narrative may provide a clue to changes in character. Patrick White's novel *A Fringe of Leaves* tells the story of Ellen Roxborough, a genteel, nineteenth-century Englishwoman, shipwrecked, captured, and enslaved by aborigines in the Australia bush. At the beginning of her trial, she carefully keeps her wedding ring threaded into the fringe of leaves which is her only covering. After her escape with Jack, the convict, she discovers passion and deep love as together they make their way through the jungle back to "civilization"—naked, exhausted, filthy.

> It occurred to her that she might continue wearing her ring since there were no blacks to hide it from; but she ended by threading it again on a runner, and knotting it as before. If asked for a reason, she might not have been able to find one unless—yes, she would have answered, "My finger is now so thin and shrunk, a ring would slip off and be lost."

By the end of her story, finally returned to a civilization she can never again see the same way, she throws away her ring into a garden where, she says, ". . . a child will find it . . . and value it as a plaything."

We know, by that gesture, that her break from conventions, which formerly bound and even defined her, is complete.

The way a character connects with an object can become a kind of signature throughout a long novel. In Canadian novelist Timothy

Findley's *Headhunter*, for example, his clairvoyant protagonist, Lilah Kemp, is often seen pushing a baby carriage. In James Joyce's *Ulysses*, the hero, Leopold Bloom, walks through Dublin with a potato in his pocket. Some objects remains merely that: an object connected to a character. Some accumulate significance as the story progresses, an aura of meanings, like the scarlet letter A in Nathaniel Hawthorne's *The Scarlet Letter*. At first, in the eyes of the populace, it stands for Hester Prynne's sin of adultery but comes to suggest also Hester's art of embroidery, her saintly nature, her "angelic" child Pearl, and other meanings.

Handle objects with care. Ask yourself after a couple of drafts: Can I do more with any objects? If I intend an object to carry meanings beyond its literal self, have I devised ways to suggest these meanings through foreshadowing, dialogue references, repetition? See *Characters; Image; Symbols.*

OBSESSIONS

Consider your obsessions. You can transfer anything in your life to the realm of fiction. It's your choice how much you are willing to use. Don't underestimate the potential value of your obsessions. Perhaps you can transfer them to a character utterly different from you, jump the fence of rational motivation (which is never the whole story) and offer a sharper insight into your character. Give it a try. See *Exposure; Secrets.*

ONGOING

From one point of view, writing fiction is a process that ends in a product: story or book. At last, concrete achievement: print on a page. On to the next project.

From another point of view, though, as long as there is a reader who picks up your book—from the New Titles shelf or the remainder bin—the process is ongoing. Gifts are still being exchanged. Substitute "fiction" for "poem" in the following; the implications of Canadian poet Alden Nowlan's poem "An Exchange of Gifts" shine forth clearly:

> As long as you read this poem
> I will be writing it.
> I am writing it here and now

before your eye.
although you can't see me.
Perhaps you'll dismiss this
as a verbal trick,
the joke is you're wrong;
the real trick
is your pretending
this is something
fixed and solid,
external to us both.
I tell you better:
I will keep on writing this poem for you
even after I'm dead.

ORDER

The order of discovery differs from the order of presentation. You may gradually uncover your story, set it in chronological order, place its parts A through Z. However, the way you present it depends on what you aim to show. What emphases do you want, what feelings do you want to evoke in your reader? As writer and teacher Dwight Swain put it in his instructional book *Techniques of a Publishing Fiction Writer*: "Show a gun, then a coffin, then tears, and you put your focus on heartbreak. If coffin comes first, then tears, then gun—the issue may be vengeance." See *Delay; Nonlinear; Sequence; Time.*

ORDINARY

The ordinary is your friend, not your enemy. However spectacular the sequence of events you narrate, its connection with ordinary lives will make it ring true for your reader. Some trace of the ordinary informs even the fastastic.

Many writers suffer now and then from the sense that their lives are just too "ordinary" to use in fiction. Don't you believe it. See *Elsewhere.*

ORGANIC

Although fiction writing involves analysis, revision, and hard thought, a successful story feels organic rather than mechanical. In *The Poetics*, discussing unity of action, Aristotle states that stories should be "complete and whole in themselves, with a beginning, a middle, and an end . . . with all the organic unity of a living creature." See *Action; Beanbag Chair; Outcome.*

OUTCOME

Though the outcome of your story may surprise and delight, it needs also to ring true, to be plausible as growing from the seeds developed in the story.

The reader must feel a correspondence between the outcome of the story and the significance of its action. If the jury's verdict at an accused murderer's trial is "innocent," the weight of that outcome needs to balance the weight of the action and concern—fictional evidence—leading up to it. The more sustained the delay, the more desirable a clearly important outcome. Do not throw away your punch line. Milk it.

OVERHEARING

Overhearing and spying are useful techniques. Either one can deepen tension in a scene and may mark, as well, major turns in the action. In Emily Brontë's *Wuthering Heights*, for example, Catherine, the heroine, supposing Heathcliff cannot hear her, confides to Nelly Dean her passionate love for him, and explains why now she can never marry him, but will marry Edgar.

> "I've no more business to marry Edgar Linton that I have to be in heaven; and if the wicked man in there had not brought Heathcliff so low, I shouldn't have thought of it. It would degrade me to marry Heathcliff now; so he shall never know how I love him; and that, not because he's handsome, Nelly, but because he's more myself than I am. Whatever our souls are made of, his and mine are the same, and Linton's is as different as a moonbeam from lightning, or frost from fire."

Heathcliff, hidden from Catherine's view but seen by Nelly, overhears this and steals out, to disappear.

In daily life, overheard bits may spark your imagination to a story. I find the following gems noted in my journal:

> "I try not to tell young priests anything in confession that I think might disturb them."

"When you fuck, it's pleasure. When you make love, it's a language. You speak."

"Landed the ultimate in catatonic jobs yesterday. Babysitting the Goodwill Donate-Mobile."

A writer's fun is to supply context.

PACING

Pacing refers to the rate at which a story moves: snappy, sluggish, or somewhere in between. When we listen to others talk, we're put off by longwindedness. Your readers will be just as sensitive. A good sense of pacing comes through writing and rewriting, and through answering critical questions: Does this story seem rushed? End too abruptly? Seem hurried? Drag? Is essentially the same scene repeated, only dressed with different settings and dialogue? Do characters seem underdeveloped, overdeveloped? Are there soft spots? Where? Is the dialogue effective? Does it include enough, too much, theatrical "business"? Is the story stuffed with exposition? Are clues spaced too far apart? Too close together?

A story needs to unfold at its own pace, a pace that suits the overall design. "Unfold" is the key word, each moment disclosing something new and significant, however slight. Revising with the above questions in mind may help you develop a sense of pacing. Studying revisions by acknowledged masters of fiction can also help.

When you feel your story is as good as you can make it, if you can find a dispassionate, honest reader, ask her to read it with two questions in mind: Where does it drag? Is there any place where you feel rushed, dissatisfied? A sensitive reader will always know. See *Juxtaposition; Time*.

PANIC

Moments of panic may strike at any time. Suddenly you fear you've created more characters than you can do justice to; you've lost the thread of your story; it feels just too complicated to manage. What if you die before you finish this task? The best remedy I know is to hold yourself steady, take a break if you need it, then go quietly back to work. If you are working on a novel, panic may attack when you anticipate the long stretch ahead. Don't look. Try to keep your task finite by sticking to a routine: so many pages a day. Once you have completed a rough draft and found your ending, panic will strike less easily. See *Paralysis*.

PARADOX

Writing fiction involves us in many contradictions and paradoxes: we must let go, we must be critical; we must be specific, we must touch the universal; we must be controlled, we must be free; we must write for ourselves, we must remember the reader.

Writing dispossesses us of our own experience. First, however, we must possess it. By writing we possess our own experience. See *Language; Strangeness*.

PARALYSIS

Right in the midst of writing, the task suddenly feels so daunting, the material so amorphous. You feel paralyzed. A failure of nerve. Can't move forward. Canadian novelist Nino Ricci called this the "death point" in novel writing. You can sometimes trick yourself out of it by moving aside, looking at some other bit of writing for a while. Or you may simply have to put writing temporarily aside. Run. Take an energetic bike ride. Don't put your writing project aside for too long, however. You may lose momentum.

Treat yourself gently. Often, when the mind focuses on something else entirely—doing dishes, taking a walk, cleaning your desk, polishing shoes, something as mundane as ironing—release will come unsought. Have you heard the tale of the centipede who moved agilely until someone asked him how he did it? The question stopped him cold. See *Questions*.

PASSIVITY

Cultivate an alert passivity, the capacity to be quiet inside, to hear what there is to hear, see what there is to see. Passivity not in the sense of inertia, but the capacity, as the poet John Keats put it, not to strain after something. See what happens. See *Negative Capability*.

PATIENCE

In the Preface to his novel *The Portrait of a Lady*, Henry James speaks of the "artful patience with which . . . I piled brick upon brick" in building that book.

Pages of print deceive. They look so fixed, so complete, as if they've been that way forever. Behind them may lie hours, weeks, years of patient work, revising, waiting. Patience is a virtue to acquire, even as you work day by day, counting pages, pushing ahead. Learning how to write takes time. See *Revising; Waiting*.

PERFECTION

Are you addicted to perfection? Such an addiction can undermine, inhibit, paralyze. It can bring you to a complete halt. Instead, charge ahead. Do not fear mistakes. Own your mistakes and move past them. It's a tricky balance to strike: to aim for the "right word," the well-structured story, the powerful narrative, yet accept, finally, less. A sense of humor helps. See *Ambition; Forgiveness*.

PERHAPS

This little word can be a useful tool for casting your reader's imagination backward or forward, for moving more deeply into the world of a character.

In this scene from Marilynne Robinson's acclaimed first novel *Housekeeping*, two sisters skip school. They walk along the railroad tracks toward the railroad bridge over a lake, the same lake into which, years before, the train bearing their grandfather plunged. Near the bridge, the young girls meet hoboes. One of the sisters, the narrator, older now, reinterpreting this experience in the narrative present, allows her imagination to spin around the sight of the two little girls and the hoboes, how she might have explained those little girls out in the bitter cold staring at the water:

> . . . I thought of telling them that our grandfather still lay in a train that had slid to the lake floor long before we were born. Perhaps we all awaited resurrection. Perhaps we expected a train to leap out of the water, caboose foremost, as if in a movie run backward, and then to continue across the bridge. The passengers would arrive, sounder than they departed, accustomed to the depths, serene about their restoration to the light,

disembarking at the station in Fingerbone with a calm that quieted the astonishment of friends. . . .

Here, and elsewhere, Robinson dramatizes a narrator whose mind spins with imaginings that she elaborates, again and again drawing out from a small "perhaps," a dizzying web of possibilities.

"Perhaps" invites the reader to participate in the narrator's exploring imagination. It's another "way in." See *As If (As Though); Feeding-In; Metaphor.*

PERSEVERE

An unwritten story is no story. An unfinished story: ditto. Persevere. See *Faith; Rejection; You.*

PERSPECTIVE

The question of perspective is always with you: What perspective do you wish to develop on the events of this narrative? With whose perspective within the story do you wish your reader to agree, disagree, or partially agree? How you resolve these questions depends on how you handle point of view. Defining perspective within a fiction relates to understanding your subject. Once you have discovered your real subject, you will highlight some elements, downplay others, refine perspective. You will also decide from what distance your narrator is to narrate the story.

In the following opening paragraphs of Southern writer Walker Percy's novel *The Last Gentleman,* for example, the narrator invites us to view the protagonist from a slight distance.

> One fine day in early summer a young man lay thinking in Central Park.
>
> His head was propped on his jacket, which had been folded twice so that the lining was outermost, and wedged into a seam of rock. The rock jutted out of the ground in a section of the park known as the Great Meadow. Beside him and canted up at mortar angle squatted a telescope of unusual design.
>
> In the course of the next five minutes the young man was to witness by chance an insignificant, though rather curious happening. It was the telescope which became the instrument of a bit of accidental eavesdropping. As a consequence of a chance event the rest of his life was to be changed.

Throughout the novel the narrator will maintain that distance from his subject, usually calling the protagonist merely "the engineer" and not even naming him until page ten. The reader is invited to observe the hero through a kind of telescope, the instrument which is itself important to the story. This carefully maintained distance affords the reader a defined angle from which to see the novel's events, characters, and developing situations.

A sudden definition of perspective sometimes illumines a character, as in this sequence from Robert Stone's novel *Children of Light*, a study of film-industry corruption and drug-induced delusion. The hero, Walker, alienated from wife and family, a cocaine addict and out-of-work actor, stands on a high hillside in Mexico and looks down at the oceanside set where the woman he thinks he loves is being filmed, naked and beautiful.

> It was very strange to see them as he did—tiny distant figures at the edge of an ocean, acting out a vision compounded of his obsessions and emotions. He had never been so in love, he thought, as he was with the woman who stood naked on the beach in front of that camera and several dozen cold-eyed souls. It was as though she were there for him, for something that was theirs. He felt at the point of understanding the process in which his life was bound, as though the heights on which he stood was the perspective he had always lacked. Will I understand it all now, he wondered, understand it with the eye, like a painting?
>
> The sense of discovery, of imminent insight excited him.

If you watch for such turns of perspective, you will discover they often occur at important narrative moments and illumine the basic theme or subject of the fiction.

PICTURE

Do you feel stuck? Sit back in a chair and let what is happening in your story appear on the stage of your mind. Close your eyes and let your sense of the outer world gradually drop off. Put yourself *into* the scene you are presently concerned with. Let yourself see details in that room. Whether these will actually appear on the page matters not at all. Furnish the room, or the ship, or the enclosure, whatever it is. A room, let us say. A dining room. What kind of furniture: light, heavily varnished, mahogany, plain? Is there a sideboard, a china closet, a dining room table, chairs? What do they look like? Is the table set? How? Flowers in a vase? Where? What kind of flowers? Can you smell them? Are they fresh or wilting?

Take your time imagining such a setting. Then place your characters in it, doing whatever they are to do. Again, let yourself see them. What is Ralph wearing? Is it what he usually wears, or is it different today. Why? And so on.

For some writers this kind of imagining is instinctive and my suggestions will seem labored. Others have to learn how to do it. Before you start to write a scene, *see* at least one part of it. The more you can see the better. You may be surprised at how much clearer the actions of your characters become.

PLACES

Fictional places, like events, always connect with people. A place may link characters to the past, hint at the future, or offer the chance to dramatize feelings in the narrative present. This can create a complex perspective on what you might expect to be an uncomplicated place. Important places are never uncomplicated for characters—in fiction or in life itself.

In a recent story, "Strange Bodies on a Stranger Shore," I tried to convey this through the narrator's voice, here delivered in first-person point of view. The scene shows a mother visiting a convent with her nineteen-year-old son. They are ushered into the convent parlor.

> What mysterious cubbyhole in the brain center secretes a sense of place, stashes it away to resurrect it alive and well, thank you, decades and lives later? Over thirty years later! No madeleine for me, no sweet taste to elicit memories of sweetness past; instead, the familiar bland austerity of an updated convent parlor to elicit, even now, something timeless, lost, lived. How could this blank faceless room, so blatantly tidy, work so powerfully to shut down a part of me deep inside—a part I couldn't ever name but always knew if it was dead or alive, a part I'd felt to be so throbbingly alive just two hours before in the raging wilderness of a hot New York City?

You may be tempted to overdescribe place and underconnect it with feelings and characters. This is always a mistake. For some writers, a sense of place comes first, as if a stage were opening for their imagination. Once characters are placed on that stage, they begin to move and respond.

Place cannot be divorced from point of view. Someone, either the narrator or a character, describes the place and implies or states a certain point of view.

Here are three very different impressions of Rome, each defined by the character doing the seeing, the narrating voice, and the entire context of the preceding story. The first, from modern Southern writer William Goyen's lyrical "A People of Grass," presents a lonely man left cold, literally and figuratively, by the glories of Rome.

> He maundered about the city of Rome all day, misplaced. It was May, cold and dark and rainy. . . . Blossoms were late, crimped by cold and the pale touch of cold sun. He had left a cold room on whose worn floor of ancient tiles were sensual figures of faded crimson grapes and purple pears that stung bare feet with chill. . . . Here in this room he had risen in cold dawns to the forlorn cry of starlings answering the toning of many bells; and through the window he saw the sunless dome of Saint Peter's that did not comfort.

The second excerpt shows Dorothea Brooke, heroine of George Eliot's *Middlemarch*, living out the first weeks of a loveless marriage amidst the oppressive Roman splendors whose history she cannot comprehend, whose art and statuary oppress her. She experiences a different Rome entirely, one which will haunt her for life. Eliot makes explicit the connection between Dorothea and Rome as she elucidates Dorothea's reaction to the glories of Rome:

> . . . in certain states of dull forlornness Dorothea all her life continued to see the vastness of St. Peter's, the huge bronze canopy, the excited intention in the attitudes and garments of the prophets and evangelists in the mosaics above, and the red drapery which was being hung for Christmas spreading itself everywhere like a disease of the retina.

In the final example Isabel Archer, Henry James' heroine in *The Portrait of a Lady*, after refusing the marriage offer of an English Lord, rests serene and a bit self-satisfied amid the solemn statuary of the Capitol in Rome.

> ... he left her alone in the glorious room, among the shining antique marbles. She sat down in the centre of the circle of these presences, regarding them vaguely, resting her eyes on their beautiful blank faces; listening, as it were, to their eternal silence. . . . a clear, warm shadow rested on the figures and made them more mildly human. Isabel sat there a long time, under the charm of their motionless grace, wondering to what, of their experience, their absent eyes were open, and how, to our ears, their alien lips would sound. . . .

For some, writing about a place does not require walking its streets. Others, like prize-winning novelist William Kennedy who brings Albany, New York, to life in his novels, ride buses, internalize place by a kind of osmosis plus research. Figure out how you work best to capture and deliver a sense of place. It may vary from story to story. See *Description; Point of View; Setting.*

PLAY

Children at play are unselfconscious, absorbed; they delight in discovery. They explore kitchen drawers, invent wonders with pots and pans. We're beyond all that, of course. Writing is adult activity. You need technique, goals, drive, patience, talent, a sense of urgency, belief in what you have to say. Yes, yes of course. But the capacity for play is important. It's the other side of adult self-consciousness. At times a sense of play, the capacity to loosen up, will lead to discoveries, a willingness to improvise. A distrust of rigidity, of rules. An imaginative stretch. Just as we use the word "play" to describe the disciplined, learned capacity to elicit from an instrument something fresh and beautiful, so a writer plays on the possibilities of language, experience, imagination, and plays, as well, with the fruits of her reflection, observation, and pain. Don't be a cramped writer. Cultivate discipline. Then be free. See *Breathe.*

PLOTTING

Some writers love to create plots, invent incident and complication, puzzle over cause and effect. Others find the prospect intimidating.

At some point, however, we all face the problem of plotting. If inventing plots delights you, go for it. If plotting intimidates you, back into it. Study your characters, reflect on their desires, their motives, their frustrations and fears. What do you wish to reveal by their actions? What incident or situation could dramatize that? How can you arrange these incidents to lead toward an appropriate and convincing end, while generating a sense of suspense and expectation in the reader?

Having answered these questions, charge ahead with a rough draft, following your characters' lead, ferreting out the implications and consequences of their choices. Some writers claim they didn't know the ending until they were there, in first draft. Others say they plan every detail, right down to the conversations characters will have. After you have finished a rough draft, the question of plot will become much less intimidating.

You can think of plot in a number of ways: as beginning, middle, end; as initiation, complication, resolution; as problem and solution; as conflict and decision; as tension and repose; as suspense and satisfaction; as question and answer; as mystery and revelation. One of these may appeal strongly to you. According to Aristotle, plot is an arrangement of incidents which "must be whole, complete in themselves, and of adequate importance." But what is wholeness in fiction, what is completeness, and how to measure adequate importance? Aristotle will not solve your practical problems in fictional strategy.

Many difficulties in plotting arise, I believe, because we may not yet know (a) our real subject, (b) an effective ending, (c) enough about the secret lives and motivations of our characters.

A few questions to ask after you've finished your rough draft. How do the parts of this story or novel connect? Are they causally connected, or do they resonate against one another to create an internal music through careful interweaving of parts? How important is chronological sequence? Is there a gathering of tension? If so, where? If I mixed up sequence, exploited delay, would tension increase? Is there conflict? If so, where? If not—what replaces it to hold reader interest?

The traditional paradigm for plot is (a) beginning, (b) complication rising to a climax, (c) then a turn (*peripeteia*), and (d) a resolution. The principle according to which you select and arrange the episodes of your story is your understanding of the story's basic action. The traditional plot pattern shows a protagonist capable of eliciting and holding our attention as he moves through obstacles toward a goal in a series of causally related events. As he moves through such arranged events, conflicts intensify. Ultimately they reach a climax or crisis, a breaking point, and the protagonist, as he survives this (or doesn't), moves to a new place.

This paradigm, based on drama, provides only one way to think about story. Many writers now challenge the adversarial/conquest dynamic behind the traditional view of plot, claiming it perpetuates a patriarchal view of the world where climax is all-important. Some contemporary fictions weave a web of associations that work in contrasting and complementary parallel lines, such as experimental writer Italo Calvino's *If on a Winter's Night a Traveler*, a novel which branches out to become ten different novels, each with its own plot that breaks off at a suspenseful moment. Calvino also develops two readers of the story lines and weaves through it all a commentary on contemporary literature.

You can learn a lot about narrative strategy, plotting, and structure by rereading a book or story backward, section by section, chapter by chapter, once you have read it forward carefully. Tricks of arrangement become visible when you are no longer absorbed by the momentum of story.

In composing realistic fiction our task is, as Henry James puts it, to create "the impression of life." This impression will not just "happen"; it must be thought out. On the other hand, rigid mechanical adherence to the schematic outline of plot may drain life from the piece.

As you plot, frequently ask yourself: Why would a reader be interested in this? What is at stake? Does it matter? Why? To whom?

A final thought about plotting: Underlying successful plots there is always the sense of alternatives. Things could have gone otherwise. The character *could* have chosen this course of action (with these consequences), but did not. This stressful confrontation might have been defused in such-and-such a way, but was not. Part of the reader's pleasure comes from an intuitive sense of what isn't said, what didn't happen. This means that you, the arranger of this plot, need to be alert to how things *might* go, *could* go. Your sense of that will grow from moving the parts of your story around in your own mind, letting them play against one another, so to speak. Although you do not spell out alternatives in so many words, that sense of ways not chosen confers a density. It contributes to the underlying sense of danger, and crucially affects the achievement of suspense. See *Narrative; Point of View; Time.*

POINT OF VIEW

Who is telling the story? From what point of view?

These seem simple questions to answer. They are not. The point-of-view decision affects how you weigh and arrange all the other elements: choice of words, setting, pacing, character, description, management of narrative time, perspective on the material of the story, the significance of its outcome, the degree of distance your reader feels from the story.

To completely discuss the subtleties of point of view would require a full book. It is a slippery and subtle topic. A few distinctions, however, are basic. Beyond that, as you write more and more, you will sense (at least in the revising process) where shifts of point of view may enhance your story, where you've been too loose about point of view, where you may have made the wrong basic choice.

A story told by a first-person narrator, as J.D. Salinger's *The Catcher in the Rye*, pulls the reader in close.

> If you really want to hear about it, the first thing you'll really want to know is where I was born, and what my lousy childhood was like, and how my parents were occupied and all before they had me, and all that David Copperfield kind of crap.

An I-narrator lends a feel of authenticity, immediacy. This degree of closeness to the reader implies limits, however. A first-person narrator has no access to the inner workings of any other character's mind.

In addition, you must decide—and then figure out how to show—whether or not the first-person narrator is reliable, intrusive, marginal or removed. Suppose you open like this:

> I first met John Compostela on the summer afternoon we visited Lake Garda. He was . . .

Here, the narrator may go on to tell the story about John, their connection, involving himself directly in the action and the relationship, or he may hold himself quite distant, the observer, simply the narrator of John's tale. Whether close to or distant from the subject observed, the situation described, a first-person narrator must stay within his own mind. He can observe, project, surmise, imagine what goes on inside John's mind, but he cannot know. He may place himself (or the author may place him) ambiguously distant from the matters he relates, as Marlow, for example, the narrator in Joseph Conrad's *Heart of Darkness*, who tells his listeners of his life-altering excursion into darkness in the Congo; or he may be the main character in the story, like Pip in Charles Dickens' *Great Expectations*, narrating the story of his own great expectations.

If the first-person narrator is in the voice of a child narrating a situation he observes but does not understand, part of the reader's pleasure derives from judging the gap between the naive narrator's grasp of what he sees and the reader's own sense of what the narrator unconsciously reveals.

In Richard Ford's novel, *Wildlife*, for example, a young son, sexually innocent, tries to fathom the implications of his father's loss of work, his parents' separation, his mother's sexual involvements. Ford uses the device of an older person narrating events of his younger life. "When you are sixteen you do not know what your parents know, or much of what they understand, and less of what's in their hearts," says the narrator. From his accumulated experience, he now reflects upon and interprets what he could not have known as a child. Even with the wisdom of experience, however, as first-person narrator, his knowing remains strictly limited.

Ford's narrator, older, goes on to consider the benefits of such constraints:

> This can save you from becoming an adult too early, save your life from becoming only theirs lived over again—which is a loss. But to shield yourself—as I didn't do—seems to be an even greater error, since what's lost is the truth of your parents' life and what you should think about it, and beyond that, how you should estimate the world you are about to live in.

Third-person narration achieves less closeness to the reader but offers more freedom to the narrator. Here, the narrator stands outside the story, refers to characters in the story as "he," "she," "they," or by name. In this opening of Henry Fielding's *Tom Jones* the narrator definitely sets his character, Squire Allworthy, at a distance and will keep him there.

> In that part of the western division of this kingdom which is commonly called Somersetshire, there lately lived, and perhaps still lives, a gentleman whose name was Allworthy. . . .

(Fielding, incidentally, will go on, elsewhere, to poke fun at his fiction, letting the reader know that this is all made up.)

The third-person narrator may connect in several ways with the story he tells. In third-person omniscient point of view, he plays God, knows everything about the events and motives of characters, moves freely into their minds and feelings, shifts time and place with ease. He may choose simply to narrate, rather impersonally, the events of the story and not comment on them, as in Ernest Hemingway's often anthologized "Hills Like White Elephants" where we are left to conclude—by reading between the lines of their dialogue—just what is at issue in this meeting between a man and a woman at a restaurant in Spain. Or the narrator may intrude his views, evaluate the motives and actions of his characters. He may even, in the manner of a nineteenth-century writer such as William Makepeace Thackeray, make comments on life in general as he tells his story, the comments being obviously or not so obviously connected to his tale.

Although omniscient narrators are somewhat unfashionable these days, American novelist Thomas Savage offered an example of omniscient third-person narration in *The Corner or Rife and Pacific*, his highly successful novel of life in the small western town of Grayling, Montana, in the first decades of this century.

In third-person limited point of view, a popular form today, the narrator, telling the story in the third person, observes limits, more or less strictly. He limits himself, for the most part, to knowing the thoughts, experience, and feelings of a single (or just a few) characters.

An example of second-person point of view is Joan Chase's award-winning novel *During the Reign of the Queen of Persia*. It is written in second person plural, narrated by two sets of teenage sisters so close to one another in age and feelings that they speak as "we." In Jay McInerney's popular novel of New York City nightlife, *Bright Lights, Big City*, "you" is the defining viewpoint, as in "You are at a nightclub talking with a girl with a shaved head." The choice of second-person point of view is rare, however, and difficult to sustain successfully— especially in a long fiction.

A caution: *do not shift point of view within a scene.* You will find fine stories that occasionally do this, but such shifting can rapidly dilute a scene.

Always review your story to decide whether you have chosen the best point of view for achieving your end. It is crucial. If you decide to change point of view, it will involve more than tinkering. It will dictate adjustments, excisions, additions, shifts of emphasis. The ease of computer correcting may induce you to touch up a bit here, a bit there. In this case, it won't suffice for effective story revision. If you start from the beginning and rewrite in the newly chosen point of view, you will feel the material shift beneath your fingers. A different point of view shifts everything. See *Questions.*

POSTERITY

Forget about it. Work for the words on the page today, see how they read tomorrow; tomorrow repeat the process. Posterity will take care of itself. See *Fame.*

PRACTICE

Practice makes publishable, though not necessarily perfect. What kind of practice works for you, however, is a highly individual choice. I keep several stories going at once. As I work on them, eventually one or two take over most of my attention. I find it useful, moreover, to be thinking about a problem in the context of a specific story rather than in isolated exercises. See *Exercises; Routine.*

PREPARE

Prepare your reader for the outcome of the story by planting clues. These may be remarks, seemingly innocent, which later take on added meaning as the reader comes to see a character more deeply. They may be images that gather implication as the story progresses, like the camera in Don DeLillo's *Mao II*, which appears rather innocently in the book's opening, but gradually suggests limitations and distortions in our late-twentieth-century ways of seeing each other and experience. Clues may be bits of dialogue that echo something that has gone before and implicitly prepare for what's coming.

Often, some of this preparation comes about instinctively as you write the first draft. Later, as you revise, cut, shape, and mull, you may thicken or thin parts. At first, you may omit crucial clues in the early pages of the story, since it's usually awhile before you understand what you're about. You can easily remedy this, once you return to the beginning with a sense of the whole. See *Clues; Questions.*

PRETENTIOUSNESS

In her book *One Writer's Beginnings*, Eudora Welty shares the opening of one of her early stories. Set in Paris, she thought it sophisticated.

> Monsieur Goule inserted a delicate dagger into Mademoiselle's left side and departed with a poised immediacy.

Ten years later she published her first story, "Death of a Travelling Salesman." Here is its first line:

> R.J. Bowman, who for fourteen years had traveled for a shoe company through Mississippi, drove his Ford along a rutted dirt path.

In the second story she is writing about the ordinary world she knew well, rural Mississippi ("rutted dirt path"), deftly supplying us with concrete detail (he drives a Ford) of a character's history (for fourteen years he has traveled these roads) and a sense that something is about to happen. Monsieur Goule, on the other hand, with his "delicate dagger" and "poised immediacy" seems stuck forever in the pages of an unreadable book. See *Finger Proud; Ordinary.*

PRIVACY

Every writer needs privacy. His rough drafts, his doodles, should be protected from another's prying eye. We need our own space in which to make our own mistakes. For some, a room is a crucial issue. A place of one's own. I began my writing career in a broom closet beneath a chapel. I could have done worse. See *Exposure.*

PROCESS

At one moment highly analytical and rational, at another intuitive, instinctive: writing is a process that requires different kinds of energy at different stages.

I see it as (1) a process of translating experience into words; (2) a process of dispossession (of one's own experience); (3) a process of dialogue—with the material one is probing, uncovering, searching out, inventing—and with oneself; and (4) a process of self-discovery. See *Self-Knowledge*.

PROMISE

When you offer a story you make many promises. You promise to tell a story that will deal with people, to offer it in scenes and to create a situation whose development will involve tension and change and offer some kind of satisfaction at the end. Remember that promise as you write and revise. At the end your reader will know if you have kept it. See *Contract*.

QUALIFIERS

In his essay "An Approach to Style," E.B. White, famous editor and essayist for *The New Yorker*, calls these little words—*somewhat, very, rather*—"the leeches that infest the pond of prose, sucking the blood of words."

The more complex your narrator, the more she may be given to using qualifiers. Be careful. You may dilute both her and your prose.

QUESTIONS

In a long, complicated story, your reader needs occasional help to keep it all straight. Questions can remind him what's at stake and provide a sneaky review of the material he's worked through. Scenes where the protagonist ponders what has preceded, reviews choices, puzzles over what to do next, help to refocus the reader. This review is especially necessary in mysteries. In this example, from American writer James Lee Burke's stunning *In the Electric Mist with Confederate Dead*, Cajun cop Dave Robicheaux reviews the case so far.

> That night I sat alone in the bait shop, a glass of iced coffee in my hand, and tried to figure out the connections between Kelly's death and the pursuit of a serial killer who might also be involved with prostitution. Nothing in the investigation seemed to fit. Was the serial killer also a pimp? Why did his crimes seem to be completely contained within the state of Louisiana? If he had indeed mistaken Kelly for me, what had I discovered in the investigation that would drive him to attempt

the murder of a police officer? And what was Baby Feet Balboni's stake in all this?

As a writer, the habit of questioning your materials, their implications, their drive, becomes basic. In his instructional book *The Art of the Novel*, novelist Milan Kundera remarks, "meditative interrogation (interrogative meditation) is the basis on which all my novels are constructed."

For some fictions, the question "Where is this going?" is crucial. For others, or at other moments (scenes), the question "What is this showing?" is more important. One question merges into the other.

I recommend keeping a sheet of paper—a different color from the paper you print out copy on—nearby while you write. As questions arise, jot them on that paper. Keep the papers in a folder to refer to, once you have a rough draft. Any questions that arise as you write are important and it's easy to forget them. Questions that occur to you will occur to at least some of your readers. As you worry over the precise word in a phrase, larger questions can easily get shunted away.

As for the really large questions of moral choice, truth's ambiguity, innocence and guilt, your task, as Anton Chekhov said, is to pose them fully, not necessarily to answer them. Think about it.

You will not satisfy your readers, however, if you leave everything open to question. You need to answer something, need to weigh the concerns at issue so that the outcome tips in one direction or the other. On the other hand, examined ambiguities, unresolved contradictions, questions that seem at first to mean one thing but the fiction redefines to suggest even deeper meanings—this process of "meditative interrogation" can satisfy a thinking reader. Any fiction that opens the reader's mind to a question worth carrying around will also leave that reader replenished and stimulated. See *Judgment.*

QUOTATIONS

We all need inspiration. Quotations from other writers can help. Collect those that strike a chord in you. They can pull you from a dark spot in writing, motivate you to continue, make you feel less alone.

REACTIONS

You create situations for your characters. They react. The reactions, especially of your protagonist, guide your reader's attitudes toward events and incidents. The connection between your characters' reactions and your reader's judgment is direct and deep. Therefore, your characters' reactions must be in some way intelligible. If they are puzzling, you must offer at least a tiny insight into why the character reacts as he or she does, an inkling that promises: "More will eventually become clear to you." See *Clues; Foreshadowing*.

READ

Train yourself to read as a writer. For some this is difficult. I speak from experience, since I surrender to fiction hedonistically, not as a detective. I must return, *reread* as a writer, a second and third time to figure out: How did she do that? How did she arrange elements to make me feel that? For a writer, all reading is rereading. This takes time. It's worth it.

Once you have read a story or novel with interest, if you've responded to it in an important way, reread it backwards: chapter by chapter, section by section. Or start in the middle. Read forward. Then backward. Study the arrangement of parts, the strategies, the clues and their pattern. They will emerge in a way they couldn't when you were simply following the momentum of narrative. See *Arranging; Design*.

READERS

Your story lives only when it is being read. In the early stages of writing, however, don't worry unduly about your potential reader. Struggle to discover what you are trying to say, how best to say it. Eventually, as you write and rewrite, you will feel yourself turning into a reader, examining over your own shoulder, testing with a reader's ear and eye and mind.

Your reader cares not a hoot about your personal life, your views, your hangups, your sufferings. What he seeks is not you, but some aspect of himself. Reading fiction is a participatory act. A reader wants to lose himself, in some important sense, to participate in another world, another life. At the same time, he seeks an act of recognition that enlarges his understanding of himself and his world.

This transaction depends on a shared universe, or two shared universes: one that you both share simply as human beings in this world, and the other that you create and open to his participation through your fiction.

You want him to pick up your book, enter your fictional world, but you want more: continued reading (please don't put down my book!); some measure of assent (yes, I can move along with you, I'm not scorning you as I read); full attention; sympathetic understanding.

Such a private, intimate collaboration: fiction reading. See *Ongoing*.

READINGS

Writers lead mole-like lives. Most of the time we are hidden, alone, facing the limits of our talents and resources, staring at the computer screen or blank page, putting these strange, tentative markings on it to create an imagined world.

Now and then we surface to give readings. They can be useful. They remind us, palpably, of the audience out there: faces that fall into interesting (sometimes distressing) grooves as they listen; eyes that seem to comprehend or not; heads that nod off.

Moreover, when we read a story aloud to an audience, small and large faults of arrangement fairly leap from the page. We get a sense of how sentences flow, how events connect, how alive the dialogue is. In the end, I believe readings serve writers as much as listeners. If we listen to ourselves and watch our audience, we soon discover whether we are making contact or mouthing thin air.

RECOGNITION

The experience of recognition lies at the heart of reading fiction. Whether your story is set a millennium ago or on some other planet, whether its figures are daily commuters to a Manhattan skyscraper or migrant laborers in southern California, some connecting point makes the reader wish to continue reading about them. Something she recognizes. Perhaps one character lives out a reader's secret desire; perhaps another says words she longs to speak but would never dare. Perhaps the web of constriction in this character's world, far though it be geographically from the place where your reader spends her days, echoes some constricting design she feels when she wakes up in the morning. The click of recognition can take place at a very specific and deep level for a reader. This is one reason to know and explore your characters' secret selves.

For a writer, the act of recognition may come crucially into play in detecting an ending. It occasionally happens, if you have worked intently enough on a manuscript, that an appropriate ending emerges simply as an act of recognition. Suddenly, what was implicit becomes clear. When that happens, milk it. Your ending is at hand. See *Echo; Ending.*

REJECTION

Every writer hates rejection. It is, however, inevitable. But writers can learn from mistakes and even sometimes resurrect cast-off parts of a story to a new, worthier life. Rejection is the tough road toward publication. Sometimes the reasons for rejection have little to do with the quality of the piece itself: the journal had too many stories, needed poetry; the subject had been dealt with in the last issue; no room in this issue for that many words, and so on.

In the introduction to his novel *Touch*, best-selling mystery writer Elmore Leonard notes that it was written in 1977 and was quickly rejected by over a dozen publishers. Finally accepted in 1978, its subject so puzzled the publisher that nothing was done until 1982 when, at Leonard's request, the rights returned to him. Finally, it was published in 1987.

On the dedication page of his detective novel, *A Stained White Radiance*, James Lee Burke thanks his literary agent who kept submitting an earlier novel of Burke's for nine years to almost a hundred publishers.

If this happens to well-known authors, why be surprised if it happens to you?

Here's one trick to reduce negative effects of rejection: When you send out a book or a story, have in mind the next place you'll submit it if it is rejected. That way you won't waste time in tears if it comes back. Into another envelope, on with the stamps.

I made special-occasion placemats out of my first dozen or so rejections. I found large transparent plastic covers into which I could slip my rejection slips and arrange them for humor and contrast. It was somehow satisfying to crack lobster claws or slice steak with my family or guests on top of formal rejection slips from *The New Yorker*, *The Atlantic*, and other journals. It helped to remove the sting. See *Affirmation; Persevere.*

REPETITION

Repetition is a technique prose writers often use instinctively. Count the number and kinds of repetitions in the paragraphs below—of sound, of syntax, of image, of sentence structure. Skillfully used, repetition confers on prose a kind of incantatory power, as in this example from Don DeLillo's novel *White Noise.*

> The other excitement was snow. Heavy snow predicted, later today or tonight. It brought out the crowds, those who feared the roads would soon be impassable, those too old to walk safely in snow and ice, those who thought the storm would isolate them in their homes for days or weeks. Older people in particular were susceptible to news of impending calamity as was forecast on TV by grave men standing before digital radar maps or pulsing photographs of the planet. Whipped into a frenzy, they hurried to the supermarket to stock up before the weather mass moved in. Snow watch, said the forecasters. Snow alert. Snowplows. Snow mixed with sleet and freezing rain. It was already snowing in the west. It was already moving in the east. They gripped this news like a pygmy skull. Snow showers. Snow flurries. Snow warnings. Driving snow. Blowing snow.

Deep and drifting snow. Accumulations, devastations. The old people shopped in a panic. When TV didn't fill them with rage it scared them half to death. They whispered to each other in the checkout lines. Traveler's advisory, zero visibility. When does it hit? How many inches? How many days? They became secretive, shifty, appeared to withhold the latest and worst news from others, appeared to blend a cunning with their haste, tried to hurry out before someone questioned the extent of their purchases. Hoarders in a war. Greedy, guilty.

The repetition of the word "snow" in different syntactic contexts carries a sense of density and driving sameness of snow itself. DeLillo "imbeds" in that vision of oncoming, inevitable, heavy snowfall a series of people gripped by fear, apprehension, anxiety, anticipation—"those who," "those too old," "those who"—creating a kind of litany. The repeated questions dramatize the interplay of inevitability and predictability which happens when heavy snowfall is predicted. It is coming, it is surely coming, but when? Dense snowfall blankets, quiets, renders still. DeLillo avoids what could have been a static description by energizing it through repeated verb forms, particularly participles, through the questions, through the specifically imagined types of people, holding all within carefully structured syntactic repetitions.

The great British writer and theorist E.M. Forster issues us into chapter two of his novel about English class tensions, *Howard's End*, with the following emphasis on syntactic repetitions:

> It was pleasant to wake up in Florence, to open the eyes upon a bright bare room, with a floor of red tiles which look clean though they are not; with a painted ceiling whereon pink griffins and blue amorini sport in a forest of yellow violins and bassoons. It was pleasant, too, to fling wide the windows, pinching the fingers in unfamiliar fastenings, to lean out into sunshine with beautiful hills and trees and marble churches opposite, and, close below, Arno, gurgling against the embankment of the road.

Repetition offers the pleasure of recognition to the reader, something like the pleasure of theme and variations in music. A sense of order without the constricting sense of inflicted predetermined design. A sense of form. Pleasure to the reading eyes and ears. Repetition implies pattern; pattern can comfort and reassure.

Repetition with no larger point to it, however, rapidly becomes boring. See *Arranging; Echo.*

RESCUE

We live encompassed by the sad fact that we cannot stop time, hold it, penetrate it, or even, really, control it. Time does us in.

Fiction writers attempt to stop time, hold it, penetrate it, illumine it from within, create the illusion of controlling it. All these things we do, consciously or not, through words. Tiny tools for such a daring task!

What do we rescue? A moment of seeing, of feeling, a glimpsed situation, the drama of tiny events, a special character. Journal-keeping arises from the sense of inevitable loss that overshadows us. Fiction writing rescues threads to weave, moments to collect, ghosts to clothe, narratives to mesh, characters to immortalize.

The wondrous thing in all this: the act of rescue becomes itself an act of creation, of transformation, the creation of a calculated lie that uncovers and creates, simultaneously, a new and deeper truth. And it even creates, in passing, a different experience of time for the reader. See *Constraints; Limits.*

RESISTANCE

Nailing yourself to a chair for several hours a day to turn out copy for which there may be no demand requires resisting many negatives. The imagination resists your prodding; words resist your design; the market resists your insights: the world is stacked against you. It resists you.

With no resistance, no battle; with no battle, no victory; with no victory over resistance—no fiction. Word by word you seduce the reader away from resisting you.

In one of his many visits to the Parisian bookshop Shakespeare and Company, James Joyce told its proprietor, Sylvia Beach, that despite his extreme eye trouble, he never dictated when he wrote. He was then nearly blind in one eye and had endured several operations. Nonetheless, he wrote by hand, always. He profited, he claimed, from the resistance his hand offered in the act of writing, and he liked to see his sentences as he shaped them, painstakingly, word by word.

RESPONSES

As a shorthand for dramatizing distinctions of character, try creating a scene where two characters respond differently to the same stimulus.

In the opening chapter of Jane Austen's *Pride and Prejudice*, for example, we are introduced to Mr. and Mrs. Bennet, parents of five daughters of marriageable age. For Mrs. Bennet, the arrival of a new young man of large fortune in the neighborhood means only one thing: a possible suitor for a daughter. For Mr. Bennet, it implies no such thing. Austen dramatizes the differences in their character largely through their response to this event. In this excerpt, Mr. Bennet responds to his wife's news:

> "What is his name?"
>
> "Bingley."
>
> "Is he married or single?"
>
> "Oh! Single, my dear, to be sure! A single man of large fortune; four or five thousand a year. What a fine thing for our girls!"
>
> "How so? How can it affect them?"
>
> "My dear Mr. Bennet," replied his wife, "how can you be so tiresome! You must know that I am thinking of his marrying one of them."
>
> "Is that his design in settling here?"
>
> "Design! Nonsense, how can you talk so! But it is very likely that he may fall in love with one of them, and therefore you must visit him as soon as he comes."
>
> "I see no occasion for that."

By dramatizing their difference chiefly through dialogue, Austen saves herself pages of exposition and character description and delineates sharply the contrast in their characters. This chapter, three pages long, repays careful study as an efficient, sharp, humorous, and searching depiction of character. See *Character(s)*.

RETURNING

Acts of returning matter in life. In fiction such acts become a means to dramatize change or lack of change in a character. A figure, now older and more insightful, returns to the places of his youth and finds them singularly unchanged. Against that backdrop his own growth becomes clearer—perhaps to himself, certainly to the reader. Or perhaps he returns to find that a world he once knew has now disappeared forever. His reaction to such a discovery can also reveal much. See *Change; Reaction.*

REVISING

I agree with Brooklyn-born writer Bernard Malamud who, in a 1987 lecture, called revising "one of the exquisite pleasures of writing." Malamud claimed to revise every story at least three times: ". . . once to understand it, the second time to improve the prose, and a third time to compel it to say what it still must say."

Some writers revise as they go along. Gustave Flaubert, we are told, kept two sets of blank pages in front of him. On the first he wrote, with wide margins, the initial version, quickly, catching ideas as they came. After a few pages, he would return to the beginning and start correcting, polishing, revising word by word, sentence by sentence. When the pages were virtually illegible with their writings-over and scratchings-out, he'd make a fair copy of the pages, writing this on the blank sheets. This he always read aloud for sound.

First words and first thoughts sometimes have an energy that can be lost through revision. You may regret throwing out a first version too quickly. Although you may drastically change the overall structure through revision, afterward take one more look at the first draft. It may hold, here and there, a phrase or word whose spark you wish to retain.

A word of caution: Computers make revising easy. This can be a boon; it can also mean loss. Sometimes the original word was better. If you didn't print out hard copy and work with that, you may have lost the focus and energy forever. Often, moreover, mere tinkering is not enough for significant revision. Rethinking structure, point of view, character arrangement, and pacing may be more crucial. Any one of these elements requires major rewriting. You may need to start over at the beginning to get the right disposition of parts, weight, density.

Here are a few questions I ask myself when I'm revising.

1. When I back away from the story, can I say to myself in some coherent way what I think it's about?

2. Is that something I believe matters humanly?

3. Is there enough visual detail to enable a reader to see the action of the story? Are the characters see-able? Does it matter? Have I sunk to clichés in dealing with them, stock figure details—the grampy with pipe and rocker, etc.?

4. Can I find a line, a phrase, an action that seems central to the meaning of the story? Does that help me understand what the story is about?

5. Is there anything—word, phrase, paragraph, scene, whole section, that could be cut and never missed? (Be ruthless. I've used scissors and paper often, moving sections about, pinning them in place with straight pins. Sounds primitive but it's useful.)

6. Do my characters' voices, their dialogue, make me see or feel what they're like?

7. Any pointless dialogue? Does my dialogue work (a) to dramatize character and (b) to move the story forward?

8. Is the sequence right? In the correct order? (So easy to get it wrong, in large and in small units.)

9. Do I feel the need to know more about the background of any character? Have I fed in information about character bit by bit as the action progresses instead of presenting it all in one lump?

10. When I read the story carefully with a cold eye, can I find images or metaphors that seem to echo one another? (If so, it's a hint toward the underlying action of the fiction.)

11. Is something resolved by the end? (The reader needs to feel *something* resolved. This can occur at any level—images, action.) Can I say what is "completed" in this story?

12. If I sit back, close my eyes, and retell the story, can I see it? Can I hear the characters speak, see them move, and feel the underlying movement of the story? Does this exercise show me anything about what's missing or overdone in the story?

13. Have I eliminated passive voice and used linking verbs—is, am, was, were—as little as possible? (Verbs are crucial to energetic prose. Look at them.) Can I cut adverbs and put the action into the verb?

14. Have I used gesture to advantage with my characters? (The way a character picks up a coffee cup can tell more about him or her than paragraphs of description.)

15. Is it clear to the reader just where people are when things are

happening? (It's easy to mess this up.) Standing, sitting, walking about, in a room? Are my characters grounded in a setting or moving about in a vacuum?

Now relax, put it all away, let it sit. After days, even weeks, pull it out and redo the final draft. I find it best, for a short story, to type it straight through, beginning to end, from memory, without a look at the last version. As a rule, what drops off was never needed. See *Questions.*

RHYTHM

Sensitivity to prose rhythm comes from listening, reading your sentences and those of others aloud, feeling them on the tongue. Rhythm is created by alternating stresses and unstresses on words and phrases, by varying long and short units—phrases, sentences, paragraphs. All of this makes visible the shape or contour of thought that lies behind print on a page. The shape of that thought depends, obviously, on the mind thinking it. Rhythm, therefore, leads directly into the dramatization of narrative voice and of character.

In the following paragraph, from Virginia Woolf's challenging novel *To the Lighthouse,* the heroine, Mrs. Ramsay, prepares to go to town. The rhythms also move us along in tune with her physical movements and the restlessness of her mind.

> She had a dull errand in the town; she had a letter or two to write; she would be ten minutes perhaps; she would put on her hat. And, with her basket and her parasol, there she was again, ten minutes later, giving out a sense of being ready, of being equipped for a jaunt, which, however, she must interrupt for a moment, as they passed the tennis lawn, to ask Mr. Carmichael, who was basking with his yellow cat's eyes ajar, so like a cat's they seemed to reflect the branches moving or the clouds passing, but to give no inkling of any inner thoughts or emotions whatsoever, if he wanted anything.

Two examples from James Joyce achieve different effects, each calculated to suggest the character and the situation of the moment. In the first, from his novel *Ulysses,* Joyce tailors prose rhythms to suggest ebb and flow of the ocean and the ebb and flow of an overactive imagination as Stephen Dedalus, would-be writer and dreamer, lies on the beach ruminating on his life.

In the long lassoes from the Cock lake the water flowed full, covering greengoldenly lagoons of sand, rising, flowing. My ashplant will float away. I shall wait. No, they will pass on, passing chafing again the low rocks, swirling, pausing. Better get this job over quick. Listen: a fourworded wavespeech: seesoo, hrss rsseiss, ooos. Vehement breath of waters amid seasnakes, rearing horses, rocks. In cups of rocks it slops: flop, slop, slap: bounded in barrels. And, spent its speech eases. It flows purling, widely flowing, floating foampool, flower unfurling.

A few pages later we will meet Leopold Bloom, main figure of the novel, described in prose rhythms that alert us immediately to this ordinary, observant, down-to-earth hero:

Leopold Bloom ate with relish the inner organs of beasts and fowls. He liked thick giblet soup, nutty gizzards, a stuffed roast heart, liver slices fried with crustcrumbs, fried hencod's roes. Most of all he liked grilled mutton kidneys which gave to his palate a fine tang of faintly scented urine.

Kidneys were in his mind as he moved about the kitchen softly, righting her breakfast things on the humpy tray. . . .

Reading your prose aloud will alert you to the implications of its rhythms and how these connect, or do not, with the fiction you are creating. See *Energy; Sentences.*

ROUTINE

The admonition to count words or pages daily sounds dreary, pedestrian. It seems far removed from the romantic notion of the writer in his garret receiving inspiration from on high, letting it flow unimpeded from the end of his pen.

Forget the garret, forget the magic pen. Moments of inspiration come, and when they do—how lovely. You need a daily routine, however, to be a productive writer. Its details may vary according to what stage you're at in an undertaking—first draft, revising, reviewing the copyedited manuscript. Nonetheless, elements of the routine remain the same. Going to the same spot each day to write, sitting at the same desk, remembering where you were yesterday, starting anew: these simple repeated steps get you over a threshold and into *writing*. I find it encouraging to keep a chart on the wall where I jot down how many pages I did that day. When I arrive the next morning, it's comforting to see that although I may have the sense of being stuck, of having spent much time puzzling rather than writing, in fact, the chart tells me that in the past thirty days I've actually produced so many pages. It's a great spur to continue.

I have also evolved a revitalizing routine for when I'm really stuck. Our town is surrounded by a vast, beautiful marsh, diked centuries ago by the first Acadian settlers. I go out there and walk the dikes for a while. I usually return with the cobwebs blown away, ready for work. Find a routine that suits you—for work and for refreshment. See *Count; Determination; Exercises; Hobbies.*

RULES

Every rule you read for fiction writing can be broken. That is the only rule. Before you break them, however, be sure you understand their value.

SAUSAGE

Incidents strung together sequentially make for dull fiction. A story structured like a string of sausage lacks density, complexity, and enduring interest. Ask yourself if you have more than one story line at work or if you have put together a sequence of scenes in which the same two characters face each other. Also consider whether the questions that lie behind the story, or one implied in the action, are questions that matter to thinking, feeling human beings. See *Density; Meaning*.

SCENE

A scene is the unit in a narrative where characters move, act and react, speak and respond. Consequently, narrative tension deepens and readers get a keen sense of characters in action onstage. At the heart of every scene lies some kind of confrontation. It may be low-key or intense, but for a scene to work something must be at stake. In short, scene brings fiction to life. Readers remember a great scene.

Most stories can be understood as a sequence of scenes linked by transitions tending toward an outcome of crucial significance for a character. The end of each scene shows your character in a different spot—emotionally, physically, or psychologically (one or all)—from where he was at the beginning. Selecting which parts of your narrative deserve to be rendered in scenes is a major part of writing fiction.

Arrangement of scenes affects readerly distance. A scene pulls the reader in close. Consider the difference between the following three pieces, all dealing with the same situation. The first is narrative summary, the second a half-scene, the third a full scene.

1. Narrative summary

Harold knew that when he came home from college with *MADE IN U.S.A.* tattooed in red, white, and blue across his chest, there would be an uproar. His father, usually quiet but deadly serious about proprieties, wouldn't tolerate it. Saturday mornings they always swam together at the local Y pool, and Harold saw no way to worm out of that ritual.

Yet, nothing turned out as he'd anticipated. They went to the pool, he changed, waited for his father's remark, nothing came, they swam their laps, showered, he waited again and finally he could stand it no longer so he broke the silence. Later he would wonder just why his father had been so muted.

2. Half-scene

Their swim together that Saturday morning was full of words that never made it to the surface.

"What do you think of it, Dad?" Harold was tempted to ask outright.

He suppressed it.

Though they showered and dressed together, his father never seemed to notice the fresh tattoo on Harold's chest. Or maybe he did and made the same decision Harold did: words better left unsaid.

3. Full scene

Harold Johnson pulled off the T-shirt and slipped out of his jeans with his back to his dad. They were at the pool for the usual Saturday morning workout.

Harold's stomach churned.

"Let's go," said his dad, and strode ahead, through the swinging doors, toward the pool. Without a look back, he dove in.

Though Harold dreaded the touch of that too-cold water on his bare flesh, he followed and jumped in quickly before his father surfaced.

Might as well delay it, he thought.

His dad surfaced. "How're the courses?" he asked, bobbing

there in the deep end. His black hair hung in his eyes. He smoothed it back and shook his head.

"Okay," said Harold, carefully keeping his chest below water.

"Passing?"

"Um-hum," managed Harold and turned to begin his ten laps.

When they reached the end of three laps, Clarence stopped and hung onto the end of the pool, waiting for his son.

"Been following the newspaper stories about immigration?" he asked, as Harold stopped swimming.

Harold was stymied. Was this a trap of some kind?

He treaded water for a moment, then replied, "Don't know what stories, Dad. Don't have much time for the papers these days."

"You know, Harry. Too many illegal immigrants in the country. Let's control the flow. You've heard about the bill that just passed in California?"

"Not really, Dad." His father was interested in politics but they never discussed it in the pool.

"Just thought you might be afraid they'd deport you, son," he said, and turned with a splash to continue his laps.

Nothing more, ever, about Harold's great adventure in self-definition. Absolutely nothing.

To manage scene selection well you need to know where your story is headed, its true subject, and its main events.

A scene can be relatively simple, two figures facing one another over some evident or hidden issue, or it may be more complex, presenting a number of figures interacting in various ways.

The following excerpt, from John Updike's short story "Still of Some Use," catches a significant moment between father and grown son. Foster, the divorced father, has spent the day cleaning out the attic of his old house with his ex-wife. They have gathered a pile of cast-off toys, games, stuffed animals, which the son will now truck to the local dump. Touched at seeing bits from his childhood piled in the truck, Tommy asks if his father wants to go with him. Foster declines, telling his son how he used to enjoy making a trip to the dump. Tommy replies:

"It's changed since you left. They have all these new rules. The lady there yelled at me last time, for putting stuff in the wrong place."

"She did?"

"Yeah. It was scary." Seeing his father waver, he added. "It'll only take twenty minutes." Though broad of build, Tommy had beardless cheeks and between thickening eyebrows, a trace of that rounded, faintly baffled blankness babies have, that wrinkles before they cry.

"O.K.," Foster said. "You win. I'll come along. I'll protect you."

Behind every scene lies the emotional charge developed in the story to that point. In the scene above, the reader senses the emotion behind the words. Unlike other castoffs from childhood, even at this stage the father can still be of some use to his son.

Great scenes are loaded with implication. Scenes can be too long, though, too explicit. It's a question of dramatizing just enough to carry the emotional charge you seek.

In the scene below, from Sherman Alexie's "The Approximate Size of My Favorite Tumor," Jimmy Many Horses, dying of cancer and abandoned by his wife Norma, lies in his hospital bed having just come back from a radiation treatment. Jimmy, a smart, ironic Native American, tells his story in first-person point of view.

"Jesus," I said to my attending physician. "A few more zaps and I'll be Superman."

"Really?" the doctor said. "I never realized that Clark Kent was a Spokane Indian."

And we laughed, you know, because sometimes that's all two people have in common.

"So," I asked her. "What's my latest prognosis?"

"Well," she said. "It comes down to this. You're dying."

"Not again," I said.

"Yup, Jimmy, you're still dying."

And we laughed, you know, because sometimes you'd rather cry.

It is possible to have only one scene in a short story. Often, however, short stories contain three to five scenes. A novel, of course, contains many more.

The thought of writing a major scene involving many people with differing agendas can intimidate even an experienced writer. The task is akin to conducting a full symphony orchestra. You have to manage a complicated score (which you, unlike the conductor, are creating as you go along), bring each character in at the right moment, on key, with enough implied emotion to clarify what's at issue, suggest more, and move the story along.

Although you will find instances that break the rule, keep to the same viewpoint within a scene. This provides clear focus and maximizes intensity. It also keeps a scene more lifelike, as a moment lived by *one* viewing character, a moment that matters.

A few questions to ask yourself after you've selected a scene:

1. How does it move the narrative forward?
2. Where does it begin and end?
3. From what point of view is it to be narrated?
4. How does this scene deepen characterization and touch the underlying themes of the story?
5. How does it connect with the preceding scene or narrative?
6. Does it foreshadow the next scene, the rest of the story or book?

See *Action; Narrative; Showing (vs. Telling)*.

SECRETS
Think of each of your characters, even the minor ones, as having a secret. Penetrate that secret. It will give them depth. The film director Robert Altman said about his movie *Wedding* that he thought of each character as carrying a secret and took it from there. There is no man or woman without a secret self that remains hidden. Plumb that—in yourself, in your characters. See *Solitude*.

SEEING
Seeing differs from merely receiving impressions. It involves the visual, yes, but implies much more: perception. This means seeing *through* the visual to what it implies, denies, or contradicts.

Therefore, when you are composing a setting or imagining a scene, be careful to supply enough visual detail to ground your readers in a place. Then ask yourself what your arrangement enables your reader to see. Any good fiction equals more than the sum of its parts. It can create for the reader a new, fresher, alternative, and perhaps deeper way of seeing a character, a situation, some aspect of life. See *Discovery; Recognition.*

SELECTION

To select the telling scenes to carry your narrative, you must discover the actual as opposed to the ostensible subject of your story. In the process of selecting, ask "If I leave this out entirely, what will be missing? Does it matter? Why? Can the reader still catch, by implication, what's going on?" See *Design; Finding Your Subject; Focus; Pacing.*

SELF-KNOWLEDGE

All writing is an act of exposure. As you reflect on your fiction, you may discover odd things about your inabilities or abilities. Is your character angry? Examine your angers. Is your character greedy? Examine your greed. Writing involves a deep look, sometimes painful, always liberating, at our own deeply entrenched flaws. There's treasure to mine there, alloyed as it is.

For example: I was raised in a harmonious home where courtesy and consideration of others mattered. I hate disharmony and open conflict. For a long time I wondered why my scenes were so often dull, unsatisfying. Finally it dawned on me that such limitations had a lot to do with my own background, training, conditioning. I was too timid to expose what really was happening in a scene. Consequently, I've often had to write scenes over and over to make the conflict sharper, and sometimes funnier. After I became conscious of what was inhibiting me, the battle was partly won.

For some, the sticking point may be using socially unacceptable language, even though it's needed for dramatizing a certain character; another may recoil from depicting explicit sex, violence. Consult your innermost hesitations to see where they come from. You may be surprised. Perhaps you'll choose to honor them; perhaps you'll work past them. In any case, such increased self-knowledge can only help your writing. See *Exposure; Freedom.*

SENSES

Cultivate awareness of every sense. It's your one way to deliver a world to your readers. Pioneering feminist writer Tillie Olsen opens her story "Hey Sailor, What Ship?" with this intense appeal to every one of the senses:

> The grimy light; the congealing smell of cigarettes that had been smoked long ago and of liquor that had been drunk long ago; the boasting, cursing, wheedling, cringing voices, and the greasy feel of the bar as he gropes for his glass.

Thomas Mann's novella *Death in Venice* demonstrates the power of smells to convey a world, an attitude, as well as a theme. "The stagnant odour of a lagoon," the sticky sweetness of overripe strawberries, the pervasive stench of disease and much more suggest the protagonist's descent into that world of putrid decay and death, suffused as it is with a rotten beauty.

In his short story "Lemonade," Canadian writer Timothy Findley, conveys the loneliness of a small boy primarily through sounds. Every morning the child sits outside his mother's bedroom door and listens for each sound as the maid wakens her and serves her breakfast. The litany of sounds brings home to the reader the acute loneliness of the child. See *Description; Enough.*

SENTENCES

Become familiar with the shape of English sentences. We are locked into a subject-verb-object world and struggle to devise ways out of that trap. When you revise, see if you've varied your sentences: long, short, simple, complex. Do they flow? Do you want them to flow? Play around with them. Have you too many of one kind? Are you developing mannerisms? Be critical. Sentences build stories. They can also quickly turn off readers. Consider the famous opening sentence of Jane Austen's *Pride and Prejudice*. She might have written: "We all know a rich man needs a wife." How much more sedate and witty is her sentence:

> It is a truth universally acknowledged, that a single man in possession of a good fortune, must be in want of a wife.

When you read, choose sentences that strike you as particularly memorable. Analyze them. Pull them apart. Try writing in other words what they communicate. What have you lost? If you do this exercise often, you will come to see how flexible and rich the seemingly rigid English sentence can become.

John Updike begins his story "The Wallet" with this sentence:

> Fulham had assembled a nice life—blue-eyed wife still present-
> able and trim after thirty-three years of marriage, red-haired
> daughter off in the world and doing well, handsome white
> house in one of the older suburbs—yet the darkness was not
> quite sealed out.

From this compressed, mildly ironic sentence (an irony of tone conveyed by "assembled" and "nice") the reader gathers a sense of Fulham's values, his social class, and the undercurrent of menace the story will go on to unfold. Updike might well have taken a paragraph to convey this information. The grammatical structure of the sentence— bracketing off Fulham's visible achievements with irony and menacing implication—serves Updike's narrative purpose well.

First drafts are often full of leaky sentences; you want them to shine as they carry your narrative brilliantly to port. See *Economy; Rhythm; Syntax.*

SEQUENCE

Do not confuse sequence with causality. As Aristotle wrote, "To happen after something is by no means the same as to happen because of it." Holding this distinction clear in your head becomes important as you make final decisions about the order of your narrative. See *Arranging; Order.*

SERENDIPITY

The word "serendipity," coined and defined in the eighteenth century by British writer and scholar Horace Walpole, contains several notions relevant to fiction writing. In a letter of January 28, 1754, to his friend Horace Mann, Walpole describes his lucky accident in finding a coat of arms in an old book:

> This discovery indeed is almost of that kind which I call seren-
> dipity, a very expressive word, which . . . I shall endeavour to
> explain to you: you will understand it better by the derivation
> than by definition. I once read a silly fairy tale called *The Three
> Princes of Serendip*: as their highnesses travelled, they were
> always making discoveries, by accidents and sagacity, of things

which they were not in quest of: for instance, one of them discovered that a mule blind of the right eye had travelled the same road lately, because the grass was eaten only on the left side where it was worse than on the right—now do you understand *serendipity*?

Walpole's anecdote implies several ideas that come together in the experience of serendipity: A seeker sets out on a journey; a series of discoveries occur which seem accidental, fortuitous—not the discoveries he sought but something new, puzzling, or enlightening, something which nonetheless to the wise eye of the seeker can be put to use. These discoveries may yield some new meanings or insights, may even redefine the direction and meaning of the journey. "Serendipity" suggests a poised balance between mysterious powers at work "out there" and the seeking eye.

This kind of experience is familiar to writers. One moment you think you know what you're after, feel you've found a pattern. Then suddenly an incident occurs, you overhear a word, see something that teases your imagination, something you sense connects with your writing. It puzzles you, tantalizes you. Ultimately, as you reflect on this and try to connect it with the pattern you're creating, you redefine the pattern itself. You have reached a new understanding of what you're trying to do.

Writing becomes an ongoing search for equilibrium between the lucky accidents of serendipity, the excitement of discovery and redefinition, the coherence of pattern achieved. It is a journey of discovery. See *Discovery; Gifts*.

SETTING

A setting often does double duty: it conveys the present situation within an immediate circle and also suggests a larger circle of time and space. It is not mere description. Setting is wedded to character, point of view, and underlying theme. It provides crucial context, grounds a character in his or her world, suggests its dimensions, immediate and long range. It's not so much the place they live in but how they come to see it that determines the limits and possibilities of their actions.

In her best-selling novel *The Accidental Tourist*, Anne Tyler charts

Macon Leary's discovery of new freedom and a new self as he abandons the framework of middle-class living and opts for the stressful charms of life with Muriel, an intriguingly resourceful woman who lives in a poor neighborhood.

> He was beginning to feel easier here. Singleton Street still unnerved him with its poverty and ugliness, but it no longer seemed so dangerous. He saw that the hoodlums in front of the Cheery Moments Carry-Out were pathetically young and shabby—their lips chapped, their sparse whiskers ineptly shaved, an uncertain, unformed look around their eyes. He saw that once the men had gone off to work, the women emerged full of good intentions and swept their front walks, picked up the beer cans and potato chip bags, even rolled back their coat sleeves and scrubbed their stoops on the coldest days of the year. Children raced past like so many scraps of paper blowing in the wind—mittens mismatched, noses running—and some woman would brace herself on her broom and call, "You there! I see you! Don't think I don't know you're skipping school!" For this street was always backsliding, Macon saw, always falling behind, but was caught just in time by these women with their carrying voices and their pushy jaws.

Tyler infuses the setting with ordinary, everyday activity and through it she shows, as well, Macon Leary's changing perceptions. See *Places*.

SHOWING (VS. TELLING)

Beginning writers are often instructed to show (through dramatic scenes) rather than tell (through narrative summary). Some telling, of course, is necessary. Exposition and summary surround scenes, linking them. But as a general rule, I guide my students toward showing as the better way of sustaining narrative interest and intensity.

In the following excerpt, created for a writing class on the spur of the moment, I tried to demonstrate how telling is turned into showing, or scene.

Telling

> Adam had always been a strong-minded baby. No one knew it better than his mother. He proved it beyond all doubt the first

morning Elaine's mother-in-law came down for breakfast after flying all the way to Caldwell from Canada to see her new grandson. She brought the usual baubles to charm the baby and to each he responded by chewing on it or flinging it or breaking it. Elaine was mortified, though secretly she thought the child quite like his father. The mother-in-law, of course, would never see that. All vices came from Elaine.

Showing

Wham—the bunny plate hit the refrigerator and broke into bits.

"Good thing I bought plastic," said Granny, trying to be game. This was the second thing the baby had thrown.

"No one uses china these days," said Elaine. "In fact I wish they'd institute an automatic baby-feeder. This stuff-it-in-when-he-isn't-looking-and-wipe-up-the-dribble routine is murder."

Adam was eyeing his grandmother, daring her. Elaine quickly shoved in the rice cereal. He looked at her outraged, but it was too late.

"Now, Adam," said Granny, having deposited the broken plate in the garbage, "wait till you see what *else* Granny brought you. We don't throw this, Adam. We set it on our tray—right there, that's right, right beside the cereal dish mommy feeds you from. See, there's the little suction cup. We just press that, and—there! Now Big Bird can watch you while you eat everything up!"

Granny pulled over the chair near the highchair so she could catch his full reaction. She was disturbed by Elaine's attitude. He was, after all, just a baby.

"The lady in the store said these were all the rage this year," she said to Elaine, who was poised, holding a spoonful of cereal, watching for her chance.

Adam stared at the little plastic muppet attached now to his tray beside the cereal dish. He looked from it to the beaming face of his Granny.

SPLAAAT!

Rice cereal all over her navy angora sweater, rice cereal coating her single strand of pearls.

"Adam!" Elaine swallowed her laughter and ran for the dishcloth. "Naughty!"

Granny had backed away, purple in the face. "I don't know where he gets it from, Elaine," she said, as she dabbed carefully at the woolly rice pudding. "I never had a bit of trouble with Joe."

Like father, like son, thought Elaine, and kept her mouth shut.

Your mother is the last to know.

In the first example we are told by the narrator of an incident between a visiting grandmother and a baby. It is past, removed in time and place; it lacks specific detail and a sense of present action. In the second example, we can feel the rising tension between the grandmother and the baby as we actually hear the plate hit the refrigerator, hear Granny's reaction, catch Elaine's fatigue and Granny's wheedling. Between the words and action, all presented "up close" to the reader, we read the tension between daughter-in-law and grandmother.

Scenes move the reader in close. For more detailed examples of narrative, half-scene, full scene, see the entry under *Scene*.

SIGNIFICANCE

For a story to be significant, something crucial must be at stake. Your reader has to recognize that something as worth the time and trouble it takes to read the story. Otherwise, as he finishes reading he will feel "So what?"

You need to believe in the significance of your material. You must bring to your material both technique and a spirit of belief. Without that combination, your treatment will lack depth. As the distinguished German-American pianist Artur Schnabel put it in *Music and the Line of Most Resistance*, his book of essays about making music:

> There is no such thing as banality in material. It is always in the spirit. A piece of wood or metal or stone can be transformed into a divine message if the right spirit blesses the transformer's hand.

How you shape and dramatize your characters' sense of what is at stake will depend on your own willingness to think about how *you* weigh what is at stake.

The transformer's hand is yours. See *Imagination; Intensify; Transformation.*

SIMILE

A simile makes an explicit comparison between two distinctly different things. The words "like" or "as" link the two things. Similes abound in our everyday speech, many of them dead—"her cheeks are like roses," "her eyes twinkle like stars"—comparisons that no longer evoke significant response. If the comparison is unusual and apt, however, it strikes the reader, makes an impression—sometimes humorously by its incongruity—and prevents her from glossing over the words.

In *A Christmas Carol,* Charles Dickens tells us Marley's face "had a dismal light about it, like a bad lobster in a dark cellar."

In his panegyric novel to his place of origin in Texas, *The House of Breath,* William Goyen finds these words to describe a winter moon:

O Charity! Every frozen morning for awhile in early winter you had a thin little winter moon slung like a slice of silver Rocky Ford cantalope over the sawmill.

Note similes that strike you as you read. It will help you develop a sense of comparison, analogy, help you to see the peculiar ways our imaginations join dissimilar aspects of experience. See *Figurative; Image; Metaphor.*

SIMULTANEITY

As with any complex process, writing fiction involves simultaneously integrating a number of skills. Skater, dancer, pianist, writer: all must develop reflexes and instinctive rhythms. The writer has an advantage however; a second (and third and fourth and so on) chance.

How neatly the printed page deceives by its oh-so-fixed appearance! Scanning your page, the reader sees nothing of the painstaking process through which you built your story. Don't *you* be fooled. Every entry in this book has gone through at least five drafts. See *Cut; Density; Revising.*

SINKING (VS. SKATING)

Surface writing will never produce convincing fiction. You need to sink into your material, not skate on its surface. You may be tempted to heap up incident, or present it rat-a-tat-tat, supposing this will generate tension, excitement, suspense, and hold a reader's interest. An example of such a plot might read something like:

> Mary is alone in the house, someone breaks in, she's upstairs, he steals three oriental rugs, kills her dog, next day police question her, locate suspect (fingerprint), suspect pulls gun, shoots cop, etc.

This will lead the reader nowhere satisfying unless you have thought about Mary, thought about the invader, their connection or lack of it, and puzzled through to what is the subject you're dealing with underneath all this incident. If all you do is skate across the surface of the story, loading it with manipulated incident, your reader will be left as cold as the metaphorical ice that holds you up. See *Events; Incident.*

SITUATION

Every story springs from a situation. Observe your own situation and those around you. Study how people deal with them.

Usually a story will show one or more of the following: (a) how characters deal with their changing situation; (b) how characters come to terms with what cannot be changed; (c) how characters act to change their situation. This interplay between situation and character is basic to the structure of fiction. Let your reader know, early on, the fictive state of affairs.

Franz Kafka succinctly and directly states in the first sentence the situation governing his haunting story "The Metamorphosis":

> As Gregor Samsa awoke one morning from uneasy dreams
> he found himself transformed in his bed into a gigantic insect.

We understand immediately that Samsa's story will be his coming to terms with his bug-existence, his coping with the implications of his plight.

Not all stories and novels state the basic situation so directly. Whatever pace you set, however, before many pages pass, let your reader know who the characters are, where they are, what they are about right now, what that suggests for the future. Working out implications will be a matter for development.

Some human situations are not susceptible to change. In these cases your story may trace an equally significant alteration: a character's change in the way he views a situation, his basic attitude toward it. See *Change; Emerging; Plotting.*

SOLITUDE

Our personal solitude is like the air we breathe—always present, invisible, life-nourishing. From it we seek relief; in it we find refuge. Clumsily or adroitly, fiction explores that human secret, a radically private place which defies description or expression. In his book *The Myth Makers*, British writer V.S. Pritchett comments on Anton Chekhov's extraordinary gift for rendering that solitude in fiction. I have found these words helpful for understanding depths of character:

> What Chekhov saw in our failure to communicate was something positive and precious: the private silence in which we live, and which enables us to endure our own solitude. We live, as his characters do, beyond any tale we happen to enact. So, in the saddest as in the most sardonic of Chekhov's tales, we are conscious of the simple persistence of a person's power to live out his life; in this there is nothing futile. What one is most aware of is the glint of courage.

Reflecting on this hidden "glint of courage" in our imagined characters may lead us to see more deeply into them. And isn't it strange that some memorable fictions, themselves constructs of words, find ways to reveal the power of silence? See *Dialogue; Seeing.*

SOURCES

A story can spring from a variety of sources: newspaper clippings, a glimpsed situation, overheard dialogue, some small remembered thing from a long buried past, a voice in the head, a word, an object noticed. What matters is not where it came from but what it signifies, the power it holds for you. Plumb the feeling attached to that source. Invent episodes that develop out of, dramatize aspects of that feeling. Real power lies at the source.

For a fiction that dramatizes a story from a newspaper clipping, you might read contemporary writer Joanne Greenberg's "Stand Still, Ute River." The story begins with a clipping from the *Denver Post* describing the resurgence of interest, business, and profit in Gold Flume, Colorado, once a defunct silver camp, now remade into a thriving ski resort. She uses the clipping to provide, in capsule form, social and historical background and then zeroes in on a present mystery in Gold Flume. See *Nugget*.

SPACING

The placement of words on a page may seem a minor matter. It is not. The way the eye takes in a page affects the kind of attention a mind will give that page. When you have everything else in the best possible order, return to your manuscript once again. See if there are pages of clotted print, paragraphs that might be broken up to give visual relief to the reader. You may wish to set off a sentence or even a word through spacing, make it stand out on the printed page. Reading aloud will help you find such spots.

SPECIFIC

Be specific in description, as a rule. It draws a reader's attention. Generalizations will turn off a reader unless they are grounded by a context sufficiently filled with specific detail to validate the generalization.

Compare: "Many disasters and mysterious happenings are caused by the earth's movement" (Copeland) and "The earth moves, shifts, goes to putty or quicksand, slops, heaves, shoots mountains." (Joanna Greenberg in her story "Introduction to Seismology.")

Heaps of overspecificity, however, can also bore. Always, it's a question of what you aim to do. In a famous excerpt from one of his letters, Anton Chekhov responds to a purple patch in a friend's story that describes moonlight at length. "No! No!" says Chekhov. "Not that way. If you want to describe the moon just mention that the old broken bottle on the side of the mill-dam was glinting in the moonlight." See *Enough; Implication; Suggesting*.

SPEED

The speed with which you produce a first draft can matter in a couple of ways: sustaining tone and momentum. Since we all change over time, if too many days go by between your start and finish of a rough draft, a new person may in fact be writing it. That will show.

Second, third, and later drafts, however, benefit from your taking time to weigh, sift, rearrange, criticize. There, speed is of no matter and the attempt to be speedy may hinder the final effect. See *Momentum*.

STATIC

Don't get caught in the trap of writing static description. Instead of trying to paint a picture, imagine what a specific character sees. This approach will provide an angle and automatic selection. Tend to your verbs. Are they static? Instead of "He is angry" show his anger by giving him a gesture or action. Instead of "She felt happy" show her dancing around the room. Are your descriptive passages too long? Perhaps you can break them into smaller passages and integrate them in scenes. See *Feeding-In*.

STORY

Story lifts us out of ourselves while leading us more deeply back to ourselves. It creates an illusion of order in a chaotic world, rational design in a world that feels absurd, resolution in a world of insolubles, release in a world of traps, transcendence in a world of limitations.

A story can entertain while it enlightens; it can satisfy while it perplexes. These may sound like old-fashioned notions. The fact is, I have yet to meet anyone, however limited or sophisticated, who does not respond to a well-told, entertaining story.

STRANGENESS

Fiction writers honor life's strangeness. The British novelist Graham Swift, in his essay "Postscriptive Therapy," suggests that telling stories arises, most basically, from the capacity to stand back, look at life, recognize how strange it is, and wonder at it. From such wondering recognition stories are born.

Then the process begins: telling the story. And what a strange process that turns out to be! Looked at from a distance, odd contradictions emerge: The effective story or novel that appears to the reader seamless, flowing, involving, and satisfying, requires of the fictionmaker a great deal of breaking down into parts, shifting around, critical distancing, judgment, and calculation. To show forth the strangeness of the world requires a very strange process indeed. See *Wonder*.

STRETCH AND SHRINK

I borrow these terms from New Zealand writer Rachel McAlpine. When you reach a climactic moment, a moment of heightened tension, resist the tendency to shortchange your materials and also your reader. Stretch that moment. Slowing down the action often increases tension.

In the example below, from Andre Dubus' haunting novella *Voices from the Moon*, Larry nervously pays a surprise visit to his former wife, a dancer, after he has worked through his rage at discovering his father is in love with her and they will marry.

> "I brought you some tomatoes," he said, and handed her the bag; she took it at its top, and the weight lowered her hand.
>
> "Come in the kitchen," she said, and her voice was all right, not impenetrable like her eyes, like her lips had been. They had shown neither surprise nor guilt, nor pity, nor dislike— none of the emotions he had imagined as he drove to the house, walked around it to her door at the back. She had finished lunch, and he recognized its traces: jellied madrilene had been in a bowl, cottage cheese and lettuce on a plate, and a small wooden bowl held dressing from her salad. A tall glass was half-filled with tea and melting ice. She offered him some, and he said Yes, that would be good and at the counter with her back to him, she squeezed a wedge of lime over a glass, dropped in the wedge, went to the freezer for ice, then set the glass in front of him and poured the tea. She turned her back to him, and exclaimed over the tomatoes as she took them out of the bag, and put the nine in the window and the three in the refrigerator. He said to her body bent at the vegetable bin: "Are you dancing?"
>
> "Only alone."

This writing is like a ballet, every movement slowed down through the observing eye, to stretch out our anticipation, with his. How will she respond?

Choosing what to stretch, what to shrink is a major challenge. See *Beanbag Chair; Scene; Time.*

STRUCTURE

You may find it more useful, as I do, to think of your story or novel as a structure rather than to worry about its plot. A house with a weak structure tips, sags, develops cracks, is untrustworthy, cannot shelter its inhabitants securely.

Discovering the structure that suits your materials can take time. A misjudgment about structure can prevent you from telling the story there is to tell. I am in the process, right now, of rewriting a novel on which I spent five years. I am convinced its structure is wrong. Tinkering will not set right a basic flaw in structure. It's a rewrite from the beginning, after a cool rethink.

STYLE

Style is not something applied afterward, detachable from the piece it supposedly adorns. It is not adornment at all. Style comes from the voice on the page; it is organic to the work. It encompasses *how the writer says what she says*. Therefore, it includes everything in your linguistic arsenal: diction, syntax, sentence structure, figurative language (or lack of it), rhythm, density, management of point of view. And it goes even deeper. It is, as award-winning writer Mavis Gallant says in her essay "What Is Style?" "the author's thumbprint, his mark."

E.B. White's essay "An Approach to Style," which appears in the classic *The Elements of Style* by White and William Strunk Jr., is a must-read for a writer. It is too long to summarize here. Its conclusion, however, I quote at length, because no entry on style can afford to omit it.

> Style takes its final shape more from attitudes of mind than from principles of composition, for, as an elderly practitioner once remarked, "writing is an act of faith, not a trick of grammar." This moral observation would have no place in a rule book were it not that style *is* the writer; and therefore what a man is, rather than what he knows, will at last determine his style. If one is to write one must believe—in the truth and worth of the scrawl, in the ability of the reader to receive and decode the message. No one can write decently who is distrustful of the reader's intelligence, or whose attitude is patronizing.

Ultimately, then, the words on the page give voice to who and what we are.

SUBJECTS

In some sense, subjects choose their writers. You may discover, as you write, that you return again and again to certain concerns. They may lie buried beneath a great variety of settings, subjects, characters, and situations. If certain subjects seem to cling to you, don't worry about it. These may be yours and no one else's. J.F. Powers—whose stories were often published in *The New Yorker* in the forties and fifties, and whose novel *Morte d'Urban* won the National Book Award in 1963—made a successful career of writing about the unlikely subject of disappointed priests. See *You*.

SUGGESTING

Much of learning to write is learning how to suggest as well as to state. How to find the adjective that not only describes but carries what you wish to suggest about a place: menace, superficiality, craziness, exoticism, newness? How to have people talk to one another in words that suggest what they're *not* saying? How to place a scene in a narrative so that it suggests, however slightly, what is to come and also reminds, gently, of what has preceded? How to make external details suggest inner natures? It is a case of making a small part, sometimes a tiny part, stand for the whole. Accuracy does matter. If you stop at surface accuracy, however, mere photographic realism, your story will never haunt a reader. One read and it's over. If you can suggest more, the story will merit rereading.

Consider the following two examples. For the first, I apologize to Anton Chekhov.

1.

The seaside resort was a sleepy place. In the good seasons, probably out of boredom or the search for something new, several of the populace regularly walked on the dock. People knew one another and could instantly mark a new arrival in town. One morning a man noticed such a new arrival. She seemed to be a lady, judging from her appearance, and she traveled with a small dog.

2.

It was reported that a new face had been seen on the quay; a lady with a little dog.

Everything spelled out in the first example, and more, Chekhov suggests in the single opening line of his story "The Lady With the Pet Dog."

In the following scene from Richard Ford's story "Great Falls," the narrator, a young boy, stands outside his house where he and his father have come upon another man visiting his mother alone, at night. At this point the father has thrown out the visitor who stands outside with the boy. The boy's father and mother remain inside.

> "I like it out here," Woody said, his head down, looking at his shoes. "Nothing to bother you. I bet you'd see Chicago if the world was flat. The Great Plains commence here."
>
> "I don't know," I said.
>
> Woody looked up at me, cupping his smoke with one hand. "Do you play football?"
>
> "No," I said. I thought about asking him something about my mother. But I had no idea what it would be.
>
> "I have been drinking," Woody said, "but I'm not drunk now."
>
> The wind rose then, and from behind the house I could hear Major bark once from far away, and I could smell the irrigation ditch, hear it hiss in the field. It ran down from Highwood Creek to the Missouri, twenty miles away. It was nothing Woody knew about, nothing he could hear or smell. He knew nothing about anything that was here. I heard my father say the words, "That's a real joke," from inside the house, then the sound of a drawer being opened and shut, and a door closing. Then nothing else.

Ford has placed this scene to maximize the power of suggestion. It suggests what has gone before and also generates a sense of dark expectancy, as the child hears the sounds from inside. In addition, the boy's sense of Woody as an alien, one who in many ways knew "nothing about anything that was here," plays against the boy's own sense of standing surrounded by details of an utterly familiar world—ditch, hiss, the creek, the Missouri, the dog's bark—yet being plunged into strangeness. A strangeness latent with menace.

SUMMARIZE

Once it's written, summarize the action of your story in one sentence. Make sure it's a sentence, that it has a verb. Stay with the effort until you're satisfied. That sentence will help you focus.

SUMMARY

Summary is a device for moving story along and covering a span of time. For example:

> ... In the ten years that followed their divorce, Agatha found that she cared less and less whether she heard from Elmer. Her recollections of his appearance grew fuzzy and vague, and she began to fashion little anecdotes about their history together that remade their years into a tellable story. ...

Summary like this enables you to synthesize events in a passage of time without having to move your hero/heroine through every doorway. Summary lends distance to the narrative and also contributes density. See *Time*.

SURPRISE

Surprise can be the seasoning on our everyday experience. Surprise developments in situations or characters bring the reader up short, usually with delight. Surprise in narrative strategy is akin to sudden modulation in music. We're into a whole new harmonic field. The elements come together in a pleasing new way. Be sure, however, you've planted enough clues to prepare your reader.

Surprises come to writers all the time in the process of writing. Influential writer Raymond Carver describes being in the midst of writing his story "Vitamins" and receiving a wrong-number phone call from a man named "Nelson." Nelson found his way into the story—and, Carver felt, improved it. Don't be suspicious about surprise. Value it. Exploit it. See *Discovery; Serendipity*.

SUSPENSE

You generate suspense by withholding information that will explain, clarify, or illumine what's happening. That's obvious. You hold back, you arrange clues, you leave your reader in the dark—a lot, or a little. Some suspense is essential to every successful story. As you write, you weigh your options for moving the story forward and then, from a pool of alternatives, you select *this* one. Curiously, that untapped pool of alternatives contributes much to the story's achieved suspense. If you have developed complex, rounded characters, your reader senses what's latent in them, their hidden sides. That unrealized substratum of story, the part that never gets told, plays against the realized action. In other words, you need to know not only what does happen but what could have happened, the road not taken in every scene. See *Arranging; Foreshadowing.*

SYMBOLS

Naive readers often assume literary symbols are one-dimensional, words with a single reference: white for purity, the cross for Christianity. Any literary symbol that works, however, carries a *range* of suggested meanings, never only one. Objects, events, characters, actions can become symbolic over the course of a story or novel by accumulating a range of meaning greater or other than themselves.

As you write, and rewrite, you will probably begin to notice meanings tied to repeated images. Gradually the thing or action or object acquires an indefinite range of suggested meanings. In the course of Charles Dickens' novel *Great Expectations*, for example, the lawyer, Mr. Jaggers, repeatedly tries to clean his hands, a gesture that comes to suggest his guilty conscience that cannot be cleaned. In the course of William Trevor's *Felicia's Journey*, a serial killer's uncontrolled eating comes to suggest a hunger of spirit that cannot be satisfied.

Repeated action can take on symbolic meaning. In "Shiloh," Southern writer Bobbie Ann Mason's frequently anthologized story about marital estrangement between an injured, out-of-work truck-driver and his body-building wife, the husband, Leroy, passes his time by constructing a full-scale log house from a kit. By the end of the story, as they make a trip to the Civil War battleground at Shiloh, he and the reader realize the connections between his pointless log-house building, his ignorance of history's meaning, and the emptiness of his marriage.

Symbols offer a route into deeper meanings in a narrative, beyond surface event. Because symbols are not pasted onto a narrative but emerge from it, so to speak, and because they encompass a range of suggestions rather than a simple one-on-one correspondence, it can take a writer considerable time to understand the symbolic implications of what he's writing. See *Image; Metaphor.*

SYNTAX

Syntax is the arrangement of words into meaningful structures. Certain writers develop patterns of syntax which can become tedious to read. Syntax has everything to do with the feel of a passage, the sense a reader develops of the contours of a narrator's mind.

Consider the syntactical arrangements of the following excerpt from experimental writer Donald Barthelme's *Overnight to Many Distant Cities*.

> When he came to look at the building, with a real-estate man hissing and oozing beside him, we lowered the blinds, muted or extinguished lights, threw newspapers and dirty clothes on the floor in piles, burned rubber bands in ashtrays, and played Buxtehude on the hi-fi—shaking organ chords whose vibrations made the plaster falling from the ceiling fall faster. The new owner stood in profile, refusing to shake hands or even speak to us, a tall thin young man suited in hopsacking with a large manila envelope under one arm. We pointed to the plaster, to crevasses in the walls, sagging ceilings, leaks. Nevertheless, he closed.

Try rearranging this syntax to get the same effects of frantic movement and wry humor. It would be very difficult to do. The energetic verbs of the first sentence, "hissing," "oozing," "lowered," "muted," "threw," "burned," several of them introducing short phrases, convey haste, purposefulness, and resistance on the part of the narrator here. We catch the implied situation, sense the tension, largely through syntax. The three-word conclusion is all the more emphatic for its placement in the paragraph and its syntactical arrangement. If Barthelme had written "He closed, nevertheless," he would have diluted the humor, the ironic impact, petering out on a four-syllable, namby-pamby-sounding word instead of the definitive "closed."

The next example, from Cormac McCarthy's award-winning novel of young Texan ranchers, *All the Pretty Horses*, shows strikingly different syntactical arrangements, a predilection for linking units with "and" to convey a kind of flat, flowing feel to a climactic moment in the novel.

> . . . he left her and rode down along the edge of the lake through the sedge and willow and slid from the horse's back and pulled

off his boots and his clothes and walked out into the lake where the moon slid away from him and ducks gabbled out there in the dark. The water was black and warm and he turned in the lake and spread his arms in the water and the water was so dark and so silky and he watched across the still black surface to where she stood on the shore with the horse and he watched where she stepped from her pooled clothing so pale, so pale, like a chrysalis emerging, and walked into the water.

This kind of syntax induces hypnotic immersion rather than surprise-induced attention.

Finally, the example below from William Gaddis' novel *Carpenter's Gothic* dramatizes activity on several levels: the moving, observing eye of the female viewer, the bird in the air, the small boys playing with the bird. Gaddis expresses all this in prose that moves rapidly, multiplies participial phrases, mirrors the rapidly moving mind and eye of the observer, forcing the reader to follow attentively.

The bird, a pigeon was it? or a dove (she'd found there were doves here) flew through the air, its colour lost in what light remained. It might have been the wad of rag she'd taken it for at first glance, flung at the smallest of the boys out there wiping mud from his cheek where it hit him, catching it up by a wing to fling it back where one of them now with a broken branch for a bat hit it high over a bough caught and flung back and hit again into a swirl of leaves into a puddle from rain the night before, a kind of battered shuttlecock moulting in a flurry at each blow, hit into the yellow dead end sign on the corner opposite the house where they'd end up that time of day.

Here, as in the first example, participles and verbs convey a sense of motion. As well, interruptions of thought (a question, a parenthesis), second-thinking ("It might have been"), a long grammatically complex structure ("catching . . . before") to show the bird going back and forth, an appositive-cum-metaphor ("battered shuttlecock"), and finally a clear, stable image ("yellow dead end sign") to signal the end of the bird's journey. This sophisticated, even eccentric grammar and syntax reward critical study. See *Arranging; Economy; Rhythm.*

TASTE

Taste, here understood as an instinctive response to works of art, depends on a person's range of exposure, education, developed capacities for response. To many, opera is mostly overblown acting accompanied by screaming. Others see country music as an insult to the intelligence. Both, however, enjoy passionately devoted audiences.

So it is with stories and novels. There is no getting around the reality of your reader's taste, nor should there be. Genre writers today have an advantage over their so-called literary counterparts: they write with a clear sense of what their audience expects. Even so, the question of taste still prevails. Some readers like violent detective novels, some like psychological thrillers. Produce the best fiction you can. If you're lucky, it will appeal to someone's taste and gradually you will build an audience. See *Audience; Promise.*

TECHNIQUE

Technique encompasses all the resources you call upon to create fiction and becomes, therefore, the instrument of discovering what you're writing about.

You cannot produce competent fiction without technique, but your work will be less than great if it demonstrates only technique. Something deeper, finally, speaks across the accomplished author's page: his style.

Have you ever watched a dizzying display of pyrotechnics on the piano and gone away feeling impressed by the dexterity, but strangely unmoved by the music? It didn't "speak"; it didn't "sing." Technique alone renders that kind of playing. The metaphors connected with voice—"speak," "sing"—suggest what constitutes style in writing. Style uses all the resources achieved by technique, yet articulates them in a unique voice, that of the author or narrator, the voice created by the fiction. You can learn technique from teachers and books. Achieved style requires practice, self-criticism, trial and error, revision, pushing through limitations of language, listening to the inner voice that generates your writing, trusting, against all odds, that you have something unique to say. See *Finger Proud; Style; Voice.*

TENSE

The tense you choose for your story has far-reaching effects. Recently, present tense has been in fashion. It can pull a reader in closer to the action. It creates immediacy, we are told.

On the other hand, fiction offers other strategies to accomplish that goal: scene, dialogue. Compare the following two examples for gains and losses secured by choice of tense in short stories. The first, from Canadian writer Douglas Glover's short story "Why I Decide to Kill Myself and Other Jokes," presents the opening scene, as Willa sneaks cyanide away from her boyfriend's laboratory.

> The plan begins to fall apart the instant Professor Rainbolt, Hugo's graduate adviser, spots me slipping out of the lab at 11 P.M. on a Sunday. Right away he is suspicious. I am not a student; the lab is supposed to be locked. But, like a gentleman, he doesn't raise a stink. He just nods and watches me lug my bulging (incriminating) purse through the fire doors at the end of the corridor.

To the immediacy of present tense, Glover adds first-person narration to dramatize the speaker and generate the promise of oncoming trouble.

The second excerpt, from Raymond Carver's "A Small, Good Thing," offers a more leisurely opening.

> Saturday afternoon she drove to the bakery in the shopping center. After looking through a loose-leaf binder with photographs of cakes taped onto the pages, she ordered chocolate, the child's favorite. The cake she chose was decorated with a

space ship and launching pad under a sprinkling of white stars, and a planet made of red frosting at the other end. His name, *Scotty*, would be in green letters beneath the planet. The baker, who was an older man with a thick neck, listened without saying anything when she told him the child would be eight years old next Monday.

Carver is obviously not seeking the immediate punch so much as a gradual immersion in the narrative which will, if this opening is a clue, reveal its secrets more cautiously.

The even more leisurely opening below, from Richard Bausch's engaging novel of an older man's discovery of love, *The Last Good Time*, highlights one benefit of using the narrative past: it invites the reader to sit back, put his feet up, relax, and enjoy.

On the outskirts of a great northern city there lived an old man who kept a small apartment, alone, because that was the way his life had gone. The apartment was one of two rooms on the second floor of an old brownstone house, and he liked it clean and neat. He was retired, he lived on a monthly pension check from the city's symphony orchestra—along with the regular Social Security payments—and he considered that his standard of living was adequate. He was not an extravagant man. He kept to himself, mostly.

You may want to pull the reader right into the story. On the other hand, you may want the more traditional effect that warms the reader up, partly by the subtle distancing of past time, the creating of another, alternative time—removed from the present moment. Experiment with tense. See *Had; Time.*

TENSION

Tension might be called a narrative knot. It arises from the conflicting possibilities pulling against one another in a story. It always seeks release. In both life and fiction it is therefore intimately bound up with a sense of expectation. You may prefer to think of plot as a focus of tensions—wound together, loosened, tightened again, and so on. A key question in writing and revising: where do tensions gather? Highlight these moments by dialogue, image, scene.

Dwight Swain, in his *Techniques of a Publishing Fiction Writer,* notes that fiction translates tension into space. Don't shortchange the possibilities of tension by cutting it too short. The reader needs some way to judge the importance of events in the story or novel. Length of treatment is one yardstick. Events alone do not generate tension; the character's reaction to events, and the implications of that, create tension. Therefore, when characters face a choice of actions with significant consequences, stretch out the narrative moment.

A rich source of tension can be the gap between suppressed and expressed thought. Shift tensions, pace their development, work to redefine them on deeper levels, like peeling an onion. Perhaps your reader is only afflicted with a twitching nose or watering eyes in the beginning. If you arrange layers of tension deftly, he may be crying by the end. See *Gap; Stretch and Shrink.*

TEXTURE

If you are feeling dense about apprehending things in the world and translating them into words and images, take time now and then simply to scribble a page of details that immediately suggest texture. I find in one old journal a list I must have made in such a dry moment: *bark, mohair, grosgrain, satin, silk, wool, waffle, oatmeal, walnut, corrugated, pussy willow, straw, velvet, ribbing, felt, piqué, strawberry.* Think of their surfaces. I recall sitting quietly and trying to imagine, to feel in my mind, their texture. Always, the search is for a key to unlock associations and imaginative possibilities.

THEME

The term "theme" confuses many writers, and with good reason. Some critics consider theme the innermost subject of fiction, its reason to be. Others might call it "the moral of the story." Others liken it to the basic premise of the story. I suspect it is not merely the subject but *what you want to say, or show, about that subject.* Obviously "what you want to say" may include layers of meaning and shifting perspectives.

Theme-hunting is less useful to a writer than it may be to a teacher, who deals with fiction as an object of study. This requires objectifying a story, breaking it into its components.

As a writer, you are involved in a process. As you work, new possibilities emerge, different ways of seeing. Your sense of a story's subject, its themes, may shift. Let's say you thought you were exploring the costs of ruthless ambition to a certain character. Gradually you come to see that you are exploring a more complex web—the balances of satisfaction and costs attached to that ambition, how these play out in the lives of several characters, and the choices this leads to. Your fiction grows deeper, your themes multiply, the dominant theme becomes more and more deeply imbedded.

The process, of course, will come to an end, a completed story. When you stand back and ask "What does it say?" you may be searching out theme. A simple statement of theme, however, *does not define a story*. Great fiction is always more than the sum of its parts. For this reason, "theme searching" can be misleading. Thematic richness is a mark of great fiction: it offers a reader more each time she reads it.

A musical analogy may help. We speak of the theme of an extended piece of music, its main melody. In the course of a symphony's progression, for example, harmonies change, new sub-themes develop, tempos shift, the composer may pull parts of his composition "away from" the main theme, but that pulling away is always deeply connected to theme. Theme is imbedded in the symphony, permeating it. In the end, the attentive listener will hear it again, enlarged and more compelling, realized now through all the developments in the composition.

Theme nests deep in a story. Too near the surface it may simply become a fictionalized agenda. You do not want to turn your story into a tract for ideas. If theme is not embedded deeply, the fiction lies open to the reader's dismissive comment at the end—"So what?" See *Beanbag Chair; Significance*.

TIME

Fictional time is elastic. A moment can be lengthened or shortened, expanded or contracted. Part of fiction's pleasure springs from this power to create an alternative to time's entrapment.

Managing this "enchantment that acts on the passing of time," as Italo Calvino calls it in his book *Six Memos for the Next Millennium*, can be a writer's despair. Five hundred pages may cover twenty-four hours, as in James Joyce's *Ulysses*, or three hundred sixty pages may cover a hundred and fifty years, as in Carol

Shields' Pulitzer prize-winning novel, *The Stone Diaries*. Nicholson Baker's brief but dense novel, *The Mezzanine*, spans only one hour. A sentence or phrase may contain years, blithely wiping away generations: "Forty years later, they . . ."

We all feel the difference between clock and emotional time. In emotional time, feelings determine our sense of duration. Happy, safe moments seem to fly by; troubled, tense moments stretch eternal. Since fiction aims to touch feelings, a writer's management of time vitally affects his fiction's power to evoke feeling.

We experience time as both elastic and *layered*. One lived moment can harbor depths of conflicting thoughts or feelings. Thus, the fictional present of a story may be riddled with intrusions from the past. In American writer Jane Smiley's story "Ordinary Life," a mother of five welcomes home a twenty-year-old son who has been in India for two years. As family members of three generations gather and gingerly re-encounter each other, we learn their history: farm, divorce, lover, children taken by father, his accident, their return to the mother, the gradual reintegration of family around her. Layers are delivered to the reader cumulatively, not chronologically, their impact penetrating the present scene of family reuniting.

Writers use several techniques to treat time. An obvious strategy is *flashback*. Here, a problem of proportion often arises. Too much flashback can stop the forward movement of your story. Another useful technique is *flashforward*. Below, two young Native American boys, Victor and Thomas Builds-the-Fire, from Sherman Alexie's moving story "This Is What it Means to Say Phoenix, Arizona," are heading to Fourth-of-July fireworks. Thomas remarks how strange that they, Native Americans, are celebrating Independence Day. The narrator concludes the scene with this remark:

> The fireworks were small, hardly more than a few bottle rockets and a fountain. But it was enough for two Indian boys. Years later, they would need much more.

The last seven words flashforward and cast a shadow of irony on the youthful fireworks of the present.

Like flashforward, *foreshadowing* suggests something yet to happen in the story. A number of fiction's elements can be used to accomplish this: image, thought, dream, vision, scene, dialogue, comment, premonition, incident. Often, a reader does not realize what events have been foreshadowed until they occur. Then he recognizes or remembers: "Aha, now I remember that hint." Foreshadowing, however, does much of its work unnoticed.

Flashforward, on the other hand, is always explicitly stated by the knowing voice of the narrator.

Time shift—forward, backward—can be indicated through separation of text on the page or simply through verbal links. If you are introducing a major time shift into your story, offer a clue to your reader, verbal or spatial, so she will know where she is in narrative time.

Simultaneity of experience also can be expressed. As I talk to you, with some layer of my consciousness I remember something, think forward to where I have to be in five minutes. But I betray nothing. Because our language functions sequentially and our grammatical structures are non-fluid, capturing this simultaneity presents a great challenge to a writer in English.

In her recent novel *None To Accompany Me*, South African novelist Nadine Gordimer presents the heroine, Vera Stark, driving her car through Johannesburg and encountering various scenes of racial violence, meeting people, talking, thinking, all the while carrying in her purse a letter from her son Ivan announcing his impending divorce. Part of the tension in this section of the novel derives from the question of when will she "take time" to pull out the letter and read it entirely? She is aware of that tension and talks to herself about it, even as she resists doing it and carries on with her surface life. See *Pacing; Rhythm; Stretch and Shrink; Syntax.*

TONE

"Don't speak to me in that tone of voice!" How sensitive we are to tone—in life and on the page. A tone of voice triggers a responding attitude on the part of the hearer.

In life we have other props to emphasize or offset tone of voice: facial expression, gesture, established mutual understanding. On the page we have only one tool: words. The opening of your story or novel will establish a tone through your narrator. Is it patronizing? Smarmy? Cold? Deliberate? Ironic? Arch? Coy? Intimate? Wondering? Self-doubting?

Some openings, particularly those written in first person—as in this example from Walker Percy's *Lancelot*—immediately issue a challenge to the reader through tone:

> Come into my cell. Make yourself at home. Take the chair; I'll sit on the cot. No? You prefer to stand by the window? I understand. You like my little view. Have you noticed that the narrower the view the more you can see? For the first time I understand how old ladies can sit on their porches for years.

Tone of voice puts the reader on guard. Is this the voice of a crazy person or an armchair philosopher?

Olive Ann Burns begins her novel *Cold Sassy Tree*, about a small American town at the turn of the century, with an intimate voice:

> Three weeks after Granny Blakeslee died, Grandpa came to our house for his early morning snort of whiskey, as usual, and said to me, "Will Tweedy? Go find yore mama, then run up to yore Aunt Loma's an tell her I said git on down here. I got something to say. And I ain't a-go'n say it but once't."
> "Yessir."
> "Make haste, son. I got to git on to the store."

We know immediately, from the narrator's tone of voice and that of the Grandpa, that we're in the world of Southern family intimacy, established daily rhythms ("as usual"), a world where obedience and respect are expected from the youngsters.

E.L. Doctorow begins *Ragtime*, his novel about turn-of-the-century America, with a much more level tone, setting a quiet stage, so to speak, in a voice that invites confidence in the narrator's steady, story-telling voice:

> In 1902 Father built a house at the crest of the Broadview Avenue hill in New Rochelle, New York. It was a three-story brown shingle with dormers, bay windows and a screened porch. Striped awnings shaded the windows. The family took possession of this south manse on a sunny day in June and it seemed for some years thereafter that all their days would be warm and fair.

This narrator's tone of voice says: I'm about to tell you a story. Sit back. Relax. I'm in control. I have the whole story in mind, as you can glean from my sly little word "seemed."

When you have completed a draft, go back and try to identify the tone of voice you hear coming from the narrator. It will affect your reader's response. See *Narrator; Voice.*

TRAITS

Character traits that stereotype—the grandpa in the rocking chair, pipe in hand—do not illumine character. On the other hand, some characters in literature live on as almost pure embodiments of traits. In Jane Austen's novel *Emma*, for example, Mr. Woodhouse, Emma's father, thinks only of health. He repeatedly judges a situation by its threat to his health. For him, any crisis can be muted by the proper amount of morning gruel.

Such characters, while not fully developed, can have a function in the total fabric of the novel. They add humor, enlarge social context, and by their very simplicity underscore the complexity of other characters. Funny and uncomplicated, they tend to stick in the reader's mind. A story or novel made up entirely of trait-embodying characters, however, would be a comic strip.

All characters, of course, have traits. These gestures, mannerisms of mind and speech, help to dramatize them. Again, it's a question of proportion. Does the way this character takes his tea suggest something more about his attitudes, his inner life? Or is he merely old Mr. Fuddy-duddy once more sipping noisily? If so, is that all I want of him? See *Characters; Gestures.*

TRANSFORMATION

Whatever the source of a story, it emerges transformed by the fiction writer's hand. Some novels are inspired by newspaper accounts, such as *An American Tragedy,* Theodore Dreiser's early twentieth-century tale of a young man's self-destructive desire for luxury and wealth, and Fyodor Dostoevsky's classic study of a murderer's mind, *Crime and Punishment.* Daniel Defoe's famous novel *Robinson Crusoe* was inspired by accounts of shipwrecked Alexander Selkirk's years alone on an island off the coast of Chile in the early eighteenth century. Some stories come from buried memories, ghosts that linger; some come from chance meetings, overhearings, glimpses, cast-off bits of other people's lives. No matter the source, a profound transformation is worked on materials. For this reason, such questions as: "Did this really happen?" "How much of this is autobiographical?" are, in the end, questions whose answers will shed no light, or very little, on the fiction itself. See *Autobiography; Buried.*

TRANSITIONS

Again and again you face the problem of transitions in composing fiction: transitions in space or time, from outer to inner world. Spacing on the page is the simplest way to signal temporal transition. Instead of two spaces, use four spaces between paragraphs to indicate a shift of time. To indicate a substantial shift of time or space, begin the new paragraph (after the four spaces) at the left margin, without indenting.

You may wish a more seamless transition, say, from the present moment to another moment in a character's memory. How you handle this depends on how intimately you have drawn the reader into the mind of the remembering character. If the reader has been following the character's train of associations, you need no marker such as "he remembered." Simply move right into the memory.

In the excerpt below, from Don DeLillo's novel *The Names*, we move with the mind of a man sitting in the dark inside a silo. He observes his immediate surroundings, then slips seamlessly into a memory of other silos.

> Owen entered one of the silos and sat in the dark. It was the smallest of the structures, five feet high, and he watched the night sky rapidly deepen, stars pinching through the haze. That was the universe tonight, a rectangle two and a half feet high, three feet long. At the lower edge of the opening he could see a narrow band of earth losing its texture to the night. Council Grove and Shawnee. The old storage elevators were frame construction until they switched to silos, see the Greek, a pit for storing grain, about the mid 1920's he thought it was. Lord the machines were wonderful, the combines and tractors, those stark contraptions flailing and bumping through the bluestem grass. He was lonely for machines. The boxy little Fords and Chevrolets. The dry goods delivery truck . . .

With "Council Grove and Shawnee" DeLillo signals a transition: we are moving from observation into memory. We follow Owen's association of silo and elevator with no difficulty. See *Moving Characters; Time.*

TRANSPOSING

Transposing in music involves moving a piece from one key to another. Not only do notes change, the key change itself contributes a different "feel" to the music: sadder, lighter, more haunting, bouncy, poignant, and so on. Excellent musicians can transpose at sight, even though it means integrating all those new sharps and flats into their playing. The capacity comes about largely through practice. The musician not only develops a synthetic sense of structure, he can imagine, as well, singing through that structure in another key.

Try transposing a whole story or a chapter from one point of view into another, first person into third, let us say. The process will demonstrate how everything shifts, how the "feel" is altered, how the whole piece is now skewed a different way, offering different insights, subject to different constraints. Often a piece that is somewhat dull in third person will come to life when transposed into first person. Or vice versa. Try it. See *Point of View; Tone; Voice.*

TRUST

Trust your reader. Trust the power of your own imagination. Hope to win your reader's trust. Reading itself requires a developed trust in the author's words. If a reader is familiar with several books or stories by the same author, she will often be both more demanding and more forgiving: "On the basis of what this author has given me before, I had hoped for such-and-such. I'm disappointed this time, but there will be more forthcoming. Maybe the next one will be better." Readers build up a level of trust in certain authors over time. See *Belief; Faith.*

TRUTH

A reader will feel a fiction "rings true" when a character's actions, the choices he makes, correspond to previous actions in the story. In his study of literary short story writing, *Writing in General and the Short Story in Particular*, Esquire fiction editor Rust Hills calls this quality the "inevitability of retrospect." As a reader moves forward, following the choices of a character, the way ahead still feels open. By the end, many possibilities of action have been closed off. The reader looks back and sees, *now*, that it was indeed "inevitable" that things would turn out this way. It "rings true."

As a writer, you are engaged in the strenuous and often baffling effort to make your lie of fiction so artful that it will ring true. At times you may feel stymied, even paralyzed, by a peculiar stress. This springs, I believe, from the deep contradiction permeating your task. We engage in an ongoing tug-of-war between, on one hand, life's messiness and fluidity, its shapelessness and fragmentariness, and, on the other hand, our attempts to give it shape, to create limited verbal structures that will yield insight. See *Paradox*.

TURNING POINT

The plot of a conventionally arranged fiction moves through gathering tension toward a climactic point. At that point, or just after it, a major change, or shift, or reversal occurs. The disappointed lover discovers he's better off; the alleged murderer, found innocent, is freed; the saint is found to be the sinner.

In *The Poetics*, Aristotle calls this point the *peripeteia*. He defines it as follows:

> A Peripety is the change from one state of things within the play to its opposite, and that too is the probable or necessary sequence of events. . . . this, with a Discovery will arouse either pity or fear—actions of that nature being what Tragedy is assumed to represent; and it will also serve to bring about the happy or unhappy ending.

Old-fashioned as it may sound, there's still a certain pleasure in seeing a character get what he deserves. The problem is to make the character and situation sufficiently complex so that judging "what he deserves" becomes part of the problem.

TWO

When you read the draft of a story that seemed electrifying as you composed it you may find it's too thin. It needs something more. Not just words and images, though. Not padding. What?

It may need to be joined with a second or third story line. What other ideas have you been shelving for a later story? Do any of these share a point of contact, of incongruous connection, even startling contrast with the single-line story you've told? Fool around with them. See where they might play off one another with interesting resonances. What emerges may eventually be far more satisfying, closer to the complexities and incongruities of life.

You can find a particularly clear example of this strategy in contemporary American writer Mark Salzman's novel *The Soloist*, which combines two clear story lines: one of a middle-aged cellist who has lost his extraordinary gift and recovers pleasure through teaching a gifted child; the second involves the same hero's movement toward self-acceptance through his experience of jury duty for a murder trial. See *Plotting*.

UNFOLDING

Thinking of a story as a process of unfolding may free you from a mechanical fixation with parts, connections, cause and effect, and all the other elements treated in this book. Think of a surprise wrapped carefully, tightly. Your task is to gradually unfold what covers that surprise (even while you are devising the covering!) until the story stands revealed. See *Plotting*.

UNITS

The concept of fiction as composed of units works against the metaphor of unfolding. Fiction *is* composed of units arranged to blend with one another, as seamlessly as possible. Well-known writer and teacher John Gardner, in his practical study of fiction-writing titled *The Art of Fiction*, contends that guided exercises help beginning fiction writers by enabling them to practice composing these units—dialogue, scene, transition, summary, etc., without being paralyzed or confused by concern for the whole. As a teacher, I've found truth in this. As a practicing writer, however, I've found it more useful to scrutinize units as units once I've got a first draft on paper. Then I analyze what's there. See *Arranging; Exercises; Structure*.

USE

Material ripe for use surrounds and inhabits us. Can you recognize it? Are you willing to use it? Can you find a way to shape it so that it speaks to another? All writing involves exposure. You must therefore come to terms with how much you are willing to use.

What is there to be used? All experience—in its complex immensity. In his book *The Art of Fiction*, Henry James refers to it as "a kind of huge spider-web of the finest silken threads suspended in the chamber of consciousness." From this "spider-web"—at times overwhelming in its prolix detail—we weave a new web, our fiction. See *Exposure*.

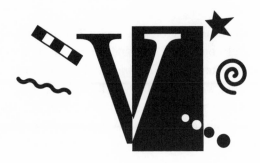

VARIETY

Variety is the spice of fiction: variety in sentence structure, pacing, character. Flexible sentence structure and arrangement inject energy into prose. As for pacing, vary the arrangement and content of scenes. Finally, characters need to speak in their own voices—distinct, idiomatic. Some good fiction writers get away with little variety in their characters' voices, it is true. They make up for it in other ways, usually a distinctive, authoritative, compelling narrator's voice. But your characters will come to life and be more convincing if each differs from the other. It's a goal to work for. Variety not only entertains, it creates surprise, a great value in life and in fiction. See *Arranging; Syntax; Voice.*

VERBS

Verbs generate power and energy. Charles Dickens excels at passages that bristle with verbal power. He is worth studying for this alone. Here is his description of old Mr. Turveydrop, the Model of Deportment, in the novel *Bleak House.*

> He was a fat old gentleman with a false complexion, false teeth, false whiskers, and a wig. He had a fur collar, and he had a padded breast to his coat, which only wanted a star or a broad blue ribbon to be complete. He was pinched in, and swelled out, and got up, and strapped down, as much as he could possibly bear. He had such a neckcloth on (puffing his very eyes out of their natural shape), and his chin and even his ears so

sunk into it, that it seemed as though he must inevitably double up, if it were cast loose. He had, under his arm, a hat of great size and weight, shelving downward from the crown to the brim; and in his hand a pair of white gloves, with which he flapped it, as he stood poised on one leg, in a high-shouldered, round-elbowed state of elegance not to be surpassed. He had a cane, he had an eye-glass, he had a snuff-box, and he had rings, he had wristbands, he had everything but any touch of nature; he was not like youth, he was not like age, he was not like anything in the world but a Model of Deportment.

Through verb forms—"pinched in, and swelled out, and got up, and strapped down"—Dickens transforms what might have been static description into a vision of a character fairly bursting with effort and strain. Dickens cannot even let a hat and gloves simply "be," but the hat "shelving downward from the crown to the brim" has to be "flapped" by the gloves. And even though old Mr. Turveydrop is standing still, that very stillness is charged with tension as he's "poised on one leg." Almost any page of Dickens will reveal such verbal energy—helped along, always, by his syntactical arrangements. See *Energy; Rhythm; Syntax.*

VERISIMILITUDE

Verisimilitude is the quality in realistic fiction that convinces the reader, feels authentic, "lifelike." Writers usually achieve verisimilitude in two ways: (1) selecting details in a scene or setting that give the reader a keen sense of that place, that action, that moment in time. This does not mean heaping up detail; it means selecting a detail that seems "right," and suggestive, for the moment. Detail includes physical movement (a distraught mother suddenly turns away from a suffering child), gesture (a would-be lover nervously touches the hand of the "other.") (2) arranging clues to enable the reader to make *connections.* Through these clues he can connect gestures, words, actions of the characters with a motive or cause—a thought, a past event, a remembered experience. Gradually, as those connections are made, the writer builds a world that is true to what we experience in life itself, only more satisfying, perhaps, because unlike life, fiction enables us to intuit or imagine wholeness. See *Detail; Dialogue.*

VOICE

A speaking voice can touch us deeply. It carries unique power. We sense immediately if we are being patronized, insulted, charmed, flirted with, invited into complicity, put down, or a host of other possibilities. Some voices mesmerize, some haunt, some scare, some bore. In life, of course, a speaking voice can be accompanied by all sorts of helping props, such as gestures, movements, facial expressions.

Fiction writers lack those amplifying props. On the printed page, words alone create voice. Readers grow familiar with the voice of a certain author. We welcome that familiar voice, respond to its predictable tone, its characteristic insights.

If a novel uses a variety of narrators, then each narrator's voice holds us, directs our attention, elicits our judgment.

Some writers find voice elusive. I believe it is a crucial element in successful fiction. Try to hear the voice coming from the page. Does it attract you? Put you off? Compel you to go on reading?

Here is the memorable voice in the opening paragraph of, "Sarah Jane's First Date," a story by my student Mary Louise "Mim" Mimmack.

> My personal fertility has been useless to me. I've been ovulating these thirty-five odd years or so just so other women can have children. Last month I either started menopause or I'm pregnant. I'm a little young for the former and unless I've experienced an immaculate conception, the latter is impossible. Put it this way, if an especially bright star appears over my house, I'm going to move.

Her voice brims with self-deprecating humor, playful ease with language and allusion, a gentle, pleasing strain of irreverence.

Sensitivity to voice implies sensitivity to levels of language. In the following example, from Margaret Atwood's novel *The Robber Bride*, a professor of military history heads for the coffee room at her university.

> She pauses at the coffee room, where two of her colleagues, both dressed in fleecy jogging suits, are having milk and cookies. Dr. Ackroyd, the eighteenth-century agriculture expert, and Dr. Rose Pemlott, the social historian and Canadianist, who by any other name would still be a pain in the butt.

The final line here playfully joins two dissimilar levels of language. It combines poetic allusion ("A rose by any other name would smell as sweet") with slang ("a pain in the butt"). That juxtaposition dramatizes the sharp-eyed, smart-aleck voice that fans of Atwood's prose have come to expect.

Voice functions much like a key in music. It sets the tone of the entire work and any variation in voice shifts that tone. You can use it like an artist uses the colors of his palette—which underlie and control all that he will do. See *Narrator; Tone.*

WAITING

Writers learn to wait. We wait to understand what we're trying to say, to figure out how to say it, to hear from journals, from editors, from publishers. We wait for galleys and page proofs, for the book to appear, for reviews. If you cannot stand to wait, this is not the profession for you. See *Negative Capability; Passivity; Patience.*

WILL

The rule for manipulating characters and for picking raspberries is the same: "If they resist, don't insist." As you move a character to do something, you may feel an inner resistance. Heed it. You have reached the point of ripeness in bringing a character to imagined life. He can now resist, nudge, subtly direct your hand. The material is speaking to you.

To persist in writing fiction, however, requires willpower. Routine. Discipline. Revision. Patience. Curbing the urge to run away from the blank page. Resisting the urge to give up too soon. We read of the prolific nineteenth-century British novelist Anthony Trollope grinding out so many words a day for his novel *Doctor Thorne*, between his bouts of seasickness on rough seas. Or Mrs. Trollope, his mother, tending a dying husband, a dying son, and writing, writing.

After a certain point, however, naked imposition of will on material becomes harmful. It can render you deaf to what's implicit. As you exercise willpower, learn as well to listen. See *Implication; Listening.*

WONDER

Every writer needs a capacity for wonder, the ability to see past worn surfaces to something else in the daily quotidian of faces met, roast beef eaten, flowers sniffed, traffic endured—something surprising, strange, oddly beguiling. At the heart of fiction lies a sense of life's strangeness. See *Strangeness; Surprise.*

WORDS

Words are our tools—slippery, evasive, frustrating. Inevitably, they betray us. Still, they're all we've got. We pitch these fragile little sound symbols into a deafening world. It's a brave act. How can words hold up?

Words hold up because they carry a power we set ourselves to discover and release. At times, belief in the power of words can be a supreme test of faith, especially since we live in a world where words are cheap and their power discounted or debased. Still, we have only these tools of the trade. Believe in them. See *Language.*

WORLDS

Readers grow familiar with the worlds of their favorite authors and the concerns that animate them. A world is built, as Henry James puts it, "Brick upon brick." Details, details. Yet all the while, animating those details, is a sensibility, a way of seeing life. Bricks may be similar, but the way of seeing is yours alone. So the world you create with your fiction is unique and personal. Think about it. See *Style; Trust; You.*

YOU

In the preface to his novel about an independent young American woman, *The Portrait of a Lady*, Henry James elaborates a memorable metaphor for the uniqueness of "seeing" which animates every fiction. He imagines a "house of fiction" pierced by a million windows. At each window

> ... stands a figure with a pair of eyes, or at least with a field-glass, which forms, again and again, for observation, a unique instrument.... He and his neighbours are watching the same show, but one seeing more where the other sees less, one seeing black where the other sees white, one seeing big where the other sees small, one seeing coarse where the other sees fine.... The spreading field, the human scene, is the "choice of subject"; the pierced aperture, either broad or balconied or slit-like and low-browed, is the "literary form"; but they are, singly or together, as nothing without the posted presence of the watcher—without, in other words, the consciousness of the artist.

You are the watcher at your own particular window onto life. No one else sees what you see. In the stress of putting together a fiction, managing its parts, weaving them together in a seamless structure, then standing back to see what it says, you may have long moments of doubt. Imagined, your fiction seemed riveting; written, it leaves you cold. Don't give up. Rethink; revise. Take a little distance from it.

No other pair of eyes looks through the same window at life. No other person has the same story to tell.

ZERO IN

What part of the story should you zero in on? Where should you distance the reader, where should you move in close?

These choices are in part instinctive, governed by your emerging sense of the story's design, and above all by your developing sense of its real subject. See *Finding Your Subject; Scene.*

ZZZZZZZZZ

How did that happen? How can you wake up your reader? See *Art.*

ABOUT THE AUTHOR

Ann Copeland has published six books of fiction, most recently *Season of Apples* (Goose Lane Editions, 1995), and her stories have been reprinted in numerous prize anthologies, including *Best American Short Stories*. She holds a Ph.D. from Cornell University and has taught creative writing at various universities for more than fifteen years. She lives in Sackville, New Brunswick.

INDEX